E 744 .W58 1963

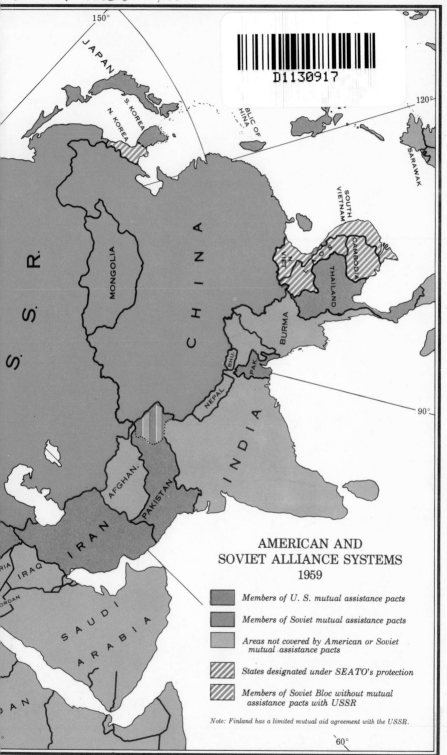

AMERICAN AND
SOVIET ALLIANCE SYSTEMS
1959

Members of U. S. mutual assistance pacts

Members of Soviet mutual assistance pacts

Areas not covered by American or Soviet
mutual assistance pacts

States designated under SEATO's protection

Members of Soviet Bloc without mutual
assistance pacts with USSR

Note: Finland has a limited mutual aid agreement with the USSR.

E 744. W58   1963

WITHDRAWN

Alliance Policy in the Cold War

WITHDRAWN

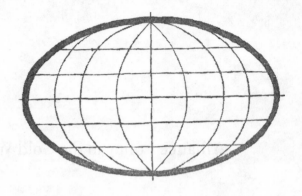

edited by Arnold Wolfers

The Washington Center of Foreign Policy Research

ALLIANCE POLICY
IN THE COLD WAR

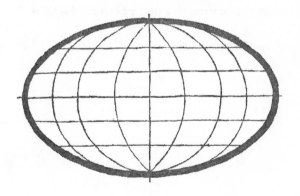

The Johns Hopkins Press

Baltimore, 1959

© 1959 by The Johns Hopkins Press, Baltimore 18, Md.

Distributed in Great Britain by Oxford University Press, London

Printed in the United States of America

Library of Congress Catalog Card Number 59–10764

Second Printing, 1963

PREFACE

THE PRESENT STUDY is the work of a group of authors all of whom are, or have been, members of the research staff of The Washington Center of Foreign Policy Research. The Center, founded in 1957, is an affiliate of The Johns Hopkins School of Advanced International Studies, in Washington, D. C. It gives a revolving body of scholars and practitioners the opportunity to engage in individual research on topics of their choice and to participate in weekly round-table discussions on matters of special interest to American foreign policy and to the development of generalized knowledge in the field of international politics.

In the fall of 1958, at a time when the aftermaths of the Suez crisis and the shock of the first launching of a Soviet Sputnik brought into focus the difficult problems posed by inter-allied relations, it was decided that "alliance policy" should be made the subject of a series of round-table meetings. At these meetings the idea and plan for this book were conceived. It is the first symposium by the members of the Center to be published in book form. Two earlier studies, the first on "East-West Negotiations" (first edition 1958, second edition 1959), the second, a set of "Military Policy Papers, December 1958," were issued as paper-bound brochures and distributed by the Center to a limited number of persons believed to have a special interest in the subject.

In 1962, another symposium on *Neutralism and Nonalignment* was published in book form by Frederick A. Praeger, Inc.

The reader is reminded that all parts of this study were completed prior to May 1959 and have been only slightly modified for this edition.

Arnold Wolfers

Washington, D. C.
January, 1963

CONTENTS

BIOGRAPHIC NOTES

ROBERT C. GOOD

Director, Office of Research and Analysis for Africa, Department of State. Formerly Research Associate of the Center; Assistant Professor of International Relations and member of the staff of the Social Science Foundation, University of Denver.

ROGER HILSMAN

The Director of Intelligence and Research, Department of State. Formerly Research Associate of the Center; Deputy Director for Research of the Legislative Reference Service, Library of Congress; Research Associate of the Center of International Studies, Princeton University, and Lecturer in Public and International Affairs at Princeton's Woodrow Wilson School. Author of *Strategic Intelligence and National Decisions,* 1956; co-author of *Military Policy and National Security,* 1956.

ERICH HULA

Presently Professor of Government, Graduate Faculty, New School of Social Research, New York; Research Associate of the Center, 1957–1958.

JAMES E. KING, JR.

Director, International Studies Division, Institute for Defense Analyses. Rhodes Scholar. Graduate from Command and General Staff School, Ft. Leavenworth, Kansas. Formerly Research Associate of the Center; country specialist (Canada), Department of State, Office of United States High Commissioner for Germany; military operations analyst, The Operations Research Office, The Johns Hopkins University; contributing editor, *The New Republic.*

CHARLES BURTON MARSHALL

Research Associate of the Center. Formerly Visiting Scholar, Carnegie Endowment for International Peace; Consultant, Committee on Foreign Affairs, United States House of Representatives; member of Policy Planning Staff, Department of State; Political Adviser to Prime Minister of Pakistan. Author of *Limits of Foreign Policy,* 1954.

WILLIAM LEE MILLER

Presently Assistant Professor of Social Ethics at the Yale Divinity School and Research Assistant of the Center, 1957–1958. Author of *The Protestant and Politics,* 1958.

HANS J. MORGENTHAU

Professor of Political Science and Director, Center for the Study of American Foreign and Military Policy, University of Chicago. Formerly Research Associate of the Center; member of the Institute for Advanced Study, Princeton, New Jersey. Author and co-author of numerous books: *Scientific Man vs. Power Politics,* 1946; *Politics Among Nations,* 1948; *In Defense of the National Interest,* 1951; *Dilemmas of Politics,* 1958; *The Purpose of American Politics,* 1960; *Politics in the 20th Century,* 1962.

PAUL H. NITZE

Assistant Secretary for International Security Affairs, Department of Defense. Formerly Chairman of the Executive Committee and Research Associate of the Center; President, Foreign Service Educational Foundation; Special Consultant to War Department; Vice Chairman, United States Strategic Bombing Survey; deputy to Assistant Secretary of State for Economic Affairs; director of Policy Planning Staff, Department of State; member of the Gaither Committee.

WILLIAM WELCH

Associate Professor of Political Science, University of Colorado. Research Associate of the Center, 1957–1958; expert on Soviet affairs.

ARNOLD WOLFERS

Director and Research Associate of the Center; Sterling Professor Emeritus of International Relations, Yale University. Author of *Britain and France between Two Wars,* 1940; co-author (with L. Martin) of *The Anglo-American Tradition in Foreign Affairs,* 1956; *Discord and Collaboration,* 1962.

Introduction

STRESSES AND STRAINS IN "GOING IT WITH OTHERS"

Arnold Wolfers

EVEN BEFORE World War II came to an end, there were unmistakable indications that a radical shift was going to take place in American peacetime foreign policy. The traditional policy of "going it alone" was to be replaced by a policy of "going it with others." This change did not reflect any expectation that a new threat to American security would follow upon the defeat of the Axis coalition and make the United States dependent on the military support of others. It was assumed, on the contrary, that after the war the United States could look forward to a period of friendly relations with all of the remaining major powers. However, considerations of national security did affect American thinking and were a dominant motive behind the break with tradition. Isolationist sentiments vanished as a result of the bitter experiences of two world wars, which, it was believed, could have been avoided if the United States had collaborated with others prior to the outbreak of hostilities. What appeared to be needed, then, was American participation in an international organization devoted to the preservation of peace and the punishment of aggression. Only later, when the Soviet threat to American security materialized, did the new policy take on the form of an alliance policy directed against a specific country or group of countries.

1

The American response to the threat of Soviet or Sino-Soviet expansion is too narrowly described by "alliance policy" if the term "alliance" is used in the customary sense of a pact of mutual military assistance. For brevity's sake, however, "alliance policy" is employed in the title of this volume to cover all efforts to prevent other countries from siding with the camp of the Soviet opponent. As used here, the term suggests an American Cold War policy directed toward the development of an extensive system of alignments in which actual military alliances form the iron core.

The scope of American foreign policy is not exhausted, of course, by efforts to defend the non-Communist world against the economic, political, or ideological expansion of Soviet control. There continue to be other objectives of American policy, purely economic and humanitarian objectives, as well as the original purpose of preventing aggression from any quarter. These have not been wholly sacrificed to the necessities of the Cold War. However, as Sino-Soviet power has grown and as the threats to the United States and other non-Communist nations have become more fully appreciated, alliance or alignment policy for purposes of defense has come to dominate the scene and must do so as long as the East-West struggle continues unabated.

That the relations between the United States and its mighty Communist opponents should have become the focus of interest and attention both to policymakers and to students of international relations is not surprising. By comparison, the relationships within the non-Communist world seemed much less important and received, therefore, much less attention. Moreover, interallied relationships in view of their great diversity appear to elude treatment as a phenomenon with characteristics of its own. On closer examination, however, one can detect—apart from some more positive aspects—a series of disruptive or erosive forces operating within the entire American alignment system, forces that make their imprint on the relationships between the non-Communist countries and especially on the relations between the United States, the leader of the coalition, and the rest of its members. The present study seeks to throw light on these relations.

Because analysts are likely to concentrate on defects rather than on achievements, a distorted picture of the alliance system might be created if no mention were made here of the evidence of solidarity within the non-Communist world and of common resistance to Soviet blandishments and threats.

Again and again, conflicts either between the United States and other free countries (as in the Suez case) or between friends of the United States (as in the case of Cyprus) have threatened to defeat attempts at building up a comprehensive network of alignments. On other occasions, the attitudes of uncommitted countries have become a cause of alarm. At one moment, it looked as if Nasser were ready to cross over to the Soviet camp and to take other Arab countries with him; at another, Tito's defection to the East was confidently predicted. Yet, in spite of all the crises, rifts, and erosive forces besetting the Free World, none of its members—the "uncommitted" countries included—have so far voluntarily joined the Soviet bloc, and none of the countries allied with the United States in postwar collective defense arrangements have allowed resentment, fear, or a change of government to lead them into a policy of neutrality, although Iraq deserted its alliance with Great Britain. Quite generally, whenever the danger signals have been unmistakable, there has been a tendency to rally around the United States rather than to defect. Therefore, while complacency might well prove disastrous in view of the many centrifugal pulls to which the non-Communist world is exposed, it would be misleading to suggest that the future offers only the prospect of continuous and irreparable disintegration.

With these qualifications in mind, it would seem proper, however, to focus attention on the sources of serious tension between nations and groups of nations on whose solidarity the future independence and security of all of the non-Communist countries may depend. Only if the stresses and strains are carefully identified and understood is there hope of discovering appropriate ways of overcoming or reducing their harmful impact.

It might be argued that solidarity, even among close allies, has usually proved a perishable asset. Wartime coalitions have rarely long survived the termination of the war for which they were formed. However, the present danger is not the dissolution of a wartime coalition, but the dissolution of an alignment intended to prevent a war that has not yet occurred. Therefore, if the present coalition were to start breaking up before the threat that brought it into being had disappeared, it would fall far short of its original purpose. The return of the United States to a policy of "going it alone" would then become a desperate but inescapable alternative. Should the Cold War come to an end or fade into the background, conceivably the United States could afford to withdraw from military alliances while continuing its policy of "going it with others" in nonmilitary areas of co-operation and within the United Nations.

An inquiry into the chief causes of the many irritating conflicts that characterize relations with and among our friends and allies must take into consideration the numerous psychological features and motivations of the human actors in whose hands the conduct of alliance policy lies. The personalities and idiosyncrasies of leading statesmen, the preconceptions and biases of influential groups, and the emotions, resentments, fixed ideas, or peculiar anxieties of whole peoples can all become divisive forces. Since the success of a policy of alignment depends on the creation and maintenance of a sense of common interest, of mutual confidence among governments, and of solidarity among entire nations, these psychological factors can exert a decisive influence on the course of events. This is particularly true in an era in which leaders of unusual authority —like Nasser, Dulles, or Adenauer—carry so much responsibility that their personal approaches to problems or to one another may make or break alliances. Moreover, where so many peoples of widely divergent cultural backgrounds and ideologies are simultaneously involved in the process of hammering out common policies, national peculiarities like Indian pacifism or American moralism may become serious psychological handicaps, while such typical national attitudes as Arab fanaticism or the complaceny of democracies may create almost insuperable obstacles to concerted action.

While the human factors go far in determining the way in which alignments consolidate or dissolve, many of the psychological elements of stress and strain that make themselves so painfully felt in the case of the present American alignments with others can best be understood as reactions to particular aspects of the environment in which the coalition operates. In fact, one does injustice to the responsible governments if one fails to recognize the vexing external conditions—some of them unique—that tend to render collaboration among the non-Communist countries an extraordinarily delicate problem.

The geopolitical approach to international relations is not popular today, perhaps because of excessive claims made by its enthusiastic exponents. It makes sense, however, in this instance to stress the very marked geographical hurdles that lie in the path of American collective defense efforts. They represent such serious handicaps to the common pursuit of security *vis-à-vis* the Sino-Soviet bloc that they could prove fatal to the alignment system if nothing were done to counter their effects.

Soon after the fall of the Axis coalition, it became evident to those responsible for American foreign policy that the Soviet Union, occupying the area Mackinder called the "heartland" of Eurasia, had emerged from the war as an expansionist power of great military and industrial potential and extraordinary dynamism. Already it had extended its control far beyond the old borders of its predecessor, the Czarist Empire. More ominous was the fact that the rising giant was surrounded by a virtual power vacuum along its entire periphery, from Scandinavia and the British Isles, along the rimlands of Eurasia, to Japan and Korea.

It was also clear that the non-Communist countries on the Eurasian mainland and adjoining islands would not be able to generate enough strength or unity within the foreseeable future to contain the Communist bloc, should it attempt to take advantage of the weakness of its neighbors as was to be expected. If there was to be established and maintained any reasonable balance of power that would give assurance of continued freedom from Soviet control to countries interested in maintaining their independence, only one nation was strong enough to provide that balance, and this nation was located on the other side of the globe. Perhaps more by instinct than by premeditated design, the United States took upon itself the task of building an alliance system that would wield the necessary counterpower.

As the potential strength of the Sino-Soviet bloc matured, the United States gradually began to realize how ambitious was its project of spanning the oceans with a defensive coalition whose holdings on the shore of the Eurasian land mass were, for the most part, easily accessible from the heartland but thousands of miles from insular America.

Under these circumstances, promises of United States assistance to countries across the oceans were not credible without additional evidence of American intentions. The only hope of effective deterrence and defense lay—and still lies today—in a projection of American power across the water barriers: the establishment and maintenance of a substantial American military presence in or close to the chief Eurasian danger areas.

Although it was an unavoidable consequence of geographical circumstances, the need for the projection of American power far beyond the confines of the United States almost inevitably places a heavy psychological mortgage on the alliance system. This deployment of forces is an easy target for hostile Soviet propaganda, which plays on such themes as "American occupation of sovereign countries" and "provocative American encirclement" of the Russian homeland. In the non-Communist countries that permitted or invited American forces to be stationed within their territories, those who for whatever reason are opposed to the alignment of their country with the United States condemn the American presence as an abnormal situation and as a threat to national independence. In fact, in the light of historical experience, it would have been more abnormal for the United States to have allowed a power vacuum to persist in areas adjoining a state whose leaders had frequently proclaimed it their duty to exploit the weaknesses of the "capitalist" enemy. Moreover, at the same time that it projected its own power across the oceans, the United States, at great financial sacrifice though with only moderate success, has sought to fill the vacuum with indigenous military and economic power, which, it was hoped, would eventually render superfluous American overseas deployment.

Whether normal or abnormal, the presence of American forces on the territory of its friends and allies places strains on their relations with the United States of a kind that was absent in former peacetime coalitions. Demands for "disengagement" or that the "*Amis* go home" voiced strongly in some quarters abroad, are symptomatic of a psychological reaction that can weaken allied solidarity. One may wonder, in fact, that this reaction has not been more widespread and why it has not evoked from Americans a response of "bring the boys home," considering that, until very recently, the United States has been so strongly isolationist.

These problems of distance between members of the alliance are compounded by yet another geographical handicap. If one visualizes the alliance system in the form of a wheel, one could say that the friends and allies of the United States are spread out along its rim, each occupying the end of a spoke, while the United States is located at the hub of the wheel. Danger to any allied country—to the end of a spoke representing the Formosa Straits, or territories south of Soviet Turkestan, or on the Iron Curtain in Central Europe—is communicated to the United States at the hub as a threat to the entire wheel and elicits a correspondingly strong defensive reaction. No similar reaction, however, can be expected from countries located on opposite spokes or on remote sections of the rim. Instead, any American military action or exercise of "brinkmanship" in behalf of an ally in immediate danger tends to strike other more remote allies not only as a diversion of American attention and strength to tasks of minor importance, but as a risky maneuver that may involve them all in conflicts incapable of being localized. This attitude may appear parochial, but it is not dissimilar to the reactions of military theater commanders who would like all support channeled to their particular section of the front, despite the necessities of an over-all strategy that is hard for them to comprehend since they have not shared in its formulation.

Illustrations of this attitude are numerous. Just after West German newspapers had deplored American inflexibility in defense of Quemoy, the Berlin crisis turned the Adenauer government into the chief exponent of Western policies of unwavering firmness. On this occasion, in turn, some Asian allies of the West may well have feared threats to their security from excessive American concentration on the problems of Western Europe. Inevitably, then, the coalition leader whose strategy must be guided by global considerations will find it difficult to satisfy both the ally who, in a particular case, is on the firing line and those allies who happen to be remote from it.

The image of the wheel helps also to explain another and seemingly paradoxical aspect of the difficulties encountered by the leader of the coalition. In contrast to normal expectations, many of the nations, especially in Europe, that are directly exposed to Soviet encroachment have consistently shown less apprehension at Soviet intentions than the United States, which, until recently, was relatively safe from foreign attack. Often, Americans have been chided for their hysteria or suspected of exaggerating the Soviet menace in order to push their allies into more vigorous armament efforts. However, if one thinks in terms of the position of the "hub power"—sensitive to threats against any point on the wheel's rim —such a power must necessarily be particularly aware of the constant pressures exerted by the Soviets, first in one area, then in another. In a sense, Turkey is closer to the United States than to Denmark, Taiwan closer to the United States than to Pakistan.

Another hindrance to allied solidarity lies in the fact that the American alignment system is plagued by an unusually drastic discrepancy between the strength and prosperity of the United States and its allies. This is a source of tension, whether the issue is the distribution of collective defense burdens, the relative influence on policy open to members of the alignment system, or American interference—however subtle—in the internal affairs of allied countries. This situation is especially delicate because, among the friends and allies of the United States in need of assistance and protection, there happen today to be many who are exceptionally sensitive to foreign encroachments on their national independence. In the case of the new states, recently emancipated from Western colonial rule, this sensitivity is a natural result of their pride in an independence won after long and bitter struggles. Some of them refuse even to accept economic aid, generously offered with no strings attached, because they regard it as a new form of "economic imperialism." Some of the larger countries that not long ago enjoyed the prestige and benefits of empire and of world-wide influence are sensitive because dependence on another power is hard for them to accept. On the whole, the graceful adjustment of the former great powers to the *capitis diminutio* that has been their fate is worthy of admiration. But the United States itself must be given credit, too, for the relative lack of serious tensions within an alignment system where inequalities are so great. Rather than showing much disregard for the sovereignty, self-respect, and wishes of its allies, the United States has perhaps erred more in allowing itself to be blackmailed by some of even its weakest friends. Certainly, Soviet allegations that the allies of the United States have been turned into satellites and used as unwilling tools of egotistical imperial ambition are not borne out by the facts. Nevertheless, whenever any of America's allies feel that they are not sufficiently consulted on policy or not given sufficient support for their views, resentments are provoked that constitute another source of stress and strain.

Aggravating this source of tension within the alignment system is the new dimension to the power discrepancy that has been added by the nuclear age. There exists today within the coalition a sharp division between the nuclear "haves" and the nuclear "have-nots." With the exception of Britain, all of America's friends and allies currently belong to the second category, and even Britain—or other countries that may follow in her footsteps—must remain so far behind the United States in independent strategic nuclear striking power that a more than quantitative gulf will separate them from the United States for the foreseeable future.

In its early phase, the introduction of nuclear weapons did not place strains upon relations between the United States and its European allies; on the contrary, it helped tighten the bonds between them. During its short-lived monopoly of atomic power, the United States was able—or was believed able—to spread a protective nuclear umbrella over what was to become the NATO area and to offer Western Europe a reliable guarantee against Soviet attack. In fact, reliance on SAC became so deeply ingrained in the minds of those people in Western Europe who gave any thought to the Soviet danger or to the possibility of future war that it outlasted for years the period of the American nuclear monopoly.

Only after the successful launching of the first Soviet sputnik in 1957 did Europeans in growing numbers awaken to the disturbing fact of United States vulnerability to nuclear attack and thus to the possibility—or probability—that Soviet and American strategic nuclear power might neutralize each other. For the Europeans, this would mean the alliance with the United States had been deprived of what they considered its major value. Gone was the assurance that the grand deterrent of American nuclear power made Europe safe from any major attack or that a minor attack on Europe, if it occurred nonetheless, would automatically trigger an American blow at the Soviet homeland.

American nuclear capabilities have also placed a peculiar strain on United States relations with Asian countries. Despite the fact that race had nothing to do with the 1945 choice of atomic targets, Asians have not forgotten that the only atomic bombs ever used in war were dropped on a non-Caucasian people. As a result, there is some fear in Asia that the United States might be less inhibited in employing nuclear weapons on battlefields outside the North Atlantic area. Whether such considerations strengthen Asian neutralism is difficult to estimate, since another factor, which we must examine, explains why so many countries today are pursuing neutralist policies.

An American policy seeking to embrace most of the non-Communist world in a network of military alliances was almost certain to run up against the insuperable obstacle of neutrality. After opposing "entangling alliances" and insisting on a policy of neutrality for their own country for more than a century, Americans should hardly be surprised by this particular obstacle, unless they assume that *quod licet Jovi non licet bovi*. At all times, weak and vulnerable countries have sought refuge in neutrality and found it a source of protection, provided that their stronger neighbors held each other in check. For the non-Communist countries today, many of whom are weak and vulnerable, neutrality again appears as the most prudent policy. The more American and Soviet power have come to balance each other, the greater the premium on neutrality. Moreover, under conditions of a reasonably stable world balance of power, a policy of neutrality or of noncommitment to either of the opposing blocs offers advantages transcending mere immunity from attack. If free from ideological or moral inhibitions, a noncommitted country can swing toward one camp or toward the other as it sees fit and can hope thereby to elicit concessions from both. Leaders of relatively minor countries—a Mossadegh or a Nasser—are well aware of the influence they can exert by taking advantage of the opportunities open to noncommitted countries.

The United States has endeavored to make the best of a world in which neutrality has so many attractions. Realizing the impossibility of convincing even a bare majority of the non-Communist countries that their best interests would be served by joining with America in pacts of mutual military assistance, the United States has come to accept genuine neutrality as the maximum degree of "collaboration" that is possible with many of the non-Communist nations of the world. Certainly, neutrality is a far lesser evil than a swing of the uncommitted countries toward the Soviet camp. The more this has been recognized in the United States, the easier it has become for Americans to accept as valuable supplements to the Western alliance system such open or tacit assurances of friendship by the uncommitted states as may be attainable. For this reason, the present study will treat as partners in the American alignment system all countries that do not either give preferential treatment to the Sino-Soviet bloc or enter into anti-Western agreements with members of the bloc. The governments of the uncommitted countries would probably refuse to be so listed for fear of being labeled pro-American or pro-Western and of provoking hostility at home and abroad as a consequence. Inevitably, relations with the uncommitted "third force" represent a particularly delicate aspect of American alignment policy.

A further source of interallied tension deserves attention: the discrepancy between the United States and other non-Communist countries in the variety of external conflicts with which they are faced. Whereas the security of the United States is directly endangered today only by the Sino-Soviet bloc, many of its friends and allies are absorbed by other dangers as well, threats to their national interests from non-Soviet quarters that often seem to them more immediate and real than the Communist threat. The Algerian rebellion struck more deeply into the hearts of Frenchmen than any hypothetical threat to France's security emanating from beyond the Iron Curtain; Pakistanis are more inclined to turn their guns in the direction of eastern Kashmir than toward the Khyber Pass.

For American policymakers, meanwhile, who are able to concentrate American efforts exclusively on counterbalancing the Sino-Soviet bloc, it is a source of concern and often irritation that the same primary focus on the Sino-Soviet danger does not prevail among all non-Communist nations. Clearly, disputes between members of the alignment system are disruptive of over-all non-Communist solidarity and run counter to American interests.

As a consequence, the preservation and, when necessary, the restoration of peace within the Free World has become almost as much of a concern to American policymakers as the conduct of the Cold War itself. While there is bound to be pressure on the United States to take sides against the "aggressor" in any dispute between its friends and allies that erupts into armed conflict, it is also clear that American partisanship endangers the likelihood that the accused "aggressor" country would later participate willingly as an active member of the alignment system. Therefore, the general tendency has been for the leader of the coalition to serve as a neutral mediator who seeks to mend the fences of the alignment system by promoting a peaceful settlement between the disputants. However, even if successful, such mediation usually becomes a source of dissatisfaction with American behavior. While the compromises of a peaceful settlement will leave fewer wounds than collective security measures against a friendly country, both sides are inclined to feel that greater American backing of their positions would have resulted in a settlement more favorable to their interests. Neither the colonial nor anticolonial powers, for instance, and neither the Israelis nor the Arab states have spared the United States from harsh criticism for not giving them full support. The damage to the American alliance policy is obvious, though inescapable.

While the nuclear age has raised the strains of power inequalities to a new level of seriousness, the "revolutionary age" in turn has aggravated and increased the possibilities of internecine strife within the non-Communist world. Two forces are operating concurrently to keep the Free World in turmoil. One is the Communist ideological and propagandist onslaught on the tenets and institutions of the West; the other is the nationalist struggle against Western colonial rule and against any remnants of that rule that keep alive the bitter memories of colonialism. Both Communists and the vanguards of colonial emancipation—who are no less fanatically dedicated to their goal—make life difficult for any government seeking to co-operate with a United States, depicted as the mainstay of the hated *status quo*. Because American policy has been forced by the circumstances of the Cold War to place more emphasis than is popular on military defense and the preservation of order, the United States is falsely identified in many quarters with social reaction and militarism, a fact not conducive to the smooth operation of collaborative policies that depend on broad public support. Under such circumstances, an effort to create a favorable image of the United States in the minds of other peoples is not a negligible part of a policy of "going it with others."

That makers of American alliance policy are faced with an impressive set of adverse circumstances does not mean that they are relieved of the responsibility for success or failure. Stormy weather and treacherous currents are no excuse for shipwrecks that able navigation could have avoided. The present study would therefore be inadequate if it sought only to chart and analyze the rough seas over which the United States must travel in its collaborative policy, however useful such a contribution to knowledge of the difficulties might be. More is being attempted here. This book is policy-oriented, and its authors are seeking to discover not only the obstacles that exist, but also the ways and means by which they may be mastered. Even if the stresses and strains imposed by conditions beyond the control of the United States are inescapable, there is still enough leeway for different courses of action to justify the contention that the final outcome will depend substantially on the wisdom of the actual policy choices and of the attitudes on which they rest.

Many of the questions raised in the preceding pages and many others pertaining to significant facets of American alliance policy are discussed in the following chapters. The authors have not attempted to present a comprehensive or integrated treatment of the subject. Instead, each writer has addressed himself to the aspect of the problem that he felt he could treat most competently. Since the study has been produced by men who represent a great variety of backgrounds and disciplines, experienced practitioners of policy as well as academic scholars, it should convey a realistic picture of the complexity and scope of alliance policy under current world conditions and should suggest some ways in which alliance policy can be made more effective in the future.

The authors of the first two chapters are concerned with the "psychological factors"; Chapter I deals with the choices between two approaches to foreign policy that affect the solidarity and cohesion of co-operating countries, and Chapter II, with deeply ingrained American attitudes that present special difficulties for a policy of collaboration with other nations. The next two chapters (III and IV) focus on the conflict that has come to light between the American commitment to universal collective security under the United Nations Charter and the subsequent commitments under the bilateral and multilateral collective defense agreements directed against the Sino-Soviet menace; Chapter III attacks the problem from a political angle, while Chapter IV deals chiefly with its juridical aspects. Two chapters then follow that examine the military aspects of American alliance policy, especially as they pertain to the present and foreseeable phases of the nuclear age; Chapter V is devoted to American force deployment throughout the non-Communist world, and Chapter VI to NATO and its particular problems. The author of Chapter VII, starting out with theoretical reflections about alliances, applies them to current American and Soviet alliance policies. The subsequent two chapters are more specific; Chapter VIII treats the novel question of how, if at all, the "fledgling states" arising from the liquidation of empires can be fitted into a system of alignments, and Chapter IX deals with the colonial issue, one of the chief worries of American policymakers. Finally, Chapter X studies alliance policy from a different angle by examining the experience of the Soviet Union in its network of co-operative arrangements with—in the Soviet vernacular—other "sovereign" nations.

I

COALITION POLICY AND THE CONCEPT OF WORLD ORDER

Paul H. Nitze

I

WHEN THE USEFULNESS or weakness of the present American alliance system is discussed, the emphasis is usually placed on common defensive purposes, or their absence. The assumption is that the nations involved are of necessity and exclusively concerned with the pursuit of their individual interests in national security and can be held together only—and sufficiently—by the conviction that a common defense effort best serves their respective needs. If one follows this line of thought, the only thing the United States can and must do to preserve or strengthen the alliances it deems essential to its own security is to impress its allies with the fact of a common danger from the East and of the effectiveness of the collective defense measures that, together with its allies, it seeks to undertake. There is, however, another way of looking at the problem, one that in my opinion offers a better if not the only chance of holding a wide peacetime coalition together.

The other approach that I am suggesting centers on the idea of world order, and thus points up the cleavage between two schools of thought on international politics and on what United States foreign policy is, or should be.

One school of thought, of which Mr. Dulles is sometimes but not always a member, tends to emphasize United States interests,

15

United States security, and the direct threat to that security posed by the hostile power and intentions of the Soviet-Chinese-Communist bloc. From this point of view allies are important to us only because of the contribution they can make to our interests and our security. The object of our foreign policy under this conception is basically defensive. It is to keep the Russian Communists and those whom they control from expanding into areas that would threaten our direct interests and our security as a nation.

The other school of thought—that which I believe to have the sounder position—maintains that United States foreign policy is, or should be, positive and not merely negative and defensive. It maintains that United States interests and United States security have become directly dependent on the creation and maintenance of some form of world order compatible with our continued development as the kind of nation we are and believe ourselves capable of becoming. It further maintains that such a system cannot be created or maintained without a protracted and creative effort on the part of the United States—an effort that goes far beyond mere holding operations against Communist encroachment.

II

Is there any historic justification for the idea implicit in this second point of view that a tolerable system of world order is within the realm of the practically possible and not merely a utopian and impractical ideal? I believe there is. At least there have been several periods in history in which a degree of world order has been maintained. That something has been done in the past is not conclusive proof that something analogous can be done in the future. It is not, however, wholly without relevance.

The century from 1815 to 1914 was such a period during which a degree of world order was maintained. During those one hundred years the balance of power among the European states operated to preserve a large measure of international stability. No single power could realistically aspire to dominate the world. England, with firm control of the seas, acted as a check on the ambitions of any of the land powers. England was not strong enough and did not aspire to dominate the European continent. She acted as a balance wheel to preserve the balance of power between the European continental land empires. No nation outside of Europe had the command of modern technology or an industrial base sufficient to make plausible a general challenge to European leadership. Economic institutions based on the gold standard and centered on the London capital market provided an economic framework within which large portions of the world, including the United States, were able to make tremendous forward strides in developing their economies. The principles of the common law and of political institutions based on the notion of public responsibility began to spread out to the far corners of the world. Above all, wars up to 1914 were kept limited as to their geographic extent and the objectives of the participants.

The two world wars and the progress and spread of modern technology shattered this system. The balance of power in Europe, and the very empires on which it depended, were destroyed. The power of England was weakened. The significance of sea power was diminished by modern weapons systems of great range and potentially overpowering destructiveness. The primacy of the European powers was cast in doubt. A strong United States and a bitterly hostile Russia came to the fore.

The second school of thought proposes that today the fundamental issue in the international arena is not merely that of United States security; it is the issue of who it is that will construct a new international order, appropriate to today's world, to take the place of the one that was shattered in the two world wars.

It maintains that, whether we were then fully conscious of it or not, what we were doing during the seven years from 1946 to 1953 was exactly that, contesting with the Soviet Union and its allies, whether it would be they, or we and our allies, who would succeed in constructing such a new system.

III

What are the main elements of the structure we were trying to erect, and to defend while it was being erected?

This new structure had to have its political, its economic, and its military aspects. It had to provide for certain world-wide functions. It had to foster closer regional institutions within the world-wide system. A unique role in this system had continuously to be borne by the United States because we alone had the resources and the will to tackle the job. And it had to be constantly defended against the hostile and destructive efforts of the Soviet-Chinese-Communist bloc, who were dedicated to the construction of quite another system.

An important part of the structure was its economic part. This had its world-wide aspects geared into the United Nations structure. The International Monetary Fund provided an institution looking toward greater stability of the world's currencies necessary for the financing of the world's commerce. The International Bank for Reconstruction and Development was to provide a pool of capital to flow to those areas needing capital and able to make sound use of it. The arrangements under GATT, the General Agreement on Trade and Tariffs, were to move toward the reduction of administrative barriers to international trade. These international institutions were reinforced by regional and bilateral actions such as the Marshall Plan, the Organization for European Economic Co-operation, the European Postal Union, the Technical Assistance Program, and the Colombo Plan. And we tried to support these international, regional, and bilateral approaches through United States economic policies generally consistent with our new role as the world's leading creditor nation and principal reservoir of capital and of technology.

In the military sphere a similar structure compounded of inter-national, regional, and individual arrangements was gotten under way. The heart of these military arrangements had to be strength at the center, strength in the United States itself. Supplementing United States strength at the center, an immense effort went into building strength at the periphery, through NATO, through the MDAP program and through our bilateral arrangements with the R.O.K., the Chinese Nationalists, and Japan. Much of the non-Communist world was tied together through a system of alliances. Even those parts of the free world outside the alliance system were given a substantial measure of protection through the strengthen-ing of world acceptance of the principle of restraint against the use of aggressive military force—and our active support of that principle.

These economic and military measures found their place within a political structure the broadest aspect of which was the United Nations Organization, but the heart and driving spirit of which was United States responsibility. A pattern of political relationships emerged, characterized by exceptionally close collaboration between the United States, England, and Canada, spreading out through close, but not so close, relationships with Germany, France, Italy, and Japan, and shading off to co-operation on certain basic matters with the uncommitted but free countries such as India and Burma.

The object was to create a structure sufficiently flexible in its arrangements that it would house the diverse interests and requirements of the entire non-Communist world. Even with respect to the Communist world it was hoped that the structure would have something to offer and would, by its attractive power, either draw off portions of the Communist world, as it did in the case of Yugoslavia, or result in a weakening of the bonds within the Communist world, as it did in the case of Poland but failed to do in the case of Communist China.

The point of view I have been outlining seemed to many to be overambitious. If it were consistently to be followed as a basis for United States policy, it would call for a protracted and expensive effort. It challenged Soviet policy not merely at a series of geographic points but overall and in its essence. It is quite understandable why many Americans have thought that a more modest policy—one following more nearly the first school of thought— would be more prudent. If we restricted ourselves to United States interests, to United States security, we might avoid getting ourselves too much mixed up in other people's business. Our policy would constitute less of a direct challenge to Russia. We had plenty to do here in the United States. Why bite off so much that perhaps we couldn't chew it?

United States policy has fluctuated between a modest view of United States interests and security and the more ambitious target of participating in the construction of a *novus ordo seclorum*. The present administration has made many pronouncements that appear to support the first school of thought. They have made other statements, however, implying that the object of United States policy should be "peace with justice." The concept of justice is hardly understandable apart from a system of order within which the principle of justice is to operate.

The issue between the two schools of thought has not been resolved. It is pertinent, therefore, to raise a number of other considerations that bear upon the issue.

IV

The issue between the two schools of thought can be examined in terms of a "we" and "they" analysis.

The proposition can be supported that one of the principal tasks of politics is to expand as far as possible the group that looks upon itself as constituting a common "we" and of narrowing as much as possible the group of those whom that "we" group must consider to be a hostile and opposed "they" group. Let us first examine possible definitions of the minimum "they" group in the contemporary international scene. We will then come back to an examination of the maximum "we" group.

In the days when Stalin ran the Soviet Union with an iron hand, it was possible to reduce the "they" group whom we considered unalterably opposed to us to a very small group—Mr. Stalin and the small group of men intimately associated with him in the Kremlin. This was made easier by the fact that Stalin seemed to think of his "we" as being largely reduced to one person, himself, Stalin, the more than royal "we." It was possible to view the Russian people and even much of the Soviet governmental bureaucracy as being the victims of Stalin's terror and a part of the common "we" opposed to Stalin's tyranny of which the American people, along with most of the people in the world, were all equally a part. It was possible to have a similar view with respect to the people of Poland, Hungary, and the other satellites—that they were part of the common "we" opposed to the small Kremlin "they."

Today it is Soviet policy to attempt to reverse the tables on us. They would like to center, focus, to reduce the "they" which they are opposing, and which is actively opposing them, to Mr. Dulles and a small group of "imperialists," "warmongering generals," and big businessmen. In the summer of 1958, when Mr. Khrushchev was writing letters to President Eisenhower proposing a meeting at the summit, he attempted to make a distinction between the American people and Mr. Dulles, and even between Mr. Eisenhower and Mr. Dulles. Only Mr. Dulles and the small group supporting him were to be "they." Everyone else, the peoples of the world, including the people of the United States, would be the "we" who wanted peace.

This change of approach in Soviet policy expressed itself in Soviet doctrine in the abandonment of the concept of "capitalist encirclement." Throughout Stalin's rule the concept of "capitalist encirclement" was used to suggest a large, numerous, and threatening "they," which justified the existence of the oppressive police state in the U.S.S.R. It was a self-isolating concept depicting the entire non-Communist world as hostile—the general "they" opposed to the small elite Communist "we." At the 20th Party Congress in 1956, a change in doctrine took place. Instead of "capitalist encirclement" they began to speak of the "zones of peace." In his March 11, 1958, election speech Mikoyan stated that the "Soviet Union long ago came out of 'capitalist encirclement' both in the geographic and political sense of this concept," and added that it was now the imperialists who were encircled by socialist ideas.

Communist doctrine has from its beginning held forth the "utopian" goal of a socialist world order, attainment of which was historically inevitable. It claimed that Marxist-Leninist doctrine gave scientific insights into the inevitable historic processes by which this world order would come into being. It is only since 1956, however, that this "utopian" goal has been translated into a more down-to-earth political goal in the sense of a conscious effort to expand their "we" group to the maximum, to narrow the "they" group opposed to their "we" group to the minimum, and to jettison or camouflage such doctrinal baggage as interferes with the process.

Just as we use the shorthand phrase "peace with justice" they use the phrase "Peace" with a capital "P" as a shorthand phrase to describe their concept of world order.

It is a world in which there are no centers of power strong

enough to challenge Soviet power, a world in which social ideas
consistent with Leninist-Marxist scientific insights predominate, a
world in which the "they" opposed to their "we" is reduced to political bankruptcy and insignificance. Order would be provided by
the "vanguard of the people" heading up into the central committees of the various Communist parties, these committees co-operating under the accepted leadership of the Central Committee of the
Communist Party Bolshevik in Moscow. Any action in support of
this concept of world order is, in their view, in support of Peace.
Anyone opposing these ideas is against their concept of world order
and therefore against Peace.

V

How does all this apply to coalition policy on our side of the Iron
Curtain? It applies in two ways: it illuminates an important aspect
of the external threat that has evoked today's coalition of the free
nations; it helps to explain why a concept of world order may be
necessary to give that coalition greater cohesion and greater staying
power.

Historically the words "coalition" and "alliance" have been used
almost interchangeably. In so far as there has been a difference it
has been that the word "alliance" more often has implied an arrangement between independent states involving treaty agreements,
while the word "coalition" has tended rather to emphasize a consensus of attitude and approach to a set of common problems.

Some people tend to emphasize the inner-community aspects of
coalition and to denigrate the external-defensive aspects. Among
the inner-community aspects they include common religion or
ideology, common cultural heritage, common interests in security
and economic progress, or common political aspirations and a concept of world order. Others assert that historically coalitions have
generally arisen as the result of a common reaction to a serious and
direct common external threat. They refer to the great coalitions
that overcame France's drives for hegemony over Europe under
Louis XIV and Napoleon, and those that overcame Germany's
drive for hegemony under the Kaiser and under Hitler. Today they

emphasize the defensive origins of the free world coalition in the face of the Soviet Union's drive for hegemony.

Both inner-community and external-defensive elements are combined in some proportion in any international coalition, in any consensus or pulling together of peoples beyond national lines. The weight of historical evidence favors the greater force of the defensive element in evoking the type of "we" consensus to which the word "coalition" is usually applied. It is the thesis of this paper, however, that the element of common aspirations and of a concept of world order can be ignored only at very great peril.

When one talks of the "coalition of the free nations," to what does one refer? The phrase refers to the common element in the attitude of all those people who feel threatened by the drive of the Soviet leadership for world hegemony and therefore feel that they are part of a common "we" seeking, perhaps by very diverse means, some other answer to their political future than acquiescence in the Soviet drive. If one accepts this answer, the term "free world coalition" has a broad but reasonably precise meaning. It then refers to an attitude of mind and it does not refer to alliances, treaties, or members of any particular organization. It does not necessarily refer to governments or nations as entities but to one aspect of the attitude of the people in those governments and nations.

If one accepts the definition here suggested, it is obvious that the word "free" contributes to the meaning of the phrase in only a limited sense. The Yugoslavs are properly to be included even though the Yugoslav government is under Communist leadership. The Spaniards under General Franco, colonial powers such as England, France, and Belgium, dictatorships such as the Dominican Republic, and various other groups politically organized in a great diversity of ways are also to be included. The common denominator, the special meaning of "free" in this context, is freedom from Soviet control and a desire to work out a political future in some other way than subject to Soviet hegemony.

Obviously any such "we" group, any such consensus, is fluctuating. It depends in large measure on the immediacy and overtness of the threat posed by the "they" that has called it into being. If that threat relaxes, or appears to relax, then the multitude of other issues, contradictions, and diverse loyalties normally tending to divide the "we" group come to the fore and weaken or break the consensus.

Sir John Kotelawala of Ceylon found that his domestic political support was withdrawn when he followed a foreign policy that was consistent with an attitude of "we" in consensus with the West and that thereby underemphasized other locally more appealing issues. Nuri es-Said placed co-operation with the West ahead of greater Arab nationalism and paid for it with his life. The "coalition of the free nations" in so far as it depends upon a common evaluation of the external threat is fragile, tenuous, and vacillating.

The coalition does, however, have a certain degree of substance. Most of the peoples and governments in the world have no desire to succumb to the doubtful mercies of Communist Russia and Communist China. They would prefer to maintain their independence as nations free to pursue their destiny in a manner characteristic of their particular nature as a people. They may not understand or desire the specific brand of individualism that we favor in the United States. But most of them desire a world in which both they and we can develop as peoples and nations each in its own manner. Most peoples and governments would therefore prefer a world compatible with the second school of thought I have outlined to one corresponding to Soviet Peace with a capital "P." They would welcome being part of an expanded "we" of which all of us are a part.

It makes a difference to them whether what we say and do includes them among those whom we consider to be "we." They are concerned when we appear to include them in an external "they" or as mere pawns to be played one way or the other as our narrow interests may, from time to time, dictate. Whenever we veer back to the first school of thought that I have been describing, and emphasize in our words and actions United States interests and United States security, we tend to make everyone outside the United States feel that they are either "they" or are mere pawns between the United States and Russia.

VI

The most difficult problem facing the formulators of United States foreign policy is that of relating and bringing into some measure of convergence policies appropriate to the coalition of free nations, the alliance system, and the United States as an individual nation.

Coalition is the widest but also the most tenuous "we." Within the coalition is a smaller group comprising the governments woven together by the system of alliances centering on the United States. Relations with some of the alliance nations, such as the weaker members of SEATO, are almost as tenuous as those with the peripheral elements of the coalition. The more solid alliance relationships, such as those binding the leading NATO countries, reflect both a greater awareness of the common threat of Soviet hegemony and more convergent political purposes and aspirations. At the center is the United States.

It is a thesis of this paper that a concept of world order is an essential element in bringing the policies relevant to these three groups into convergency. The alliance structure is today divided on a number of important issues. Should one look on alliances as being unlimited commitments for mutual support, or should one look upon them as limited commitments for specific support under specific contingencies? What is the role of consultation and leadership in today's alliance system? What specific policies should we be following with respect to the crucial issues of the day, nuclear deterrents, the future of Germany, the future of Arab nationalism and Arab unity, and the question of negotiations with the U.S.S.R.? How can the alliance system be adapted to promote those policies?

To the first question, the question of whether the alliances are to be looked upon as unlimited or as limited and specific commitments of mutual support, the usual American answer is somewhere in the middle. The legal obligations of the treaties that bind us together are limited and specific. The North Atlantic Treaty obligations are limited geographically and are related primarily to the military defense of the North Atlantic area. But obviously the concern of the member countries goes much deeper than the formal and specific legal obligations of the treaty. Whatever injures or weakens France, or Germany, for instance, injures and weakens us all. And whatever injures or weakens the United States, to some degree injures or weakens the members of NATO. In specific instances the French view, for instance, generally is that both French and United States interests would be served by following the course of action suggested by France. The United States view is that French interests, the interests of the alliance countries as a whole, and the interests of the United States would be best served by following the course of action suggested by the United States.

One approach to resolving conflicts of this kind is to consider the questions of consultation and of leadership. In the absence of prior consultation, no resolution is possible. But even if there has been adequate prior consultation, differences of judgment will usually continue to exist. How are these differences to be resolved? Should the presumption be in favor of the nation with the greatest immediate involvement, or should the presumption be in favor of the nation with the largest eventual responsibility for the consequences?

A preliminary answer to this question can be given by suggesting that the United States should lean as far as it can in the direction of assuming a presumption in favor of the judgment of the country whose interests are most immediately involved and that the country whose interests are most immediately involved should lean as far as it can in favor of the judgment of the country having the largest eventual responsibility for the alliance system as a whole. If the United States were to insist that it is the leading power in the alliance and that its judgment should therefore always prevail, there would be little hope for the alliance. On the other hand, if France, for instance, were to insist that its interests are more immediately involved with respect to Germany, with respect to Africa, and with respect to the Middle East, and that its judgment as to these issues should always prevail, it would be similarly doubtful whether the alliance could prosper. But this is only a preliminary answer. Something more than mutual forbearance is required if the alliance is to continue in the face of such divisive issues as Suez, Cyprus, and the defense of Quemoy.

It is my suggestion that a concept of world order is necessary both to hold the alliance system together and as a basis for harmonizing the relations between the alliance system and the "coalition of free nations."

A concept of world order makes it possible to raise the debate between members of the alliance system above a mere discussion of whose interests in a given situation should be controlling. With such a concept it is possible, at least in principle, to deduce criteria for judging the answers to most of the more divisive problems—criteria that are based upon a higher set of interests than those of any single country or group of countries. No such supervening criteria can be found in the narrow interests of England, of France, of Germany, or of the United States. Even the interests of the NATO nations as a group constitute an inadequate basis on which to advance convincing arguments in a situation where the interests of non-NATO members of the coalition are also involved.

A question arises as to the degree to which a de Gaulle, a Mossadegh, or a Tito is moved by considerations deduced from a conception of world order. The answer is that such a man is not necessarily moved to the point of agreement when the chain of reasoning flowing from such a concept runs counter to the interests or ambitions he is pursuing at a given moment. He and his supporters are, however, weakened in the conviction and force with which they pursue a contrary line. Those following the main line, the line consistent with the concept of world order, feel drawn together and are given greater heart. Obviously that drawing together of those following the main line must be backed by all the more usual forms of power and influence if that line is to prevail. It is the thesis of this paper, not that a concept of world order is a cure-all, but that it is an essential element in an alliance and coalition structure sufficiently flexible, powerful, and directed to compete successfully with the Soviet-Communist system.

VII

The objections to a policy pointed toward a system of world order can be roughly separated into two categories. One category includes various ways of saying "it can't be done." The other category includes various ways of saying "it shouldn't be done even if it were possible." Sometimes the two categories are combined.

Among the arguments that can be included in the first category is the proposition that in politics no permanent solutions are feasible. In answer it should be pointed out that what is proposed by a concept of world order is not necessarily a permanent solution nor one that will avoid all political problems. If a system of world order were to provide a reasonably stable framework for as much as a century, as the system described in Section II did from 1815 to 1914, a great deal would have been accomplished. This did not provide a permanent solution nor did it eliminate the necessity to deal actively and continuously with a host of important political problems. What it did do was to hold these problems within tolerable and supportable bounds.

Another objection advanced within the first category is that the effort required by the United States would be greater and of longer duration than the awareness and fortitude of the American people will support. This is a serious objection. It is possible, however, to underestimate the awareness and fortitude of the American people provided that the demands made upon them are seriously based in the logic of the situation they face in the world.

The most usual variety of the "it can't be done" objections is the argument that, even if the target sought is approximate and indefinite as to duration and even if the American people are prepared to support an expensive and long drawn-out effort, the exterior world is too complex, too divided, and too unpredictable for any even approximately stable system to be imposed upon it. In answer, the question can be asked whether even today's world does not contain some elements of order. Further, it can be asked whether a world wholly lacking in principles of order will not prove to be inherently unstable and thus tend to its own destruction. That some approximate system of world order compatible with Western ideas is impossible can hardly be demonstrated except by reference to a pseudoscientific faith such as Marxism-Leninism with its belief in the inevitability of the obverse outcome.

The more interesting category of objection is the second category—that which says we should not pursue a concept of world order even if its achievement were within the realm of the possible. Among the arguments that fall in this category are those that emphasize the point that any such ambitious target on our part is bound to increase tensions with the Soviet-Communist world. Many of the European advocates of "disengagement" fall within this category. They would rather seek some area of permitted freedom within an over-all framework basically consistent with the Soviet concept of a world order than face the risks involved in challenging it. Mr. Gomulka and his wing of the Polish Communist party appear to have made this choice as a result of the disastrous experience of the Hungarians in their attempt at an alternate solution. The position of the British Labor party and of many in the Social Democratic party in Germany appears to tend in this direction. In answer to this objection one can only point out that though the risks in contending this issue with the Soviets are high the consequences of not contending it are also high.

The most sophisticated form of objection within this second category is that which argues that an either/or answer to the issue between a Soviet system of world order or a system compatible with Western ideas can be avoided through a resolution at a higher level. Mr. Walter Lippmann, for instance, suggests that the present bipolarity between East and West can be reduced or eliminated. A new system containing a multiplicity of centers of power could then arise, which would permit the reconstitution of something approaching a traditional balance of power situation. In answer it can be pointed out that such a reconstituted balance of power structure would, in a nuclear world, require firm restraints on the unlimited use of force. If it did include such restraints through a solution other than Soviet predominant power and Soviet hegemony, it would in fact approximate a system of world order compatible with Western ideas. If this is to come about without a more clearly oriented United States effort along the lines suggested in Section III, one must assume a serious and persisting split between the Russian and Chinese Communists.

VIII

In conclusion let us return to the point made in Section III that United States policy has fluctuated between a modest view of United States interests and the more ambitious target of participating in the construction of a *novus ordo seclorum,* the motto that appears on the Great Seal of the United States. On balance I believe the informing principle of United States foreign policy has been closer to the second than to the first. What then is required is not so much a bold new conception of the aim of our policy as a clearing away of the obstructions that have, from time to time, obscured and diminished our vision.

2

THE AMERICAN ETHOS
AND THE ALLIANCE SYSTEM

William Lee Miller

THE UNITED STATES' new role, as leader of a great Free
World coalition, has requirements that are not exactly congenial to
traditional American political and moral attitudes. We Americans
are now rather suddenly given a responsibility for which neither
our past experience nor our present ideas and values have equipped
us very well. To put the matter too simply, a United States that
has not been accustomed to think "politically" now has an intensely
"political" task.

Part of the story is America's long period of noninvolvement in
world affairs, but another part of it is the way Americans, for many
other reasons, have come to think about the political realm—or not
to think about it. It is rather as though an invader, more-or-less
out of the system and more-or-less without experience in the imperial art, had suddenly come into control of the Roman Empire.

But America's role in the Free World is even more complicated
than any such imperial position and more complicated than that of
a participant in traditional European balances of power. Just at the
time that America has stepped into world responsibilities, the nature of those responsibilities has undergone drastic change. Americans have had to try to learn, simultaneously and in a hurry, those
old things of traditional diplomatic wisdom that others knew but

she did not, and those new things, like the rules for psychological warfare and economic aid, that nobody knew.

The suddenness with which the United States came into this role has added difficulty to a situation already difficult enough. Less than two centuries after she herself was but a collection of remote colonies, America has become a superpower upon whom all the old colonial powers depend. Less than fifty years after she stepped upon the international stage, in a "splendid little war," she moved to the center of that stage, where wars are no longer little or splendid. Less than ten years after a probable majority of Americans could still support the isolationist side—against all international involvement—in the debate over the events before World War II, the United States was the center of history's most far-reaching set of alliances—and that in peacetime. If Great Britain acquired her empire in a fit of absent-mindedness, the United States acquired her alliance system in a frenzy of activity. In less than ten years after the initial decisions of 1947, the United States had acquired forty-two peacetime allies; most of the alliances, and all the main outlines of the system, were worked out in the mere three years between the Truman Doctrine and the outbreak of the Korean war.

Institutions and attitudes require time to change and develop, but in this American case that time has not been granted. We have not had much time in which to develop a diplomatic corps to handle the perennial problems of alliances or a public to understand them, and we have not had much time, either, to develop the principles, skills, and attitudes to manage the *new* problems of *this* alliance system. In the same decade we have had to try to develop the ideas, train the people, and shape the institutions, to take on all the old problems of a world power and also all the new ones created, for example, by the economic dimension of the world struggle, by the war for the "minds of men," and by the immense destructiveness of nuclear weapons.

It has obviously had to be a busy time in the practical line. Along with that, it has had to be a busy time in the intellectual and ethical line, working out a changed understanding of the world and of our current responsibilities.

First, let us discuss the objective conditions that America faces as Free World leader; second, the subjective attitudes with which she meets those conditions; and third, the kind of ethical reasoning that is thereby seen to be needed.

I

The point made by every part of the objective situation is that the coalition leader must be able to think and act with "historical" wisdom or with "political" understanding.

This is evident, first, in the nature of the United States' relation to the Free World coalition. Her will is more dominant than it would be were she but one partner-nation in a company of equals —more even than a first among equals; but at the same time she is far from being an imperial power, ruling by fiat over subordinate peoples. In either of these cases her course would be less difficult, because initially and primarily she would need only to consult her own will and proclaim it. But the United States is not granted the relative simplification that comes either with unambiguous power over others, or with unambiguous delimitation of responsibility solely to one's own national interest. Instead she has the power and responsibility of the coalition leader, yet she does not have unqualified authority to shape the coalition's policy. The United States is technically one ally in a set of alliances, but actually a superpower with many lesser affiliated powers. She has in fact a large impact on her associates, but she is debarred by her own tradition and the nature of the association from the more blatant impositions of her will.

America is unmistakably the most important maker of decisions in the coalition. This follows in large part from her power and wealth: she is the first and chief nation with nuclear weapons, shielding the allies under her grand deterrent; she is the Free World's primary entry in the technological race over space satellites, missiles, nuclear submarines, and the rest; she is the major source of economic aid, loans, technical assistance, from the first loans to Britain in 1947, and the Marshall Plan, down to the continuing foreign aid programs of the present time.

The United States is, actually, the one link holding the whole complex of alliances together; several of the key relations, as with Nationalist China, with Japan, with South Korea, and with the Philippines, are bilateral treaties with the United States; the European, Asian, and South American parts of the whole are not linked except through the United States' membership in NATO, SEATO, OAS, and ANZUS, and through their common dependence on United States policy and resources.

It is the United States that bears the central threat and the universal responsibility; other powers, and the lesser ones particularly, relate themselves to the Communist world in their own limited interest and perspective, with less involvement in the global pattern. Pakistan is more worried about India than about China or Russia; France has to be more involved with her own problem in Algeria than with the common problems of the world-wide anti-Communist coalition.

There is another, less measurable but quite important aspect of the matter: the "ideological." In her own eyes, and also in those of allies, uncommitted nations, and enemies, the United States embodies and promotes in a special way the social-economic structure and ideology most directly antipathetic to the Communists: her "capitalism" is purer, her "democracy" more strictly at odds with collectivism, her "American way of life" more thoroughly and aggressively set over against the Communist view. In everyone's eyes she is the Soviets' and the Chinese Communists' number one enemy.

As the principal nuclear power, as the purest capitalist power, as the universally responsible Free World power, the United States stands on the front line in this coalition. Where in World War I she could be seen as a power on the periphery, coming in late to the fray to save the day, and where even in World War II she could wait for an unambiguous aggression against herself before entering the war that others already were fighting, by the time of the Korean war no such separate and delayed action was possible. Quite the contrary. Now the United States was the power making the key decision and doing most of the fighting, the front-line power urging others into more active help. Instead of being pulled in, she was doing the pulling.

But despite this preponderant power, and this major responsibility as "leader," the United States cannot proceed with her allies by anything approaching authoritative decree. She must send Admiral Radford and Assistant Secretary Robertson with the request to Chiang that he evacuate the offshore islands and then acquiesce to his enraged negative. She must come to the NATO Council to argue with reluctant allies over missile bases and agree, quite against her own will, to precede the setting up of the bases with new efforts at "negotiations" with the Communist power. In almost all allied countries anti-Americanism plays an important part. She must concern herself with the internal politics of her allies, and sometimes for example she seems heavy-handedly to intrude into Italian or German elections, because the alliance, and her own policy, have a stake in the outcome of these free elections.

The United States, with this mixture of an imposing leadership and a greatly qualified and sometimes suspiciously regarded authority, must continually engage in an interallied politics of a most complicated kind.

The necessity for political discrimination on the part of the United States is evident, secondly, in the inclusive and variegated nature of this alliance system, at whose center the United States must stand. The arrangement is full of tensions, real and potential, which American policy cannot ignore.

a) The alliance includes both colonial powers and colonies. The United States must hold with those who have, or had, a colonial empire, like England, France, and Holland, and must also deal with a large collection of their present or former colonies. She cannot take the unambiguous stand against "colonialism" and for national independence that some at home and abroad recommend; neither can she stand unqualifiedly beside her European allies in their colonial troubles. She must stand with, but not wholly with, a France, and with, but not wholly with, a Bourguiba.

b) The alliance includes both allies and enemies from World War II. Great Britain and West Germany are two indispensable parts of the North Atlantic alliance, and the United States must mitigate the remaining British antagonisms toward their former enemy and both adjust to and partly resist the reluctance on the part of some in Britain to commit themselves deeply to West Germany's defense. Earlier, she had to press for German rearmament, against the powers with bitter memories.

c) The alliance includes both democratic states and dictator-ships. Not all the states in the alliance, or receiving aid from the United States, can have the kind of internal politics about which the democracies can be enthusiastic. Those with less responsibility can be more perfectionist about this, but the United States often must take what allies it can get; often it must deal with the Rhees and Titos, with old South American strong men and new Asian military dictators, not because we like them, but because they are there. At the same time the United States is blamed for alliances with such leaders and states.

d) The alliance includes both more-or-less safe states, and more-or-less endangered states. This classification, of course, is not a stable one, but shifts with the shifting crises of the contest with the Communist power. The pattern, however, repeats itself: those who are immediately threatened or embroiled (Chinese Na-tionalists, South Koreans, West Berliners, Lebanese) want a firm, uncompromising, or aggressive stand when their country is in dan-ger that other, more remote allies and friends may find dangerous, adventuresome, and unnecessary. The United States, to which in every case the conflicting appeals are primarily addressed, must stand in between, mediating and judging the conflicting claims.

Many more conflicts and differences among our allies might be listed, to the same effect: the Asian against the European; the satisfied against the unsatisfied; the nonnuclear against the nuclear. Ancient rivalries and new conflicts play continually within and upon the system, and the United States must constantly act toward par-ties in dispute. She must work out a solution of the Trieste ques-tion between her Italian ally and her Yugoslavian beneficiary; she must deal both with Israel and with Arab nations (allied and non-allied); she must stand with her ally Pakistan but not against the important uncommitted nation of India.

The point about all these struggles is that the United States can neither ignore them nor take one side consistently and unambigu-ously. She cannot say, as a lesser power might, that the complex Cyprus dispute is not her affair. Neither can she alienate Greeks or Turks or British. She must continually act, not on a single prin-ciple, but toward viable compromises and solutions among con-flicting friends. As leader she cannot avoid decision, action, and blame; even for not acting and not deciding she is blamed. The whole operation obviously needs the utmost political skill.

The complex and political nature of the present American situation may be indicated, thirdly, by reference to the way nuclear weapons figure in it. Their existence greatly increases both the interdependence of the nations in the alliance and the delicacy of the relationship. They obviously raise to unprecedented heights the stakes resting on key decisions: it may not be too melodramatic to say that the fate of civilization is involved; in any case, possibilities of destruction and death in all nations, quite beyond anything hitherto experienced, are tied in with the decisions about these weapons and about the world politics in which they are now a major ingredient. Everyone's skin may be threatened; every nation's national substance may be endangered. In such a situation there arises a complex pattern of attraction and repulsion both toward the weapons and toward the chief allied nuclear power. A nation may be attracted toward a nuclear development of its own, as in France's case, not only because nuclear weapons mean power, honor, and a fuller sovereignty in general in our time, but also because in particular a nation so equipped can now itself make the key decision, to defend itself with these weapons and to pull its allies into the fight. But there is also a repulsion toward having nuclear weapons and thus making oneself a potential target for the enemy's nuclear strike; this was evident in the 1957 NATO Council discussion of the missiles for Europe.

Similarly, there is a two-fold worry about American decisions and nuclear weapons: a worry that their suicidal destructiveness will cause the Americans not to strike when one's own nation is attacked; a worry that the Americans will use them too precipitately in some other case in which one's own vital interest is not involved. The interallied discussion of these matters necessarily reflects, discreetly, subtly, in muted tones, something of a pristine ethical situation: each one desiring to save himself, but each also desiring to include the others in his own fight; each desiring that someone else take the greater risks. In such a situation, the leading power has decisions to make of the utmost subtlety and difficulty.

Nuclear weapons also make a discriminating policy necessary

in that they make absolute decisions catastrophic, and require therefore the ability to relate force to policy in the most careful way. Sheer power no longer is decisive; the psychological release of all-out war no longer is an acceptable alternative. Instead, objectives must be carefully limited, measured, "costs" of policies carefully assessed, the use and threat of force carefully related to discriminating analysis of Communist intentions, of allied convictions, and of our own purposes. In short, the easier, absolute "moral" decisions are no longer allowed, and the hard, changing, mixed and uncertain calculations of "politics" are inescapable.

II

We Americans are not oversupplied with the kind of "historical" or "political" wisdom our situation now requires. Perhaps the now rather familiar indictments of our "legalistic-moralistic" approach or of our "escape from politics" have not sufficiently given credit for the adaption Americans *have* made to the new international responsibility; perhaps the indictments sometimes imply that this country should somehow exhibit a degree of political sophistication never seen on land or sea. Probably the faults that are listed are not exclusively American, and probably there are unnoted virtues mixed in with those faults. Nevertheless, there is still much truth in the indictment.

One can understand how Americans came to have *their* characteristic ways of fleeing politics (which are not necessarily more marked or worse than the ways in which other peoples may do the same). Both historical conditions and ideas played a role. Among the former, one could list the long period of relative isolation; the absence of the deepest kinds of national tragedy—defeat in war, for example; the success and continuity of the political system; the building of an economy of abundance that could bypass, with increased production, problems of scarcity with which other nations have to struggle; the absence of the remnants of the feudal order, such as the more fundamental class divisions. "Equality of condition," Tocqueville's central conception, helps to explain much about American attitudes. And the ideas that are inseparable from these conditions and experiences tend in the same direction: the "colossal liberal absolutism," as Louis Hartz calls it, that accepts as self-evident the individualistic ideas of the classical liberal creed; the empiricism that, as Henry Kissinger says, wants to wait till all the facts are in and act with certainty; the puritan and sectarian tradition that emphasizes clear moral lines and the individual's change of heart. All of these influences tend in the same direction: toward a neglect of "history" and of "politics."

By this we mean, first, just an underestimation of the *collective* base of life, in this nation overwhelmingly dedicated to "individualism." We mean, second, the overlooking of the pervasiveness of power, in this nation trusting mightily in persuasion, moral exhortation, majority votes, good will, and the rule of law. Thirdly, we mean an underestimation of the impact of interest on the minds and actions of men and nations and an overestimation of the harmony that is actual and possible among those interests. Then, fourth, there is of course our too great optimism about man's ability to understand and control the elements of history ("the impossible takes a little longer") and our too simple and shallow view of those elements. Americans tend to make a simple transfer from the more exact fields of science and technique, in which they excel, to the inexact world of politics, in which they do not. They have a hard time living with imponderables and with unresolved situations. The American's experience and ideas incline him to overlook the complexity of history, the variety of human nature, and the ubiquity and persistence of power and interest.

When we say "unhistorical" we mean an attempt to reduce or to elevate history—the realm of freedom-and-necessity and of the unique-but-conditioned event—to something else: to nature, with its necessary laws of cause and effect, which science can discover; or to a spiritual-individual realm, of some pure and inward freedom. In either case, one loses the contingency of history.

When we say "unpolitical" we mean the attempt to treat politics as something else: as a natural process or instead as a realm subject to pure moral decision. In either case, the real and distinctive mixtures of politics—of ideal mixed with interest, of will qualified by other wills, of freedom within limits, of purpose qualified by power and power qualified by purpose—are overlooked.

The attitude that we describe in these broad, sweeping terms really is, of course, just a coloration and not a pure and consistent picture. And certainly it is better to err on this American "unpolitical" side than on the opposite side of a cynical, utterly pessimistic, and thoroughgoing *Realpolitik*. The different American ways of escaping politics have in common an implicit desire for a single, clear, "right" course of action, with a certain outcome and without risk, ignoring the inevitably mixed, unpredictable, and risky course of history. They have in common also an inclination to ignore the limits of our power and freedom, making it particularly galling to an American to admit that there are many important things America just cannot do. Peculiar problems are bound to arise for American alliance policy and American leadership in the alliance as a consequence of such an attitude. They are particularly serious because the nonpolitical coloration affects the outlook of both conservatives and liberals, of both internationalists and nationalists.

We can see the problems, first, in relation to the whole basis of alliances; second, in relation to particular allies; and third, in relation to various courses of action within the system.

There is some continuing restiveness about the whole alliance system, though perhaps not now as much as in the past. At the outset of the containment policy and the beginning of the building of the Free World alliances, in 1947, there were the two opposite strands of criticism, the more internationalist and the more nationalist. These continue to the present. To some extent they are polar opponents, but to an extent they also actually share some underlying attitudes of the unpolitical kind we have been describing.

For the more thoroughgoing internationalist, the collective self-defense system has appeared to be an impure thing, a compromise, a renewal of the old, evil "power politics." It appeared to be a direct contrast to the universal collective security program of the United Nations. Internationalists of this stripe protested against the Truman Doctrine in 1947; some (though by no means all) participated in the Wallace protest of 1947-1948; they objected to the creation of NATO; they continue to protest against "bypassing the United Nations" today. Many have believed, moreover, that a world government is possible. The United Nations may represent to them something of the inclusiveness and something of the rule of law that they desire, but not as fully as they would like. The collective self-defense system is quite another matter. It is particular, not universal; it is directed against a specific enemy, not against aggression in general; it is obviously motivated more by self-interest and self-protection than by a disinterested attachment to a principle; it includes a prominent military element. Therefore, it is an undesirable thing.

The nationalists also have been disgruntled by the coalition, but for different reasons. One continuing expression of the American attitude we have described is a kind of cocky unilateralism, a feeling that we can do what we want and that we should "go it alone." This American nationalism has in it elements that mark that phenomenon everywhere: a strong, sensitive sense of the nation's honor and glory; a certain xenophobia; a love of display of the nation's power. In addition, the American version is more affected than most by a strong sense of national separation, uniqueness, freedom, and power. The same spirit could support, in one moment, the isolationist alternative, too much withdrawn (nonintervention before World War II, Herbert Hoover's "Fortress America" in the "great debate" in 1950) and in another moment an adventurous, expansive semi-imperialist policy, too little restrained (unconditional surrender, the "American Century," General MacArthur's expansionistic impulses). A common denominator of the apparently contradictory policies is the desire to exercise an unsullied and untrammeled national will. The nationalist spirit is restive with real allies, because they obviously place restraints upon us. Mixed in with that is a dislike of the foreigner, anyway. Usually, too, the nationalist wing is the more blatantly anti-Communist and pugnacious, inclining more toward preventive war and surer of our unbeatable strength; allies appear to be unnecessary and restrictive, and also somewhat soft and weak-willed in the contest with the Communist power.

These two extremes, tending for contrary reasons to oppose the coalition, actually have some underlying attitudes in common. They share the uncalculating neglect of the specific correlation of forces in the real world—the one by consulting only its ideals, the other by consulting only its image of the national glory. They share a desire that the nation act in a single "pure" way, rather than on a mixed and compromised course, acting partly in response to allied needs and pressures. They share the desire to resolve by some decisive act the unresolved problems of history. All these impulses find our alliance system as a whole quite unsatisfactory.

But the more simple and extreme positions are no longer as powerful as they once were. Now the relation of attitudes to the alliance is more refined. The struggle concerns aspects of the alliance rather than its whole justification. Part of the dispute concerns preferences among allies. Just as we noted above that different allies may disapprove of each other, so within the major power different factions may approve and disapprove different sets of allies. The more internationalist persuasion, accommodated in part to a collective defense system, may nevertheless find repugnant the dictatorships and "reactionary" regimes attached to it. The alliance, in this view, should have a purer ideological content. Some members of the so-called Free World, said one complaint, are in no sense free. In such a complaint there is too much ideology and too little realization of the limits on the power and freedom of the United States. There is too little recognition that the alliance must be based not so much on compatibility of social structures as on a common interest in resisting the Communist empire. That narrow interest in security is not very elevated in ethical theory, to be sure, but it does have its own justification and importance in the real world. At least some justification for the term "free" can be found in the common desire for freedom from Soviet control and for some understanding of the need for "impure" allies in the measures necessary to defend *that* freedom.

But if the internationalist has disapproved of Franco and Chiang and Rhee and South American dictators and Arab potentates, and maybe sometimes of Adenauer, the nationalist has preferred these very allies to others who in his view are less staunchly anti-Communist. His implicit tests are not only solid anti-communism, but also pro-Americanism, and strength. England and France may sometimes appear to him to be too "soft" in regard to the common enemy; certainly the courting of India, and of other uncommitted nations of Southeast Asia, does not appeal to him. Really, he too has an ideological, and an unpolitical, way of testing our allies and friends.

Similar patterns of principled opposition appear also in regard to other questions of the conduct of the alliance. They appear, for example, when we consider the relative weight of our own national will and the relative merit of our own unilateral action, as against those of our allies. Some internationalists have an automatic and principled preference for collective action, the more collective the better. Action "through the United Nations," in this view, is always morally preferable to action through NATO or other alliances, and then, in turn, action with allies is automatically preferable to unilateral action. There is an ethical presumption in favor of action by collective international agencies that too easily assumes that collectivity in itself is necessarily a good. Latter-day American internationalism, having in some measure abandoned the vision of a universal system as an immediately relevant goal, may have shifted some of its vision to the Free World pattern of alliance, assuming that multilateral action is automatically an ethical gain.

One may say that the Free World system is justified from the realistic side too much in terms of national interest, and from the idealist side too much in terms of collectivity as a good. The important ethical judgment rests with the justice of the cause itself, rather than whether it is pursued multilaterally or unilaterally.

Similarly, the principled American internationalist may over-value the opinions of allies or uncommitted powers, as against the conclusions of his own government: how Indians and other Asians feel, or sometimes how the English and French feel, can too automatically be given first place. Some residual wisdom is thought to be there, some disinterested insight, that is not available over here. This appears especially with reference not to governmental opinion in the nations in question, but to popular opinion; the allied publics are part of that "world public opinion" to which frequent appeal is made. On the other hand, the nationalist might seem almost to make it a principle never to consider seriously the opinions of the others, but to prefer to go ahead in our own way.

With reference to the conduct of the alliance there is a similar division concerning the military and economic-political aspects respectively. Some idealists too automatically prefer economic "aid" to military, and some realists the reverse. Both have their rather *a priori* estimates of what is needed and of what both Americans and allies really want. The discussion over what to *call* our aid, for the purpose of congressional action and popular support, is an interesting case in point. Some held that congressmen and other Americans are more likely to approve military than economic aid; therefore, the phrase and category of "defense support" was devised, to include some essentially nonmilitary items under this military rubric. Others have held, however, that the reverse is true: more aid ought to be given and administered as economic aid. Some go further and want as much foreign aid as possible divorced not only from military considerations but from any policy considerations whatsoever: it should be taken away, not only from the Defense Department, but even from the State Department, and made something like a disinterested outpouring of beneficence.

The views we have been criticizing are thus reflected in both sets of attitudes about America's postwar system of alliances—and in both for the wrong reasons. One way to summarize these wrong reasons is to say they seek and presuppose a *purer* action—a pure disinterestedness, or a pure national act, in a pure solution that finally resolves the ambiguities and limitations of history—than is ever forthcoming in world politics.

III

We have already suggested, by implication, the kind of ethical reflection that is appropriate to the American role as leader of a Free World coalition. In such a "political" situation no "nonpolitical" morality—no ethic of single principle—will do; such a morality, in fact, causes quite dubious acts and attitudes, as critics of American policy often point out. Nothing is more likely to separate us from our allies, and make the complex situation unworkable.

The first thing to do is distinguish between real moral claims and traditional moral words, between genuine ethical reasoning and familiar ethical language. The second thing to do is to discourage the use of the latter in diplomatic discourse.

Dean Acheson is surely right, despite the outpouring of critical letters he apparently received, when in the lectures published as *Power and Diplomacy* he said he would deal with policies in reference to their specific purpose and effect, without resort to the language of morality. In that language he might especially include the general words of sweeping praise and blame, words like "moral" and "immoral," "righteous" and "unrighteous"; he might also include the simple opposition between "principle" and "expediency." The reason for omitting such language is that it has built into it a mistaken understanding of the ethical problems of politics. Drawn from ordinary personal relations, such language implies a morality of absolute, clear lines: a single, simple, widely accepted and easily known morality, which all should follow. It categorizes the world into neat, clear rights and wrongs; it divides the "moral" acts from the "immoral" acts, the nations that follow a policy of righteousness from those that follow, presumably, a policy of unrighteousness. Thus it vastly oversimplifies the moral and factual issue, and implies the wrong kind of ethical method for these complex situations. It tends to a dichotomous view, dividing the world into black and white, good people and bad people, which then makes the one so viewing the world unable to view critically the results of actual alternative policies. It overinclines the viewer to draw a sharp and final line, to condemn whole nations in moral terms, and to view his own society with relative equanimity. In short, it inclines toward oversimplification and self-righteousness. Also, nations like, say, the neutrals, when it is implied that neutralism is immoral, are immediately put on the defensive against those who (as it seems to them) view the world so self-righteously.

The use of such language implies that the political problem is one of morality against immorality, principle against expediency, when in fact we are regularly in situations in which some moral claims stand against others, some principles (mixed with certain interests) against other principles (mixed with other interests). The situation is never pure and neat; it is not simple but many-faceted, because the values to be brought to bear upon it are not single but multiple.

It is particularly important for a major power in our alliance not to speak in a "moral" way, implying self-praise and the coercion of its partners into its own single, simple moral frame, or seeming to endorse some allies, on principle, against some others. It is important that such a power refrain from speaking continually in admonitory tones. In fact, one of the irritants in the Free World coalition today is the moralizing by the chief diplomats of the United States. Such language is annoying and even a little frightening, because it implies that the great power in question has not really grasped the complex and historical character of its role, the differences between its own situation and that of many of its allies, the differences among allies, and the relativity of its own viewpoint.

Part of this just has to do with words. There is confusion between labeling oneself as "moral" and actually being moral—actually behaving in a responsible fashion in relation to values. The point is to try to do what is empirically best, rather than to label oneself as "righteous," to do what is conducive to the worthier result, on the whole, rather than to keep ascribing a goodness to one's actions.

But then there is also more to it than words. There is the real question about how one *does* think about ethics and world politics when one is the responsible leader of a civilization-protecting coalition, against a civilization-threatening totalitarianism, in an age of civilization-destroying weapons. These dramatic and near-absolute stakes should encourage—not an absolutistic ethic—but a carefully discriminating and responsible ethic. There should be sensitivity and a careful weighing of consequences, rather than an unbreakable set of principles.

The broad argument with which one rejects the views that begin with abstract law, ideals, principles, and moral order could be put this way: *fit an ethic critically to the world, instead of trying to fit the world ideally to an ethic.* Look to the world and criticize actions and policies within its real limitations.

Direct one's criticism to alternatives in the real world rather than to imperfections measured against an abstract moral standard. The moralizer is always measuring acts against a pure and perfect standard, finding alliances (for example) unworthy; he does not take up into his ethic the appraisal of the real alternatives, and therefore in acting in relation to his perfect standard he may cause results in the world quite contrary to his intent.

"Alliances" are rather suspect among such folk; they represent either too much international entanglement or too little. Alliances are impure because particular and defensive and exclusive by nature, because essentially creatures of power politics, and because the particular allies almost always leave something to be desired, by the strict standards of the "moral" men. Each particular, real ally, unfortunately, seems to fall short: the worst of them are dictatorships, and even the better ones are colonial powers, or unpurged former enemies, or socialist, or something. But to apply perfectionist standards with the idea that thus one was "moral" is the wrong way to proceed. One falls into the abyss that always yawns nearby, when the moral impulse comes into politics: being irresponsible in the name of being pure.

Try to confine one's evaluation of national policies to the specific and limited aspects of one situation. General sweeping commitments to "freedom," against "aggression," against "colonialism," for "liberation," for "justice" and "peace" cause cynicism when it is seen that they often cannot be honored. Declaratory policy, indicating only moral appraisal and not the intent to act, can have, as in the "liberation" case, unfortunate results. Overgeneralization is one curse of conscience in world affairs. Each specific case is sufficiently different from the others to make one chary about extending one's judgment very far beyond that case.

Direct one's evaluation to the effects or consequences of acts, rather than to questions of the quality of motive or character. A political ethic is pre-eminently an ethic of consequences, as Max Weber saw. The quality of intentions and motives is so far divorced from the merit of actions taken, in the complex world of international politics, as to be irrelevant to one's appraisal of the case for the purpose of acting and shaping policy.

Direct one's criticism to the creation of future conditions rather than to punishment and reward for past acts. Have done with the idea of international "criminals" who must be punished, of outlaws who are "condemned." The tangled world situation does not allow for the kind of moralistic desire to punish reprehensible behavior that has been an element, for example, in America's China policy.

An ethic for world leadership would take up into its idea of the good or right action the actual conditions of the world. It would be tied to the actualities of politics, in recognizing the diversity of interest of which politics is made up and in recognizing politics as the art of the *possible*. Choices are limited by actual conditions; ideals, desirable to speculative ethical reflection, are not possible of realization in the real world. The necessities of national survival, the limits of power, the anarchy of international life, the absence of a world-embracing moral order: all these elements, and more, limit the action a nation may take.

But if the real world sets limits, it also leaves possibilities. If a lack of power removes moral claims, a possession of power imposes them. The given facts of the historical situation create patterns of responsibility. Among the given facts in the present situation are America's great power, the interdependence of nations generally, the great dependence of other nations on the United States, and the global threat of the totalitarian Communist empire. America's moral role in that situation is not to proclaim crusades or to seek certain and final answers, but to pay careful and discriminating attention to the responsibilities of her position.

3

COLLECTIVE DEFENSE
versus COLLECTIVE SECURITY

Arnold Wolfers

THE RADICAL CHANGE that took place in American foreign
policy at the close of World War II—when the United States
shifted from a policy of "going it alone" to its new policy of "going
it with others"—has been widely discussed, explained, and ac-
claimed and may therefore seem to require no further discussion.
Yet, attention here is to be directed once more toward the new
policy not because the wisdom or necessity of the shift is to be
questioned, but, on the contrary, because troubles may arise along
the new path that, if not properly handled, might compel the United
States to return to the old policy of isolation out of sheer desperation. There may seem to be no cause for worry. Rarely has a foreign policy enjoyed as much public support as the new policy of
collaboration has. Hardly have any isolationist rumblings been
heard despite many disappointments and many harsh words against
the United States from most of the "others" with whom the United
States set out to collaborate. However, if the present unqualified
dedication to the new policy were to lead into serious dilemmas
and provoke widespread disillusionment, a swing of the pendulum
to the other extreme could not be ruled out. The following discussion will not cover all of the pitfalls on the road of collaboration
with other nations; it will be limited, instead, to those arising out of

49

the collective security system of the United Nations, widely heralded as the chief instrument of an up-to-date policy of "going it with others."

I

Before entering upon the particular case of the United States, I shall take up in a general or theoretical way the problems posed by a nonisolationist course of action under conditions as they exist in the contemporary world. Without seeking any precise definition of the terms—which will not prove necessary—I shall take an "isolationist" course to mean a policy of national security that neither relies on commitments by other nations to give assistance in defense nor involves the country in such commitments to others. The alternative—a policy of collaboration—then is one in which promises of future assistance, usually mutual and military in character, form one of the cornerstones of national defense, second in importance only to national armaments.

Prior to the establishment of the League of Nations in 1919, nonisolationist countries—including most of the major powers—based their collaborationist policy on treaties of alliance and related pacts, also known under the name of pacts of mutual assistance. As I shall hope to show, such alliances and pacts continue to represent the chief instrument and an indispensable means of every policy of collaboration for defense. Starting with the League of Nations Covenant and revived after World War II under the Charter of the United Nations, however, a second and clearly distinguishable course of collaboration, operating through a different instrument, has come into existence side by side with the traditional alliance; it is known as "collective security" and is generally considered the chief function of the United Nations. The question is whether the two types of policy and instrumentalities can be relied upon to work in constant harmony with each other, or whether there are possibilities of clashes between them that might seriously endanger the national security of the countries caught between their conflicting demands.

There are some striking similarities in substance between these two types of collaborationist policy. They have recently acquired a similarity in name, too, which is confusing because it tends to obscure their divergence. Both in the case of alliances, now usually called collective defense arrangements, and in the case of collective security under the United Nations, countries commit themselves to assist others against attack. In both instances, then, the victim of an attack expects his own defensive strength to be supplemented by the strength of other nations. And yet the two policies differ fundamentally in respect to both intent and modes of action, so that the cases in which they are complementary and helpful to each other are largely a matter of happy coincidence.

Nations enter into collective defense arrangements to ward off threats to their national security interests, as traditionally conceived, that emanate from some specific country or group of countries regarded as the chief national enemy, actual or potential. The motive behind such arrangements is the conviction that the creation of military strength sufficient to ward off the specific threat would be beyond their national capacity or would prove excessively and unnecessarily costly in view of the opportunities for mutual support and common defense.

The peculiarity of collective defense arrangements consists, therefore, in the fact that they are directed against an opponent known to the partners of the pacts, though he may not be named in the pact for reasons of diplomatic caution. One further peculiarity following from the first is that the allies can define in geographical terms the danger they are seeking to thwart and are thus able to make their military preparations and work out their strategy in advance of any conflagration. For example, when France and Russia in the 1890's—later France and the Soviet Union—were parties to an alliance, they were promising to assist each other against Germany with armed forces suited to and deployed for the particular purpose. Similar pacts and arrangements—some bilateral like our pact with South Korea, some multilateral like NATO—are so familiar today that no further elaboration is necessary. It is also obvious that such collective defense arrangements against specific opponents, when entered into by countries devoid of offensive purposes, are aimed primarily at deterrence, deterrence of the country against which the common strength and determination of the allies is visibly pitted.

Collective security belongs to a different and presumably better world, as Woodrow Wilson once said, which explains why it is so dear to the idealist who wants nations to have at least a foothold in the better world right now. In contrast to alliances, it is not the goal of collective security arrangements to provide their members with strength against their national enemies, or for the defense of their national interests, unless one redefines the terms "national enemy" and "national interest" in accordance with the philosophy upon which collective security rests. Collective security is directed against any and every country anywhere that commits an act of aggression, allies and friends included. The theory holds that "any aggressor anywhere" is in fact the national enemy of every country because, in violating the peace and law of the community of nations, it endangers, if indirectly, the peace and security of every nation. It is further argued that every country, as a consequence, has a "national interest" in protecting every victim of aggression, even if, in so doing, it may have to turn its back on its immediate national opponent or antagonize a reliable ally.

Whatever the merits or demerits of such a system of all-round protection against aggression—about which more will be said later —there is one difference in the effects of collective action under the two systems that needs to be stressed. Few of even the most forceful exponents of collective security expect it to assure the deterrence of all aggressors at the outset. Instead, they place their hopes on the success of a kind of learning process in which the punishment of one or more actual aggressors will deter subsequent would-be aggressors from deeds that would provoke "police action" against them. By itself this delay in the immediate effectiveness of the collective security system rules out any prestabilized harmony between collective defense and collective security. After all, during the period of the learning process with its indefinite duration, nations may be attacked or annihilated by their chief national opponents because they have diverted their strength to a struggle with some other aggressor or have antagonized and weakened an indispensable ally. There are other types of clashes that may occur between the two lines of policy, but it is worth while at this point to inquire into the tendency, at least in Western countries, to regard collective security and collective defense as supplementary and as mere variations of one and the same policy.

This assumption of harmony has several roots. One is of a legal character. The United Nations Charter in Article 51 explicitly permits collective self-defense—or, briefly, collective defense—which it calls an inherent right of nations. In the Covenant of the League of Nations, there was no such provision, a fact that caused a country like France embarrassment since she sought national security very largely through alliances. While she insisted that her alliances were merely "underpinning" the collective security system, others considered them incompatible with the League Covenant.[1] It was understandable, therefore, that France and the Soviet Union, allied once more against Germany, should have been particularly eager at San Francisco that the United Nations Charter legitimize alliances, which it does under the name of "collective self-defense," a provision supported by the United States, although for different reasons.

A second factor that tends to make the two lines of policy appear not only compatible but practically identical is of a semantic nature. If confusion were intended, nothing could have promoted it better than to describe alliances or coalitions as "collective defense arrangements," thereby joining them with collective security through the use of the same term "collective." It seems not unlikely that confusion was in fact intended, at least in some quarters. One can see why American statesmen should be particularly inclined to use the two terms as synonymous, often applying the term "collective security" to such collective defense arrangements as NATO and SEATO or even to such bilateral military pacts as the one concluded with South Korea or Nationalist China. Consciously or unconsciously, they are seeking to make these arrangements more palatable to a people they believe to be adverse to alliances as the "power political" instrument that Woodrow Wilson condemned as a chief cause of war. One would think, however, that the time has come to combat what popular prejudice against alliances may still exist. If a country's security is in serious danger and popular support for its defense measures is badly needed, the true value of alliances and related pacts of military assistance—all of which serve

---

[1] See the discussion of the problem in Arnold Wolfers, *Britain and France between Two Wars,* 1st edition (New York, 1940), pp. 167ff.

the same purpose as national armaments—should be widely recognized and accepted without moral qualms or inhibitions.

Finally, the self-deluding expectations in Western democratic countries that collective security and collective defense will regularly support each other grew out of the particular historical circumstances under which collective security was introduced and activated between 1919 and 1956. Collective security was first written into the law of nations at a time when aggression by the autocratic governments of the Central Powers was foremost in the minds of the peoples of the West. Later, when in the early thirties collective security became a live issue, it was again directed against nondemocratic countries: Fascist Italy, Nazi Germany, and autocratic Japan. Finally, when collective security under the United Nations Charter was first put into operation, the aggressor was North Korea, a member of the totalitarian Communist bloc. Thus, all through the period from the establishment of the League to the war in Korea, it was natural for many people in Western democracies to assume that committing themselves to deter or punish "any aggressor anywhere" meant in fact committing themselves to oppose nondemocratic aggressors who were their national enemies anyway. As long as this coincidence lasted, collective security and collective defense were indeed directed against the same opponent, and the two concepts supplemented rather than contradicted each other.

For France, the happy dream of a kind of prestabilized harmony between the two policies came to an end as early as the Ethiopian War of 1935, which was the only occasion on which the provisions for collective security in the League Covenant were applied. On that occasion, France was called upon to participate in a leading capacity in collective action against Italy just after she had allied herself with Italy against her national enemy, Nazi Germany. Some might argue that France had only herself to blame for her dilemma, inasmuch as she had allied herself with a nondemocratic and therefore potentially aggressive country, but such an argument carries little weight today when a limitation of collective defense pacts to the few truly democratic countries would almost certainly spell defeat for the West. But there were other more recent events that struck further blows at the illusion of harmony.

Soon after the Korean war had rekindled the hope that collective security under the United Nations would of necessity be directed against nondemocratic countries belonging to the Soviet bloc—the same countries, therefore, against which all Western collective defense arrangements were directed—the Suez crisis brought a rude awakening. The "aggressors" on this occasion were two of the leading democracies of Europe, and democratic Israel. The three countries resorted to war against Egypt in the very fashion that their own leaders and publicists, no less than those of other countries, had persistently labeled as "aggression" and condemned as a crime. No longer was there any necessity for proof that action "against any aggressor anywhere" might mean action against closest friends or allies even though they be democratic. Instead of supplementing each other, the two policies of collective defense and collective security crashed head-on as far as the West was concerned: countries committed to both had to choose between their conflicting commitments.

But the clashes that may occur between the two types of commitments to collective action are not limited to the kind of clash illustrated by the Suez or Abyssinian crises. Instead, there are three different kinds, all of which pose serious problems for countries caught in the dilemma.

So far, both under the League and under the United Nations, only the one just mentioned has actually occurred: the case in which nations are called upon to participate in collective security action—even in the mild form of condemnation—against a friendly or allied country on whose support they depend for defense against a recognized national enemy. When faced with the choice of either losing the support of Italy or defaulting on collective security, France chose the latter course. In the Suez crisis, the United States took the opposite line, upholding the principles of collective security despite the damage that might have resulted for two of her most essential alliances. Fortunately for the United States, the outcome was not calamitous because the three "aggressors" did the exceptional thing of restoring the *status quo ante* despite the absence of collective military sanctions. The members of the United Nations can hardly expect to resolve the dilemma as easily on every occasion.

A second type of clash may arise from the participation of a country's national enemy in collective security action against a third power. To take a fictitious example: if Greece were condemned for committing an act of aggression against Turkey and punitive action were recommended by the General Assembly of the United Nations, Bulgaria, as a member of the United Nations, would have the right to participate in "police action" against Greece and might do so with enthusiasm. In the course of such collective action, her troops might occupy Thrace, thereby upsetting the balance of power between East and West in the vital area of the Eastern Mediterranean. Who would venture to predict that the Bulgarians in such a case would withdraw from territory they had long coveted once the United Nations decided to call a halt to collective action and invited its members to restore the *status quo ante?* Instead, it would be in line with historical experience to expect that the military situation at the close of hostilities would profoundly affect the territorial provisions of any subsequent settlement. The results of initiating collective security measures in this hypothetical case, therefore, would probably be favorable to Bulgarian interests and damaging to the West. This example illustrates one of the dangers a country might face at a time of serious tension if the universal collective security system led national opponents to take part in common military action against a third power.

The third type of clash will not appear serious to people who are confident that their own country will never commit an act that many nations would condemn as aggression. Surely, few American statesmen have been worried that they were restricting their own freedom to act in defense of American security either by their constant efforts to strengthen and broaden the scope of collective security under the United Nations or by their success in popularizing the idea of "police action" against every aggressor. Yet, as Britain—once an equally staunch proponent of collective security—discovered to her sorrow in 1956, a policy that emphasizes the principles of collective security can, under certain conditions, prove a dangerous trap. If what is condemned as "aggression" were necessarily an act similar to Hitler's military invasion of Poland in 1939 or even to Britain's initiation of war against Egypt in 1956, some countries might well feel satisfied that they will never commit such follies or crimes nor risk, therefore, being accused of aggression. But if earlier events under the League of Nations were not enough to prove that the definition of aggression and the identification of the aggressor are most difficult problems and may often become highly controversial political issues, recent developments under the United Nations should be driving the point home.

Even in the era in which a country's expansion would usually take the form of an armed attack across national boundaries, it was often uncertain which of the belligerents had first attacked or which could be held responsible for the hostilities. One can recall the heated and prolonged controversy after World War I on the "war guilt" question.

With the dawn of the Cold War, with conditions of revolutionary upheaval and ideological conflict, the issue of defining aggression became a subject of new controversy. Now, states like the Soviet Union or the United Arab Republic have been relying on methods of extending control beyond their national boundaries that are more subtle than "armed attack." In response, an even more elusive concept, "indirect aggression," has been developed and come to be equated with the traditional type of aggression.

This extension of the meaning of aggression has had the unintended effect of leading to new and possibly more frequent situations in which the identification of the aggressor rests almost entirely on the sympathies, ideological predilections, fears and alignments of the United Nations members who are called upon to vote on the issue. One might easily imagine cases in which a nation that has decided to send troops into another country to help it defend itself against "indirect aggression" arrives to find that it is faced with a government installed by rebellion. This new government might seek to resist with its armed forces what it would call foreign military intervention, condemning it as an act of aggression. Especially at a time when it is not rare for two governments to exist side by side, both claiming to represent the same country and each, moreover, recognized by large groups of nations as the legitimate government, it is no longer possible to predict on which side the General Assembly might place the blame for aggression: on the side responsible for "indirect aggression" or on the side responsible for "military intervention." This uncertainty is greatly enhanced by the fact that "outside support" or "instigation" of a rebellion, as well as military "intervention" for its suppression, are terms referring to a wide variety of actions which lend themselves to an equally wide variety of judgments or rationalizations regarding their relative "aggressiveness."

Therefore, whether a country powerful enough to undertake military action is vulnerable to condemnation for aggression depends not simply on the danger that mad or vicious men will take over the reins of policy. Its vulnerability will depend no less on what collective defense measures it may feel compelled to take for its security. Here lies another source, then, for possible conflict between collective security and collective defense.

Despite the possibilities of such clashes between the policies of collective defense and collective security, it cannot be concluded, as a general proposition, that nations would do well to give up their commitments to one or both of these policies. Many states cannot forego collective defense because they lack the power of defending themselves without outside assistance; many may find that withdrawal from the collective security system in order to avoid the possible future embarrassment of conflicting commitments would cause them losses they dare not take. Because there is not likely to be any general answer that would fit the best interests of all countries, the possible solutions to the problem will be discussed in relation to the particular situation of the United States.

II

Once the outstanding exponent of an isolationist foreign policy, the United States has become involved in collaboration with other states on a scale and with a thoroughness that is unprecedented in history. As a consequence, the vexing problems that can arise from the contradictions between the two different collaborative policies may bear down on the United States with particular weight.

In the closing phases of World War II—when the Roosevelt administration decided that the United States should break away from its isolationist past, a move that gained broad public support— neither the administration nor the public had any intention of involving the country in a system of alliances or what today are called "collective defense arrangements." Instead, isolation was to give way to "collective security." Any policies smacking of old-time alliances would have found little favor at that time. A few advocates of the United Nations may have seen in a collective security system a kind of continuing alliance of the victors of World War II by which to deter and hold down the one-time Axis powers, or an alliance of the great powers that would enable them to control small mischief-makers. But, despite the veto provisions of the Charter, which excluded collective security action against the great powers and their clients, the general view was that the United States was committing itself to a policy designed to prevent or to fight aggression anywhere.

Even at San Francisco, where the United States joined with the Soviet Union and France in their demand that collective defense be explicitly sanctioned by the Charter—as it was by the inclusion of Article 51—the United States was not contemplating entering into the traditional type of military alliances. The United States, it is true, had signed the Act of Chapultepec in the spring of 1945. But this act prepared the ground not for an alliance but for a regionally circumscribed system of collective security for the Americas, directed against any country, inside or outside the group of signatories, that was deemed to have attacked any state in the Western Hemisphere. However, the Act of Chapultepec shared with the Franco-Soviet concept of alliances one essential feature: its signatories, like allied nations, insisted on the right to take common military action against a country they considered an aggressor without waiting for the Security Council to identify the aggressor or to decide on the action that should be taken against him. Thus, by a happy coincidence, the United States helped make compatible with the United Nations collective security system the concept of collective defense on which its own subsequent alliance policy was based.

The American position, and with it the American policy of "going it with others," underwent a second and highly consequential change when involvement in a life and death struggle with the Soviet bloc became an accomplished and recognized fact. Now the danger was no longer the abstract "aggressor anywhere," but the very concrete potential aggressor beyond the Iron Curtain who was soon to require the concentration of almost the total power of the

United States together with the power of a large array of allies. From that time on—except for a continuing reluctance to call alliances by their traditional name—the old American aversion to alliances evaporated. In fact, the United States now became the architect and leader of the most widespread and intricate system of alliances any country has found it necessary to establish in peacetime.

As a further consequence, the United States now became engaged in a double-track course of commitments: committing itself simultaneously to collective security under the United Nations and to numerous collective defense arrangements that were not subject to United Nations authority. It became vulnerable, thereby, to the adverse effects of any clashes that might arise between its two policies of collective action—particularly vulnerable, in fact, since it had become more deeply involved along both lines of policy than had any other country.

Before considering ways and means of eliminating or minimizing the adverse effects of such clashes, it is necessary to gain some idea of the relative importance of collective defense arrangements, on the one hand, and of collective security, on the other, as instruments toward the attainment of American foreign policy goals. It stands to reason that if one is less important than the other, it will have to bear the brunt of any concessions that may be necessary in order to free United States policy from the consequences of dangerous contradictions.

If one considers the position of the United States in the world today, the paramountcy of collective defense should hardly be open to question. The task of balancing the power of the Soviet bloc, as a minimum and necessary goal of American foreign policy, is a formidable one. Its successful accomplishment would probably transcend the power of the United States acting alone, even if the American people were prepared to make unlimited sacrifices. It is certainly a task that no country would voluntarily consent to undertake alone as long as other states are ready and able to share it. For this reason, pacts with other countries intended to assure the United States of allied support in the struggle with the Soviet bloc are presently one of the two pillars on which American national security is based, the other being the American national military establishment.

The character and significance of the support the United States can expect to receive from its partners in collective defense arrangements are not readily recognizable in every instance. Though far from negligible, the military forces that other states are maintaining at their own expense for defense against the Soviets are on the whole disappointing. But there are other contributions, besides military assistance in the literal sense of the term, that other countries are able and willing to make for the cause of Western security. In its remoteness from the confines of the Soviet bloc, the United States continues to be dependent on its ability to operate from territory beyond the seas. Many countries are making heavy sacrifices in terms of national pride, sovereignty, and safety against nuclear attack by placing their territory at the disposal of the United States, whether for the deployment of troops or for the establishment of air bases and missile-launching sites. Even when a country merely decides to place itself under American protection, accepting the United States as the guarantor of its security, it may thereby contribute to the purposes of the alliance system by making itself accessible to the military forces of the West while denying itself and its resources to the Soviet camp.

In speaking of mutual military assistance, one is moving within the realm of the classical alliance, or what may be called "collective defense" in the narrow sense of the term. Mutual military assistance forms the core—though not the whole—of the American system of pacts and agreements. It alone can serve to block Soviet military expansion. However, despite its continued importance, it is not enough. Even from the point of view of American and Western defense, agreements with other nations that contain no military provisions have become necessary. The Soviet bloc has not been slow to discover that, in the absence of opportunities for military expansion or in addition to them, there are other methods of gaining control over foreign governments and countries and thus of upsetting the world balance of power. The Communist drive for economic, ideological, and eventually political control over other states is hardly more easily contained than a Soviet military drive. Here, too, the support of other nations against the Communist threat is essential. In fact, if the "others," who are the direct targets of such nonmilitary expansion, refused to co-operate in warding off attacks on their independence, there is little the United States could do to meet these attacks. It was logical, therefore, that after realizing the new dimensions of the struggle, the United States should have extended the scope of its pacts and agreements with other states beyond the confines of a traditional alliance system. It is more accurate to speak of an American "alignment system" when discussing the United States collective defense effort.

There is no need to discuss in detail the kinds of arrangements that fall under the heading of alignments and do not constitute pacts of mutual assistance. The many agreements between the United States and other countries for economic and military aid and for support against subversion are well known. But it is worth pointing out that even "uncommitted" countries—which by definition are unwilling to enter into formal pacts of any sort—can be drawn into the alignment system by what might be called tacit agreement that they will remain genuinely neutral and will not grant special favors to the Soviet Union.[2]

Ties with uncommitted countries are bound to remain extremely tenuous, however. It has become customary in the West to speak of the Free World as if all of the non-Communist nations were aligned with one another in a common cause. But the term is the symbol of an aspiration rather than of a reality. Ever since the Cold War started, one of its chief features has been a bitter East-West struggle for the "in-between world." Early hopes have long been dashed that a policy of military containment would not merely arrest the tide of Soviet military expansion at the Iron and Bamboo Curtains, but also prevent the spread of Soviet influence to new areas. In many parts of Asia and Africa, a Soviet alignment system is in competition with the American system. The result so far has

---

[2] The aftermath of the Eisenhower Doctrine demonstrated how difficult and politically inexpedient it may be for some governments to enter into formal pacts with the United States that would tie them to one of the "military blocs." Although the doctrine was nothing but a unilateral American declaration, any Arab government that expressed approval of the doctrine was open to attack at home for "allying" its country with the United States.

been to leave some non-Communist countries leaning toward the Soviet bloc, others vacillating between the two sides, still others remaining strictly uncommitted, and, finally, others favoring loose ties with the West. Under these circumstances, the United States as the leader of the West has particularly cogent reasons to fear any situation in which it is compelled to antagonize non-Communist countries, as may happen if collective security commitments are invoked against one of them.

There is a certain irony in the way in which the process of antagonizing friends or allies tends to work. At times, the United States has more reason to worry about actions that antagonize a doubtful friend than about those that hurt a trusted ally. The "friend" may have more opportunity or more inclination to change over to the Soviet camp, or, by threatening to do so, may be in a better position to blackmail the United States. However, alliances—even with nations that depend heavily on American protection—are also vulnerable to the divisive effects of unwelcome American participation in collective security action. Unlike some of the uncommitted nations, like Egypt or Yugoslavia, France would hardly think of accepting Soviet military aid, not to speak of switching camps, if antagonized or humiliated by the kind of action under collective security that the United States took at the time of Suez. Yet, her government might not be able to assure continued French solidarity with the West if large sectors of the French public, out of resentment, were to join the ranks of those Frenchmen who already prefer nonresistance to the Soviets to the horrors of war.

It can be said, therefore, that American participation in United Nations collective security action against any one of its many partners—allies, friends, and neutrals—might lead any one of them to beg out of the alignment system or at least to become an unreliable, worthless, or even dangerous member of it. Whether there is any way in which the United States can protect itself against the possibility of arousing the sensitivity of its friends and allies to moves they consider inimical will be discussed later. Attention must first be directed to the American collective security commitments under the United Nations Charter.

If the collective defense system has become a chief mainstay of American national security, for the foreseeable future at least, its survival is worth any price in risks and sacrifices that is lower than the price of "going it alone." This being so, it will not be easy to find arguments justifying commitments under collective security that, potentially, have a disruptive influence on American collective defense arrangements.[3] However, the services the United States may expect from its participation in the United Nations collective security system need to be given careful consideration before we turn to a discussion of methods of preventing serious clashes between the two collective policies pursued by the United States.

There are cases in which collective security can serve as a valuable supplement to the American collective defense arrangements. Occasionally, it is the only available instrument with which to draw some uncommitted or neutral countries toward an attitude of partisanship and moral support for the United States and its allies and in favor of their actions of collective defense. Korea is a case in point. Since American intervention on behalf of South Korea was widely interpreted as representing "police action for the world community" and was placed under the auspices of the United Nations, it was easier for countries like India to side with the United States on the issue of North Korean aggression and to sympathize with its intervention in the war. Some countries were even willing to go beyond the mere condemnation of North Korea because in their opinion the war constituted United Nations police action. Here, the United Nations played the role of a kind of loose Free World alliance in accordance with the expectation mentioned ear-

---

[3] Readers may suspect that the present author will find such justification particularly difficult if they know that he has taken a dim view of collective security ever since its inception under the League of Nations. See his treatment of the subject, *op. cit.*, pp. 331 and 191ff., as well as his article on "Collective Security and the War in Korea," *Yale Review,* XLIII, No. 4 (1954), 481-496. For a thorough and critical analysis of collective security by other authors, see Kenneth W. Thompson, "Collective Security Reexamined," *American Political Science Review,* XLVII, No. 3 (1953), 753-72; Howard C. Johnson and Gerhart Niemeyer, "Collective Security—The Validity of an Ideal," *International Organization,* VIII, No. 1 (1954), 19-35; Ernst B. Haas, "Types of Collective Security: An Examination of Operational Concepts," *American Political Science Review,* XLIX, No. 1 (1955), 40-67; also George Liska, *International Equilibrium* (Cambridge, Mass., 1957), pp. 81-118.

lier: that collective security and collective defense would be in harmony with each other.

The Korean case may repeat itself in the case of other satellite attacks on non-Communist countries. However, in the event of aggression by the Soviet Union itself, the situation in all probability would be different. Even if the countries that created the United Nations at San Francisco had not been assured—thanks to the great-power veto in the Security Council—that they would never be called upon to take action against a major power, it is hard to imagine that, merely because they were partners in the United Nations collective security system, they would dare to assume the risk of condemning the Soviet Union as an aggressor or recommending its punishment. As a matter of fact, the conduct of most of the members of the United Nations at the time of Red China's intervention in the Korean war speaks for itself in this respect. Their readiness to take sides against the North Korean attacker did not reappear in the face of the danger that action against Red China might set off a major conflagration.

One can conclude, then, that collective security may be useful to the United States and its allies in deterring or stopping Soviet satellite countries, but it would obviously be folly to rely on it as a means of arresting the Soviet Union itself. Even in respect to the former case, it would be well to reckon with the possibility that events since Korea—the rise of Soviet and Red Chinese power and the new danger of two-way nuclear war—may have dampened the inclination of many countries to take hostile steps even against relatively weak members or associates of the Soviet bloc. It is necessary, therefore, to search for other advantages to be derived from commitment to United Nations collective security that are less far-reaching than gaining additional allies in a war.

Because the American policy of alignment requires that dozens of countries remain on good terms not only with the United States but also with one another, the pacification of the entire non-Communist world has come to be a goal of American foreign policy, second in importance only to the containment of the Soviet bloc itself. Therefore, to the extent to which the threat of sanctions under United Nations collective security provisions serves to deter non-Communist countries from undertaking aggressive action against one another, the United States stands to gain from the restraints thus imposed on its friends and allies. The importance of this service is hard to estimate. It is impossible to say how effective such deterrence has been or is likely to prove in the future, because there is no way of telling what wars would have occurred in the absence of these provisions. It is quite likely that fear of provoking the United States by flagrant violation of the peace acts as the main deterrent and would operate even if the United States were not committed under the Charter to take part in collective action against aggressors.

There is another line along which the collective security system may affect the United States, but here only hindsight will tell whether its impact on the whole is helpful or harmful to the United States. The fear of being accused of aggression in the United Nations General Assembly, even by a minority of its members, may place restraints on the United States itself. Whether it has done so in the past is hard to judge. If such restraints were operative at the time of the Lebanese crisis in 1958, preventing a "march on Baghdad," they were probably imposed more by the fear of Soviet reactions than of any displeasure of the United Nations. However, for better or for worse, defensive action, particularly against what the United States regards as "indirect aggression," is rendered more difficult by the fact that "world opinion," opposed to any steps involving the risk of war, may in the name of collective security be turned against the United States.

The services discussed so far that collective security can render to the United States can hardly compensate for the danger and losses that may arise from clashes with American collective defense. Therefore, if continued participation is justified, or even indispensable, the reason must lie elsewhere. The fact is that promotion of the idea of collective security has created a psychological situation in which the United States cannot turn its back on the concept, not because of what collective security can accomplish and actually has accomplished, but because of what millions of people inside and outside the United States believe it may achieve in time. It has come to be the chief symbol of hope that international relations someday will be brought under the rule of law and that a community of nations will develop in which there will be no more war.

A reputation for dedication to such a system and for leadership in its operation has become an asset that the United States could forego only at a high cost in terms of appeal to foreign peoples and also of public support for its foreign policy at home.

Thus, by a kind of irony, a collective security system that may seriously interfere with the alignment system has become an important ingredient of the latter because of the place it holds in the minds of people throughout the world. With suspicion of American intentions rife as it is throughout the non-Communist world, withdrawal from the collective security system, however carefully explained, would be interpreted in many places as a move dictated by American aggressive or imperialist aims. Many friends would be lost and much antagonism aroused if it could be said—and be made a topic of Soviet propaganda—that the United States was betraying man's hopes for peace and lawfulness.

III

From what has been said about the two lines of collective policy, it follows, then, that the United States must remain saddled with its two-track policy and its simultaneous commitments to collective defense and collective security. While a collapse of the collective defense system would be a calamity of the first magnitude and would allow no alternative except a return to a highly hazardous and extremely costly policy of "going it alone," withdrawal from collective security commitments and exclusive reliance on collective defense would also be imprudent methods of escaping the dilemmas of the two-track policy.

How serious are these dilemmas likely to be in the particular case of the United States? There can be no doubt that a direct conflict between the American commitment under the United Nations Charter and its commitment to allies and friends under the alignment system can become a reality. Yet, if attention were limited to the Suez experience, one might be inclined to minimize the potentialities for serious trouble. While one could not imagine a severer blow to the American collective defense effort than would have resulted from an actual break with Britain, America's most important ally, and with France, such a break did not in fact occur.

However, there are a number of reasons, which may never be du-
plicated, why the break was avoided in this particular instance.
Britain, France, and Israel gave in to the demand of re-establishing
the *status quo ante* before any more compelling action than condemnation was recommended or taken. One need only imagine the
gravity of America's dilemma if Britain and France—or even Israel
alone—had persisted in their military efforts and if the United
States had been unable to prevent a United Nations vote recommending coercive measures against the "aggressor" or "aggressors."
Moreover, in the Suez case, the American decision to favor its
collective security commitments and to join in condemning the
"aggressors" did not antagonize the entire British and French
peoples, large sectors of which were no less hostile to the invasion
than was the American government. Many realized, too, that the
United States had pulled the rug out from under Soviet intervention and, for the time being at least, prevented a radical shift of the
Arab countries in the direction of the Soviet camp.

It is easy to imagine situations that would lack these redeeming
features. To take a fictitious illustration: if France were to be condemned for launching a military attack on Tunisia and if she persisted in her action as constituting defense of her own territory,
another American decision in favor of collective security might
leave France with no alternative but to get out of NATO. Here,
then, would be a case in which the collective security commitment
would lead to an almost irreparable disruption of the American
alliance system in Europe and thus of the Western policy of collective defense against the East.

The potential threat to American security from American involvement in the second type of clash—that is, the dangers posed
by the participation of its national enemy in United Nations "police
action"—follows from what has been said earlier. Whether or not
the United States decided to join in supporting action recommended
by the United Nations, the existence of the collective security system would open the door to Soviet military action beyond its borders. If Britain, France, and Israel in 1956 had not complied in
time with the recommendations of the United Nations General Assembly, there was nothing to prevent the Soviet Union from taking
the lead in military sanctions, arrogating to its armed forces the title

and function of a "police force of the community of nations." The collective security provisions of the Charter would legalize such Soviet military action, which might completely upset the world balance of power. One cannot help pointing to the grotesque contradiction between a collective defense system directed against a national opponent and a collective security system that may call for military action by that same opponent against an indispensable ally in the collective defense effort.

Finally, one cannot rule out the possibility that the United States could become involved in the third type of clash: that is, American collective defense action opposed by other nations in the name of collective security. Restraints imposed upon the United States in its efforts to stop or defeat what it considers "indirect aggression" were mentioned earlier. Under the Truman Doctrine—though not under the Eisenhower Doctrine, which speaks only of "overt armed aggression"—the United States proclaimed its intention of supporting "free peoples who are resisting attempted subjugation by armed minorities or by outside pressures," whether by "direct or indirect aggression." The United States confirmed this intention by its action in Lebanon. If American military assistance for this purpose reaches a threatened country before its government has been overthrown, as was the case in Lebanon, there can be no question either of American aggression or of an American initiation of international hostilities.

But it takes little imagination to visualize a situation in which the dispatch of military forces would coincide with the overthrow of the native government and lead to hostilities with the armed forces at the disposal of the new rebel government. In such a case, there can be no assurance that a majority of the United Nations members would see eye to eye with the United States in deciding which of the two belligerents was to blame for the hostilities or for their continuation. Even if no formal condemnation of the United States occurred, the American position might be gravely damaged by the present world-wide inclination to pin the label of aggressor on one party to every military encounter—an inclination that has been fostered by years of collective security propaganda. The choice might be between losing a friend or an area deemed vital to American security and arousing the opposition, if not open hostility, of large numbers of nations belonging to the American alignment system. The dilemma would be particularly serious for an American government that had sought to present the United States as the chief champion of collective security.

IV

If it is true, then, that serious embarrassments are in store for the United States on its double-track road of going-it-with-others, the question of how to meet the problem becomes one of immediate importance.

One way out is usually open: a course of action known as "muddling through," which means trusting one's ability to avoid major damage by *ad hoc* maneuvers taken on the spur of the moment. Sometimes there is no better solution, but it is useful even then to anticipate the kind of difficulties that may lie ahead so that improvisation, or *ad hoc* adjustments, will not aggravate rather than remedy a distressing situation. It need not be left entirely to instinct, for example, to decide whether it is wiser to antagonize ally "X," at the risk of losing him, than to run counter to the views of a large body of opinion in the General Assembly. A continuous and careful check on the value of ally "X" to American defense policy and an equally careful scrutiny of the respect and authority enjoyed by changing majorities in the General Assembly may prove helpful to future decisions.

However, there is no need to resign oneself to the hazardous game of improvisation. Even though continuing along the line of both collective security and collective defense, the United States can modify the execution of its two policies of collective action in a way conducive to greater harmony between them.

The fact that the alignment system needs to be preserved—in fact, continuously and substantially strengthened—does not imply that every member of the system is essential to American security and cannot be antagonized. Even if there were no collective security system, the United States could not always escape the necessity of having to choose among its friends and allies. At one time, for example, it looked as if the Cyprus crisis might create the need for such a choice irrespective of whether questions of aggression and collective security were to arise. If the United States wants to be in a position to participate on occasion in the condemnation or even punishment of a non-Communist country, it must be prepared to get along without that particular country.

While not every ally is dispensable—if France turned her back on NATO, the chance of defending Europe, slim enough as it is, might disappear completely—the United States, in some cases, might compensate for the loss of a weak, half-hearted, or unreliable member of the alignment system by increasing its own armaments or its economic and military aid to the remaining members. Excessive fear of losing friends opens the door to blackmail. Moreover, such fear may be predicated only on an unwillingness, often allegedly dictated by limitations on American solvency, that in fact stems only from limitations on the readiness to raise and pay higher taxes. The United States cannot afford to tell every blackmailing country to go over to the Communists if it pleases, as has sometimes been proposed, since the support of some nations is strategically indispensable. Nevertheless, the present boundary line separating East and West is largely accidental, after all, and therefore allows for some flexibility. If the United States was able to survive the loss of Czechoslovakia and of continental China, it would be sad indeed if it had now become so vulnerable to defections and loss of prestige that it could not make up for the loss of less important countries, particularly if the loss consisted merely in their shift from alliance to neutrality.

Flexibility may help in yet another direction without requiring sacrifices at the expense of collective defense. The United States will not always lose a friend or ally if, in pursuit of collective security action, it antagonizes a non-Communist government. The government in question and its policy may be so unpopular with its own people that American opposition to its policy—even action against it—will win more reliable support for the United States in the long run than could be obtained by surrender to its demands. However, the narrow limitations on this type of flexibility need to be stressed. Only too frequently the choice today is between a government that is unpopular at home but strongly pro-Western and one that gains most of its popularity by its hostility toward the

United States or even by its pronounced partisanship for the Soviet Union.

All in all, only a minimal alleviation of the dilemmas discussed here seems possible through modifications of the American policy of collective defense and alignment. It becomes all the more important, therefore, to look for practical changes in the American policy toward collective security that may offer a solution. Fortunately, there is more room for modification in this area.

Since American security is dependent upon the continuation of her alignment system, the United States has a major interest in avoiding situations in which it has to take sides against any member of this system, whether to condemn, stop, or punish it. Under these circumstances, it should be the objective of American policy within the United Nations to discourage rather than to promote a policy of labeling as the aggressor one of the parties to every violent international conflict. Some of the weaker would-be aggressors may be deterred by fear of condemnation or punishment, but the price of this deterrence is high. If it fails, and if the "police force" is called into action, all of the dangerous consequences discussed earlier threaten to unroll themselves: an essential ally may be antagonized beyond repair; hostilities may spread far beyond the confines of the original theater of conflict; the Soviet bloc may be given an opportunity to take "police action" beyond its borders; the United States itself may be accused of initiating the trouble. It is suggested, therefore, that American efforts to turn the United Nations into a "strong reed"—efforts to which the other members of the United Nations have given lip service at best—may backfire. The fact that the United States has engaged in such efforts should not be in doubt. American initiative has been directed, for example, toward a reinterpretation of the Charter that will permit the veto-free General Assembly to recommend police action and that will make such recommendations binding upon the members of the United Nations. The United States has even insisted that it has the right and the intention to enforce the principles of the Charter against an aggressor in cases in which neither the Security Council nor the General Assembly is prepared to recommend police action.

The possibility of dangerous clashes between collective defense and collective security commitments can be minimized by a reversal of the present trend of American policy, namely by an effort to push into the background rather than to emphasize the concepts of "enforcement of the peace" and "police action." These concepts should better be reserved for cases of unmistakable and flagrant initiation of war across recognized national boundaries and be considered the *ultima ratio* of American and United Nations peace strategy.

If taken alone, modifications in the tenor of United States collective security policy along the lines suggested might be mistaken as a sign of a general decline of American confidence in the United Nations as an instrument for the prevention of war. Such a view would be based, however, on an excessively narrow conception of the ways in which the United Nations can help promote peace, a misconception fostered over the years by official and unofficial American pronouncements. Because the major emphasis has been placed on the collective security or "enforcement of peace" functions of the United Nations, the role the world organization can play as a mediator and conciliator on the road to compromise and peaceful settlement—as well as the importance of such mediation —has received scant attention and credit. In practice, the chief services the United Nations has been able to render to the peace of the world have been in this noncoercive field and specifically in its efforts to bring the parties to a dispute to some form of accommodation or truce. These efforts include the dispatch of observation teams and the policing of borders or strips of territory undertaken in agreement with both parties. Therefore, if the value of the United Nations to the cause of world peace is not to be jeopardized, and if the intentions of the United States are not to be misunderstood, it is imperative that any reduction in American zeal for the identification, condemnation, or punishment of aggressors be accompanied by conspicuous efforts both to strengthen the role of the United Nations as a mediator and conciliator and to convince world opinion that the best services the United Nations can render in the field of pacification lie in the pursuit of such a role.

The United States has a special stake in elevating respect for United Nations mediation above that for "enforcement." It has little need, if any, for the assistance of collective security in its great struggle with the Soviet bloc; in its national armaments and collective defense arrangements, it has more reliable means of deterrence and defense than anything collective security could provide. In addition, the reliability of these arrangements will suffer if collective security is not prevented from throwing roadblocks in their path. And within the non-Communist world, all the way from North Africa through the Middle East to Southeast Asia and the Far East, where impassioned antagonism and violence are erupting again and again, mediation by the United Nations offers the most promise of preventing a split or breakdown of the American alignment system. Not that mediation is a panacea: it has failed conspicuously on more than one occasion, whether undertaken by the United Nations or by the United States itself. Also, it may hurt American interests if the majority of the members of the United Nations, fearful of war, expect the United States to make most of the concessions. But collective security may fail, too, even when it enjoys the complete support of the United States. It failed as a deterrent prior both to the Korean war and the Suez adventure; and, when put into practice, it means war rather than peace, though such war be called "police action." The United States will have done all it can for both its own protection and that of its friends and allies if it succeeds in maintaining a reliable collective defense network backed by adequate national armaments and if, in addition, it gives strong support to United Nations mediatory and conciliatory efforts within the non-Soviet world while preserving United Nations collective security as a last resort.

4

THE EVOLUTION OF COLLEC-
TIVE SECURITY UNDER THE
UNITED NATIONS CHARTER

Erich Hula

IT WOULD BE difficult to gauge the extent to which disappointment in the United Nations contributes to the malaise that manifests itself so clearly in current American discussions on foreign policy. There is no question, however, but that this disappointment has some share in creating and fostering the general discomfort. True, there has recently been no marked increase in the perennial discontent caused by the failure of the United Nations to live up to the expectations that we originally placed on it as a collective security organization. We seem to have resigned ourselves to the modest role it is actually capable of playing. At any rate, we have ceased to look upon it as an instrument that could conduce to our military security. Realizing that the ideal of an international community of power, organized upon the pattern of the national community, is beyond reach, we have turned to the device, employed in traditional diplomacy, of balancing power against power. We try, accordingly, to ensure the global equilibrium between our forces and those of potential enemies by means of national armaments and defensive alliances, and, in general, by lending our individual support, military or otherwise, to the potential victims of aggression. Though we have thus been thrown back, very much to our own dislike, upon the conventional methods of protecting the national interest, the maintenance of international peace and security, the end for which the United Nations was established, remains the lodestar of our actions. It is for this reason that we are sincerely convinced that our policies serve ultimately not only our own interests but also the interests of the international community as a whole. For this reason also we felt certain that our obligations under the Charter could not possibly prove burdensome for us in pursuing our peaceful objectives. But there is no denying that recent experience has somewhat shaken us in that certainty. Nor can there be any doubt that the growing realization of the difficulty of bringing into harmony the rules of the game of power politics, which we are unfortunately compelled to play, with the principles of a system that was intended to end this game, is producing feelings of uneasiness about the United Nations that differ in kind from the usual sentiments of distress due to its limited effectiveness as an instrument of peace.

We became keenly aware of that difficulty for the first time in the Suez Canal crisis of 1956-1957. Neither the North Atlantic Treaty nor any of the other collective defense arrangements to which we are party obligates us, admittedly, to lend our allies military or any other assistance in case they themselves resort to the use of force prohibited by the Charter. In fact, those agreements, being all subject to the higher law of the Charter, do not even obligate us to remain neutral in such a case. The British-French military action against Egypt did not present us, therefore, with a legal dilemma, properly speaking. But the political dilemma for that reason was not any less perplexing for us. The landing of armed forces on Egyptian soil, preceded by bombardment from the air, was undoubtedly prima facie a violation of the Charter. The political objective of the British and French, however, was none other than to protect vital interests of their own as well as the *status quo* in the Middle East, in the maintenance of which we were hardly less interested than the United Kingdom and France themselves, considering that these two countries are the main pillars of our alliances.

Thus, in terms of balance of power politics, the attitude for us to take would have been to lend the two Western governments our diplomatic support, though not necessarily without exercising a restraining influence upon them. To be sure, it is questionable whether the British-French action, leaving aside the moral issues involved, was good power politics or whether it would have been good power politics for us to back them. It is indeed arguable that concern for our relations with the rising Arab nations, and for the Russian competition with us in currying their favor, were equally relevant elements in a realistic evaluation of the situation and the ways in which we might meet it. But the fact of the matter is that the ideology on which the collective security system of the United Nations presumably rests left us no choice but to take sides against the two Western powers and thus to imperil the very alliance that is meant to give us the security the United Nations system does not provide.

Hence we found ourselves voting in the United Nations, together with the Soviet Union, for the immediate withdrawal of the French-British forces from Egyptian territory. Nor might it have remained a matter of merely voting against our principal allies had they not actually desisted from pursuing their precipitate course, thus sparing us the prospect of confronting the dilemma in its most cruel form. Since our participation in sanctions against the United Kingdom and France almost certainly would have had disastrous effects upon our whole defense posture, one wonders whether we could have afforded to run so formidable a risk rather than to shrink from the commitments of the Charter. In fact, from the very moment we submitted the case to the United Nations we purposely refrained from proposing an explicit moral censure of the alleged aggressors, and thus tried to soften the diplomatic defeat we helped to inflict upon them. This moderation must undoubtedly be credited, among other factors, with the quick healing of the wounds the Western alliance had suffered from that unfortunate incident. The ease with which friendship was restored among the three Atlantic powers could not, however, dim again our awareness of the problems that are liable to arise whenever the universal abstract commitments of collective security happen to cut across rather than coincide with our particular concrete alignments.

Another recent experience to suggest that the obligations of the Charter might after all be more burdensome than we had assumed was the Middle Eastern crisis of 1958, which focused on Lebanon and Jordan. It was of a less serious nature than the Suez crisis, but the lesson it taught was hardly less significant. In the first place, it was an American action this time, the landing of our Marines on the shores of Lebanon, that aroused strong opposition in the United Nations. This reaction was far from surprising in so far as it was based upon political objections. True, we were sincerely convinced that we had to comply with the request of the lawful Lebanese government, friendly to us though not formally allied with us, to assist it against domestic subversive forces aided from abroad, not only because we had ourselves a stake in maintaining the Middle Eastern *status quo* but also because we felt our action was required in order to assure respect for the purposes and principles of the Charter. But it was nonetheless not unlikely that our own appraisal of the situation and our choice of the means of meeting it would be challenged, and not merely by members of the Soviet bloc. In fact, the political necessity and wisdom of the action were also seriously questioned by large sections of American public opinion itself.

What we hardly expected, however, was that the legality of our action in terms of the Charter was to be questioned, and again not only by members of the Communist bloc. The Charter implicitly forbids intervention, in the sense of coercive interference, by one state in the domestic affairs of another. Such intervention is obviously inconsistent both with the principle of sovereign equality and with the prohibition of the use of force. But the Charter does not preclude the assistance of one government to another at the latter's request. The right to request and render assistance against domestic subversion, recognized in general international law, is today, in fact, even more indispensable than it has been at other periods, since indirect aggression plays an exceptionally large role in the current international struggle for power. In a revolutionary age like ours, domestic subversive forces are more often than not supported, if not instigated, by foreign governments bent upon extending their dominion or at least their influence. Nor is it reasonable to argue that governments that are threatened by domestic subversion and possibly indirect aggression should rely exclusively upon collective protection by the United Nations instead of resorting to the traditional method of seeking the assistance of a friendly power. For the United Nations is hardly less problematical as an instrument for dealing effectively with indirect aggression than with direct aggression. We have proved, at considerable risk, by our policy in the Suez crisis that we do not propose to revert to the doctrine, applied and upheld by statesmen and international lawyers of former times, that intervention in the affairs of another state against its will is lawful if it is intended to preserve the balance of power. But we have made it equally clear in the Lebanon case that we are not ready to accept the view according to which our commitments under the United Nations Charter forbid us to lend military support to those potential victims of indirect aggression that request such aid.

The experience of the Suez and Lebanon cases may easily repeat itself. Indeed, it is likely that the difficulty of harmonizing our own policies with those of the world body will increase rather than diminish, owing to the steadily growing membership of the United Nations and its changing political complexion. Moreover, the weakening of our diplomatic position in world politics must unavoidably lessen our influence inside the organization. The disappointment about this trend will be the keener because initially we swayed the councils of the United Nations as no single power ever was able to sway those of the League of Nations. The development might even give new impetus to those who want to get along without the United Nations, hoping vainly to escape from the ugly realities of current international politics by turning away from the mirror reflecting them. Such counsel should not be heeded and in fact is not likely to be. But we certainly have good reasons for re-examining our actual commitments under the Charter and the degree of freedom of action they leave us for securing our national existence by alliance policy and other devices of traditional diplomacy. Since the same obligations are incumbent upon us as upon other members of the United Nations, the question can also be asked in general terms: What is the actual law of collective security?

To speak of the actual law of collective security is to imply that it is not necessarily identical with the written law of the Charter. The application, or for that matter the nonapplication, of legal rules is apt to modify their original meaning or even to affect their validity. The Charter has been subject to the law of change no less than any other constitutional document, international or municipal. But we must nonetheless go back to the original legal conceptions underlying the Charter if we want to appraise the subsequent development correctly. There is another reason for analyzing once more the philosophy of Dumbarton Oaks and San Francisco. We are often tempted, by idealistic or by practical motives, to take or declare as law what in truth is only the ideology, or rather a specific ideology, of collective security, superimposed upon the legal content of the Charter. In fact, the discrepancies between a political idea and the norms by which it is translated into a legal system could hardly ever be greater than they are in this case.

The political idea and the technical term of collective security imply that all members participating in the system enjoy equal protection against aggression launched from any quarter whatsoever. One may wonder therefore whether the legal system conceived at Dumbarton Oaks and presented to the conferees of San Francisco as a genuine collective security system actually deserves this designation. The Dumbarton Oaks Proposals and the law of the Charter based upon them were in many respects more reminiscent of the philosophy of the European Concert of Powers than of that of the League of Nations, the historical prototype of a collective security system. The Charter system of San Francisco was not meant to be universally applicable. The monopoly of the Security Council in all matters relating to the enforcement of international peace and security and the requirement of unanimity of its five permanent members made collective action against any of the great powers practically impossible. The lesser powers were thus left unprotected against the gravest danger threatening them, aggression by a superior power. It could be little consolation to them that the great powers themselves could not expect the assistance of the organization against one of their peers. Like the European Concert, but unlike the League of Nations, the collective security system of San Francisco was designed to enforce peace among the smaller nations only. The proponents of the Charter felt—and rightly so—that the organization would hardly be capable of deterring a great nation from aggression. They also were inclined to think—though mistakenly—that the chief threat to the new international order was likely to be the renewal of aggressive policies by the Axis powers, defeated in World War II.

The collective security system of the Charter was and still is deficient in yet another important respect. The scope of the substantive protection it offers to members of the United Nations, within the limits of the protection it offers, is legally narrower than the protection afforded by the Covenant of the League. The members both of the League and of the United Nations were and are bound to respect the territorial integrity and political independence of other nations. But only the Covenant imposed upon its parties the additional obligation of preserving one another against external aggression. No positive guarantee of territorial integrity and political independence, be it as an obligation of the several members or of the organization itself, was incorporated into the Charter of the United Nations, although suggestions to that effect were made at San Francisco. It is hardly surprising, therefore, that the minor powers wondered how much worth they could attach to the collective protection they were promised against aggression, considering that at the same time they were denied a guarantee of their existence and possessions. In view of the deliberate omission of a positive guarantee, it is all the more significant that the Charter does not even stipulate the nonrecognition of territorial acquisitions or of other advantages obtained in defiance of the prohibition of force. Proposals submitted to the San Francisco Conference that the Charter should subscribe to the principle *ex injuria jus non oritur* failed of acceptance.

The fact that the Charter, as a spokesman of the smaller states bitterly remarked at San Francisco, was to contain "no clear declaration that the security of individual members is the objective" was not the only reason the minor powers felt disturbed. They noticed other symptoms as well that seemed to point to a system of collective security in which the territorial integrity and political independence of its members, not to mention their lesser rights, might be considered expendable. In fact, they were inclined to see in the future Security Council under the domination of its permanent members an instrumentality for effecting settlements on the Ethiopian or Munich model.

Politically speaking, their fear of a concert of the great powers that would actually be capable of taking common action was as unrealistic as was the hope of those who tried to revive what Lord Salisbury once called "the federated action of Europe," now on a global scale and in such democratically modified form as the spirit of the twentieth century required. But one can understand nevertheless, even today, why the legal concepts underlying the collective security system of the Charter should have disturbed the smaller nations. The primacy of peace was stressed so strongly that one could very well wonder whether the organization would not feel tempted, if not entitled, to neglect considerations of law and justice for the sake of peace. One can appreciate this anxiety all the better because the Charter also seemed to be leaning in the direction of a highly dynamic conception of peace that favors the peaceful change of the *status quo* where it is needed in the interest of peace. It can hardly be denied, moreover, that the Security Council was intended to possess sufficiently broad powers, legal and physical, to effect policies based upon such a philosophy.

The tendency to overemphasize the value of peace was particularly striking in the Dumbarton Oaks Proposals in which references to international law and justice, as standards to be observed by the organization in its several activities, were almost completely lacking. This tendency is still visible in the Charter itself, though to a lesser extent. For the minor powers were not entirely unsuccessful at San Francisco in their efforts to inspire into the Dumbarton Oaks Proposals, as one of their representatives put it, "something like a soul-power." The Charter provides that the organization should strive for the settlement of international disputes "in conformity with the principles of justice and international law." But it is significant that an Egyptian amendment according to which the United Nations should be bound by the same requirement when discharging its enforcement function under Chapter VII of the Charter was rejected at San Francisco.

The dynamic conception of peace, too, is less conspicuous in the Charter than in the Dumbarton Oaks Proposals. In Chapter VI of the Charter, the Security Council is given only recommendatory powers when engaged in the adjustment or settlement of international disputes or situations. But it was felt all the same, and not merely by the smaller states, that the Security Council might also make use of the compulsory power it was to possess in the case of enforcement measures to impose its own terms of settlement upon the parties to a conflict. Instead of simply applying existing law, the Security Council might change it and create new law, thus exercising legislative power for all practical intents and purposes. In other words, like the members of the European Concert before them, the permanent members of the Security Council might consider themselves entitled to assert, through the instrumentality of the Council, the legal power to regulate important matters concerning other states, including territorial and even domestic constitutional questions, without being subject themselves to a higher authority. That the Charter lent itself to such an interpretation of the powers of the Security Council and at the same time did not stipulate a positive guarantee of the integrity and independence of the member countries, seemed to indicate that the organization was intended to assure the peaceful evolution of the international political order through collective procedures rather than the strict maintenance of the *status quo*.

Any device to secure the peaceful revision of treaties and of other conditions causing grave international friction is highly commendable. There can be no permanent peace even in a national community if its members insist on absolute rights and deny to the government the authority and power to control and limit them. All that the members of a national community can legitimately claim is that they participate in some form or other in the operation of the government and that the exercise of governmental authority and power be subject to the law. As the United Nations was originally conceived, the small nations' share in controlling activities and decisions of the organization was far from equal to that of the great nations. Moreover, the Charter can hardly be said to contain the constitutional safeguards required for a government of law. Its authors purposely refrained from inserting in the

Charter what might be called an international bill of the rights of states. Out of the seven principles, enumerated in Article 2, which shall determine the conduct of the organization and its members, only two are formulated in terms of rights of states, namely, the principles of sovereign equality and of the exclusion of domestic matters from United Nations jurisdiction. The five other principles set forth the duties they must observe in their relations with one another and with the organization. Last but not least, the statement of principles concerning the rights and obligations of members is sufficiently broad to permit a flexible interpretation. This flexibility could be expected to work in favor of the several members rather than of the organization in case the latter should fail to acquire the authority and power with which the fathers of the Charter tried by legal means to endow it. But it is hardly surprising that the smaller nations asked themselves, nonetheless, what the weakness of constitutional safeguards for assuring a government of law would mean for them, particularly if the Security Council should develop into a supranational government.

We have so far discussed the general legal notions underlying the collective security system envisaged in the Charter and have come to the conclusion that they differ greatly from those upon which the League of Nations was based. They resemble, instead, *mutatis mutandis* the ideas underlying the nineteenth century European Concert of Powers. To what extent can the same be said of the enforcement machinery and the character of the enforcement measures for which the Charter has made provision?

Such successes as the European Concert had in maintaining international peace were undoubtedly due to the potential military power that it could mobilize to enforce its decisions. The actual display and use of collective force were left to improvisation, however. The same held true for the sanctions of the League. The United Nations was to be far more advanced than any collective peace system preceding it, in that the availability to the Security Council of armed forces would be assured by previous military agreements concluded between the Council and the members of the organization. Nor was the participation of smaller nations in the proceedings and measures of Chapter VII to be permitted to cause undue complications and delays. Contrary to the League system, which left the decision on the *casus foederis* and on sanctions in the hands of the several states, the enforcement system of the United Nations was to be highly centralized. The determination whether enforcement measures should be taken, and if so what kind, was to be the exclusive prerogative of the Security Council in which the great powers were to be dominant. The Council was also to determine whether all or only some of the members of the United Nations should participate in a particular collective action. The latter provision subsequently became the basis of the legal contention that, contrary to the League, the status of neutrality was not necessarily incompatible with the obligations of United Nations membership; the same conclusion might also be drawn from the legal character of the enforcement measures in general.

A sober analysis of the peculiar character of enforcement measures under the Charter is more suggestive than anything else of the wide discrepancies between the legal content of the Charter, as it was conceived by its authors, and the ideological layer superimposed thereupon.

The Concert of Europe, and in fact also the League, operated at a time when, according to a widely held view, the sovereignty of the state implied its practically unlimited right to go to war. True, the Covenant established some restrictions on that alleged right, but essentially they were merely procedural limitations. Only the Kellogg Pact and, following it, the Charter, took a further step toward prohibiting war and any use of force regardless of the substantive reason for resorting thereto. Once the use of force is considered a contravention of law, except in self-defense, it is only natural—in view of the moral opprobrium attaching to it and of its disastrous consequences in human terms —to look upon the breach of the prohibition of force as a crime and to interpret collective action against such a breach as a criminal procedure serving a punitive purpose. One might hope, moreover, that the deterrent effect of a prohibition of war and force upon a potential aggressor would be still greater if he could expect not only to be repelled by the united counterforce of the international community but to be publicly condemned as a criminal. The founders of the United Nations could have been tempted to adopt the punitive conception for still another reason. Thinking of the Security Council, acting under Chapter VII, as a kind of supranational government, they would have been only consistent had they construed the enforcement power of the Council in analogy to the punitive power of a municipal government. They were less anxious, however, to be consistent than they were to devise a legal procedure that would suit the structure of international society and best serve the interests of international peace, the paramount purpose of the United Nations.

It is significant that the prohibition of force is stated in the Charter in the form of a general principle and in words the meaning of which has been controversial among statesmen and international lawyers ever since 1945. Article 2, paragraph 4 obligates all members to "refrain in their international relations from the threat or use of force against the territorial integrity or political independence of any state, or in any other manner inconsistent with the Purposes of the United Nations." The reference to territorial integrity and political independence and to the purposes of the United Nations has been interpreted to imply that it is the intent rather than the objective character of an action that makes the threat or use of force unlawful. To be sure, such interpretation does not deprive Article 2, paragraph 4 of the Charter of its normative character, but it does suggest the lawgiver's intention to assure that the concrete meaning of the norm should be established in close relation to the particular circumstances of each case in which its violation is alleged. There is another indication to the same effect. Article 39, which charges the Security Council to decide whether enforcement measures are required, does not repeat the formulation of Article 2, paragraph 4. It provides, instead, that "the Security Council shall determine the existence of any threat to the peace, breach of the peace, or act of aggression." Accordingly, the Council is not bound to consider every breach of the prohibition of force as an act calling for enforcement measures. On the other hand, the Council may deem enforcement measures necessary even if Article 2, paragraph 4 has not been violated. In fact, the "threat to the peace," in the meaning of Article 39, need not arise from any contravention, whether of the law of the Charter or of general international law. It is its political and not its juridical nature that makes a specific act or situation a "threat to the peace" and thus liable to the Council's jurisdiction. It fits into this picture that the Charter knows only measures and no sanctions. In other words, it uses a term with connotations of administrative rather than criminal law to designate all coercive United Nations actions regardless of whether they have been called for by a lawful or unlawful act.

The spirit in which the enforcement system of the Charter was conceived is illustrated most strikingly by another feature of Article 39. It charges the Security Council with the determination of "an act of aggression" but not of the aggressor. The distinction would be too tenuous for any far-reaching conclusions if it had not, from the twenties onward, played a considerable role in the discussions on the definition of aggression. It is a distinction, in fact, to which two legal and political conceptions of collective security, the punitive and the diplomatic, must be related. While the allocation of the legal responsibility for an act of aggression is an essential function of the collective security organization according to the punitive school, the diplomatic school insists that it is not the proper task for an agency of collective security to perform. The restoration of peace, the chief purpose of collective action, and the adjustment of the dispute that has led to armed conflict, will be delayed and made more difficult if the organization assumes the role of prosecutor and judge in addition to its police functions and its conciliatory functions. The wording of Article 39 as well as other features of Chapter VII of the Charter prove that its authors were leaning in the direction of the diplomatic school. Far from constituting a criminal code, the rules of the Charter relating to the enforcement system of the United Nations could rather be called a mere legalization and formalization of the diplomatic conceptions and procedures characteristic of the concert system of collective intervention practiced by the European Pentarchy in the nineteenth century.

Since the political assumption of continued close great-power co-operation proved fallacious, the framers of the Charter failed to receive due credit for what one might call their constitutional realism. The restriction of the enforcement system, practically speaking, to conflicts among minor nations; the limited scope of the substantive interests to be protected; the stress on peace and the dynamic conception of peace; the flexibility of the legal principles to be observed by the organization and its members; the type of enforcement machinery and the legal character of the enforcement system; the importance attached to the conciliatory function—all these features testify to the wisdom of the constitution-maker in setting limits on the obligations of the organization and its members that are consonant with its physical power and with the willingness of its members to co-operate. One may wonder, however, whether the same can be said of the subsequent attempts to develop the constitutional system of the United Nations along lines somewhat closer to Wilsonian concepts of collective security. Ironically, it was the United States, the chief architect of the Dumbarton Oaks Proposals and of the Charter, that took the lead in reinterpreting and remolding the original system.

It is less surprising that the United States assumed leadership in such reinterpretation than that it should ever have become the proponent of the Dumbarton Oaks scheme. American democratic traditions, in general, and traditional espousal of the rights of small nations, in particular, hardly predestined the United States to advocate an authoritarian and oligarchic type of international organization. There is nevertheless a close connection between the promotion of this type of organization and certain traditions of American foreign policy. We know on the authority of the late Harley A. Notter, the official historian of American *Postwar Foreign Policy Preparation,* what dilemma confronted the planners in the State Department when they were preparing draft constitutions of the international organization that was to be established. "While strong pressures toward striving for a federalized international organization—or government—were being exerted," Notter remarks, "there was also at this period a possibility that the dominating American opinion of the years before the war in favor of political isolationism might reassert itself. Uncertainty regarding Senate consent to ratification of any proposed agreement in this field was ever present." [1]

In other words, the task of the draftsmen in the State Department was to be no less than to devise a system legally more advanced toward genuine international government than the League of Nations had been, while ensuring at the same time that this more radically internationalist scheme did not offend anti-internationalists inside and outside the Senate. The task could be performed only by means of a legal construction that would assure to the United States, together with other great powers, a special privileged status within the system of international government and would reduce the residual risks involved in American membership still further by limiting the liabilities of the organization itself. The type of United Nations constitution that the American government promoted and successfully steered past all diplomatic hindrances to its final adoption at San Francisco met those conflicting requirements most satisfactorily. The Charter not only provides for the nucleus of a world government; it also incorporates, as has been rightly observed, virtually all of the Lodge reservations to the ill-fated Covenant of the League of Nations. [2] Thanks to the veto in the Security Council, the United States retained, in particular, the traditional right of a sovereign state to be its own interpreter of its legal obligations, including its obligations under the Charter. In other words, we were to be our own judges, not only of our obligation to participate in collective enforcement measures but also of those rules of conduct by which the Charter tries to control and restrain the actions of all nations.

The realities of United Nations politics in the first years of the organization's existence did not by any means bear out isolationist anxieties about the consequences of American membership in a universal political organization. The leadership that had devolved upon this country as a result of World War II assured it a com-

---

[1] *Postwar Foreign Policy Preparation 1939-1945.* U.S. Department of State Publication, General Foreign Policy Series 15 (Washington, D. C., 1949), p. 113.

[2] Leo Gross, "The Charter of the United Nations and the Lodge Reservations," *American Journal of International Law,* 41, No. 3 (July 1947), 531ff.

manding position in the United Nations. Without exercising undue pressure, the United States, in all of the organs of the United Nations, including the Security Council, could count on sweeping majorities in support of its policies. Ironically, American actions were frustrated only in the Security Council, owing to the very device that was intended to stifle, and actually did stifle, isolationist opposition to the ratification of the Charter. While it had been originally assumed—and, in fact, not by isolationists alone—that for the sake of our national interest we needed some form of minority protection as provided by the veto, we now began to realize that we stood to gain rather than lose by relying on the untrammeled operation of the majority principle in the General Assembly.

However, considerations of expediency alone do not account for our tendency to shift the constitutional balance from the Security Council to the General Assembly. No less decisive was our idealistic urge to apply to international politics, at long last, the principles and procedures of domestic democratic government. Even assuming—as actually one could not assume—that there was a reasonable chance of continued American-Russian co-operation in the postwar period, the two superpowers could have kept such co-operation going only by a policy based upon the mutual recognition of spheres of influence and the give and take of exasperating diplomatic negotiation. How much more than by such devices, always distasteful to us, were we bound to be attracted by the avenue open to us in the General Assembly, where issues on which we could not agree with the Russians could be submitted to the judgment of the world's "town meeting." The submission to the General Assembly of the unsettled question of Korea in 1947 is the most notable and, in terms of its consequences, the most momentous example of such a policy.

Nor were we the only ones who tended to elevate the General Assembly to a status of equality with, if not superiority to, the Security Council. The central position of the Council in the constitutional structure of the United Nations was most strongly opposed by all minor nations at San Francisco. Not satisfied with the concessions to which the Sponsoring Governments finally agreed at the Conference, the minor nations made it clear that they would renew their efforts to broaden the powers of the democratic body once the organization had started to function. They were all the more pleased, therefore, when the United States joined forces with them in trying to assure the ascendancy of the General Assembly. But they soon realized—in fact as early as 1947 and 1948 when dealing with the Korean issue—that there were risks involved in moving the Assembly up to a higher plane of world politics, namely the risk of being drawn into the vortex of power diplomacy.

To paraphrase Canning's famous dictum, the American decision to throw the Korean question into the lap of the General Assembly was an attempt to use the new world organization to redress the balance of the Far East. Or, to put it differently, it was an application of the Concert idea in reverse. To be sure, the judgment on the Korean question was to be handed down by the Assembly as the general representative organ of the United Nations, acting on behalf of the organization. In legal terms, it was the world body as a whole that was to recommend what practically amounted to an authentic interpretation, or rather revision, of the great-power agreement on Korea, concluded at Moscow in 1945. Speaking in political terms, however, the American initiative meant nothing less than calling upon a combination of great and small powers to settle an important question—in fact one of the hot issues of the Cold War between West and East—without the consent of one of the great powers whose vital interests were certain to be affected by the decision of the Assembly.

The 1947 submission of the Korean question to the General Assembly was undoubtedly a well-intentioned attempt to effect the peaceful change of an intolerable political situation the continuance of which threatened to cause grave international friction and that actually soon resulted in armed conflict. But unfortunately it had one drawback; it did not really settle the Korean question. Contrary to the "executive" concert of great powers, the "parliamentary" concert of the General Assembly can only debate and vote but not compel. Scoring parliamentary triumphs is no substitute for the settlement of an issue by the great powers. In fact, it may aggravate matters by deepening the rift between those governments whose agreement is indispensable to the solution of the question. It was for this reason that some members of the Assembly followed the American lead in the Korean case only with unmistakable misgivings. They felt particularly uneasy about the American-sponsored endorsement by the Assembly of the South Korean government as the only lawful government in Korea. This action, they thought, could easily be construed as a moral commitment on the part of the United Nations to preserve the territorial integrity and political independence of South Korea.

If the United Nations was unable to break Russian resistance to a change of the *status quo* in Korea through pacific procedures as sought by the West, it did have a substantial share in successfully preventing the Soviets from changing the *status quo* in their favor through a war by proxy.

In 1950, as the Korean war raised American influence in the United Nations to a point never to be reached again, it also brought about an important change in United Nations law, initiated by the American government. For all practical intents and purposes, the reform measure of 1950 amounted to a far-reaching change of the constitutional character of the United Nations system of collective security, affecting the rights and obligations of its members, although it was enacted in the form of a simple act of the Assembly, the famous "Uniting for Peace" resolution.

The measure, which was hailed in the General Assembly as a "turning point in the history of mankind," did not yield all the results its proponents hoped to attain and had results, which they hardly foresaw, that were not pleasing to them.

According to the resolution, decisions on enforcement measures —so far an exclusive function of the Security Council—were henceforth to devolve upon the General Assembly in cases in which the Council, for lack of unanimity of the permanent members, failed to exercise its responsibility for the maintenance of international peace and security. The purpose of granting conditional enforcement power to the Assembly was obviously to circumvent a Russian veto that would preclude United Nations action against the Soviet Union itself or any country supported by it. But the American government, when initiating the measure, pursued a still more ambitious objective. It was a new attempt to create a collective security system technically more advanced than that of the League of

Nations. The resolution envisaged the establishment of military enforcement machinery that would make effective the Assembly system of collective security. In purely technical terms, the new system was devised along the same lines as the stillborn Council system envisaged in Chapter VII of the Charter. But the political character and purpose of the system established by the resolution was to be basically different from that of the Charter. It was to be an instrument in the hands of the parliamentary concert of the General Assembly instead of in the hands of the executive great-power concert of the Security Council. For years thereafter, we were to press the General Assembly to implement the technical provisions of the "Uniting for Peace" resolution. But they remained a dead letter no less than the corresponding provisions of the Charter. The Assembly refused to carry out a policy that it feared would transform the collective security system of the Charter into what in fact would amount to an alliance against the Soviet Union.

Be that as it may, we certainly initiated and sponsored the reform of United Nations law, to be accomplished by the "Uniting for Peace" resolution, primarily with a view to the exigencies of the Cold War. We hoped that an extension of the system of collective security to cover conflicts among great powers as well as those among minor powers would deter the Soviet Union from moving on to a hot war. Therefore, we did not find the price that we had to pay too high for obtaining additional protection against aggressive intentions of our Russian adversary. In order to make possible the circumvention of a Russian veto in the Security Council, we also implicitly abandoned our own veto right and that of our allies. Thus in a sense we extended our obligations beyond what they were under the Charter. We ceased to be our own judges, either of our obligation to participate in collective enforcement measures or of the rules of conduct contained in the Charter. In fact, neither we nor our chief allies were to be protected thereafter from becoming ourselves the object of enforcement measures. This seemed to be a well-calculated risk. After all, contrary to the Security Council, the General Assembly has only recommendatory powers. But what seemed even more reassuring was the fact that, with our commanding position in the Assembly, it was not likely that we would ever be outvoted. It did not take us long, however, to realize that we had underrated the impact of the other Cold War, the one between the colonial and anticolonial powers, both on the operations of the Assembly and on the political dynamics of the collective security system.

The Western proponents of the "Uniting for Peace" resolution found satisfaction in seeing it applied to cases to which it had been tailored, as to the case of Chinese Communist intervention in Korea and to the case of Hungary. The Suez and the Lebanon cases, however, showed that the new system could also be used against the West. The irony of this development is impressively suggested by the change in Soviet attitude toward the "Uniting for Peace" resolution. The Soviet Union, which originally opposed its adoption most violently both on constitutional and on political grounds, has since discovered that the General Assembly system can be made to serve Russian interests too. It has therefore come around to accepting the change of United Nations law, tacitly at least. Thus, if our sponsorship of the reform measure of 1950 actually was intended to span and tighten our particular alliances by an all-embracing American-led alliance in the legal form of an abstract collective security system, the plan has undoubtedly miscarried, and not only because its technical implementation failed to materialize. As the Suez and Lebanon cases show, the operation of the system that we initiated is apt to strain our inter-allied relationships and make us vulnerable to interference by the Assembly with our own actions, lawful as they may be. The fact of the matter is that the Assembly system of the "Uniting for Peace" resolution, which we designed as a means of strengthening the Western defense position against the East, can also be used by the anticolonial powers, and by the Soviet Union, both against the colonial powers and against us. Brief as the history of the organization of collective security is, it clearly suggests that members tend to use the abstract system, contrived as a protection of all against each and every other state, for the purpose of building and cementing an alliance against a concrete state or group of states. But it also suggests that, given the complexity of inter-national relations, such use of the system is not likely to be successful.

This is also borne out by the experience of the Korean war to which we must return once more. The legal and political issues to which the North Korean aggression gave rise in the organs of the world body are important in their bearing upon the whole conception of collective security.

The United States, which apart from South Korea bore the chief military burden of collective action against the aggressors, also determined the policy to be pursued. American political leadership remained unchallenged, except by the Soviet bloc, throughout the war. But it cannot be denied that the United States found it increasingly difficult to maintain the harmony of views that prevailed in the United Nations during the first weeks of the collective action. While practically all non-Communist member governments approved of the decision to repel North Korean aggression, they were at variance as to the ultimate purpose of the United Nations action.

The chief question on which they disagreed was whether the collective action was to be confined to restoring the *status quo ante* and terminating hostilities—postponing the settlement of the issues underlying the armed conflict—or whether the United Nations was authorized, if not committed, to go beyond a mere police action and employ its enforcement power to solve the Korean question on United Nations terms. In taking the latter view, the United States could claim that the Charter authorized the Security Council, by implication at least, to exercise legislative authority in removing threats to the peace. However, the political presupposition for rendering effective a legislative fiat of the United Nations, namely, agreement among the great powers, was unfortunately lacking in this case. It could therefore be argued—and it was argued by critics of the American policy—that insistence on the farther-reaching objective, a change of the *status quo ante,* would delay the restoration of peace, which according to the Charter was the primary purpose of enforcement measures.

In terms of the Charter, American policy could be questioned for still another reason closely related to the decision to go beyond a mere police action. The Charter system of collective security rests upon the diplomatic conception, as we have called it. In fact, the United States itself had stated at the San Francisco

Conference that the United Nations when taking enforcement measures ought not to assume the role of a prosecutor or judge but concentrate its efforts on the restoration of peace. American policy in the Korean case, however, was from the beginning inspired by the punitive notion of collective security. The punishment of the aggressors was declared an objective of the enforcement action and served to justify its continuation beyond the purpose of restoring the *status quo ante*. One may doubt whether this policy actually contributed to the prolongation of the armed conflict. But it certainly did not facilitate its termination. Be that as it may, it is far from surprising, realistically speaking, that enforcement measures, taken in the context of a conflict that was ideological as well as political, should assume a punitive character. The temptation to resort to the punitive notion will always be strong, regardless of the legal conceptions on which a collective security organization is founded. It will be almost irresistible in a case like the Korean war, which was part of a world-wide political and ideological struggle.

It is not surprising, either, that the resistance against being drawn into that struggle should have grown among United Nations members once the aggression was checked. In fact, the formation, in the second half of the fifties, of the third force in the General Assembly, insisting on its neutrality in the ideological and political Cold War between West and East, can be traced back to the later days of the Korean war. The nations that try to stay outside the Cold War wanted the United Nations to deal with the fighting in Korea in terms of a conflict among the actual belligerents only, and to steer clear of involvement in political and ideological warfare against the Soviet Union and communism. They shunned a policy of lining up the organization against Soviet Russia and its ideology, not only on principle but also because they feared this might lead to the widening of the local conflict into a global war. The United States and its close associates in the Korean war were no less conscious of this danger nor were they less eager to avoid it. However, they were firmly convinced that the real aggressor was Russian-led communism, and they therefore felt that it was the task of the United Nations to inflict upon this aggressor a crushing diplomatic defeat.

But the respective positions were to be different when armed conflict arose in the context of the other Cold War being waged between the colonial and anticolonial powers. In the Suez case we did not shrink from meeting our commitments under United Nations law, but we were not inclined, for good reasons, to interpret them as broadly as the anticolonial members felt we should. While the latter wanted the United Nations to deal with the conflict in terms of the political and ideological cause for which they stood and to identify itself with that cause, we confined our efforts in the United Nations to securing the termination of hostilities and the restoration of the *status quo ante*.

The constitutional development of the United Nations reflects and is due to the political pressures brought to bear upon the organization by the two Cold Wars in which the members of the international community are engaged today, the one between the great powers and the one between the colonial and anticolonial powers.

According to the Charter, it was the Security Council, dominated by the great powers, that was to be the center of authority in the organization. Though its collective security functions were limited to minor conflicts, its legal powers within those limits were to be broad and its physical power sufficient to give them effect. When owing to the Cold War between East and West the concept of an executive concert of the great powers failed to materialize, we tried to shift the center of authority and power to a parliamentary concert of great and minor powers. It was hardly a realistic scheme from the beginning and became even less so when the extension of the collective security system to major conflicts was not followed by the establishment of military machinery commensurate in physical strength with the legal powers of the parliamentary concert. The claim of the General Assembly to speak on behalf of the organization as a whole rested exclusively on its moral authority as a democratic body. But the validity of that claim was not generally recognized; and moreover it was open to the objection that the Assembly was an essentially political body, acting in accordance with considerations of political expediency rather than of moral principles.

The expectation that the concentration of authority and power in a parliamentary concert would enable the United Nations to discharge its functions effectively as a collective security body was not well founded for yet another reason. As the scheme of Dumbarton Oaks and San Francisco was inspired and based upon the pattern of the Grand Alliance of World War II, so was the scheme of the "Uniting for Peace" resolution patterned upon the political constellation in the initial period of the Korean war. Not only was the democratic bloc in the Assembly at that time overwhelmingly strong numerically; it also seemed sufficiently coherent to serve as the foundation for a lasting system of collective security. However, the coherence actually was due rather to the fear of imminent Russian aggression than to a true community of views and interests. The Russian danger at that time overshadowed all other questions, even in the eyes of the anticolonial members of the United Nations. But this is no longer the case. On the contrary a growing number of member nations regards the United Nations today primarily as an instrument to further the emancipation of the colonial peoples and to eradicate the last vestiges of Western power and influence in the world. But quite apart from the colonial issue, the lines of the bipolar structure of the contemporary world are not as clear at the close of the fifties as they were at the beginning.

The weakening of the political coherence of the General Assembly forecloses the hope for an effective system of collective security built upon the Assembly that would permit great and small nations alike to dispense with the traditional devices of power-diplomacy. But it is not likely to end the sway of the collective security ideology and its successful use for diplomatic purposes. For instead of replacing traditional diplomacy, as it was hoped, collective security—or the idea of collective security—has itself become a diplomatic weapon in the struggle for power. This does not detract from the moral value of the idea, which is indeed inspired by man's eternal longing for a peaceful and just international order; it only means that the idea shares the fate of other lofty ideas, namely, employment for combative purposes. It has become part of the art of diplomacy to judge the adversary's actions in the inflexible terms of the idea of collective security while basing one's own actions on the more flexible law of collective security.

There exists no strictly legal obligation for a member of the United Nations to agree to enforcement measures or to participate in them. True, the Security Council was to possess the legal power to order such participation. However, the exercise of this power was made dependent upon the conclusion of special military agreements between the Council and member nations. No such agreements were ever concluded. The General Assembly, on the other hand, was given only recommendatory powers by the Charter and can only recommend action even under the "Uniting for Peace" resolution.

The legal situation scarcely differs with regard to the binding authoritative character of the act by which the Council or the Assembly, respectively, determine the existence of a threat to the peace, a breach of the peace, or an act of aggression. While the determination by the Council must be considered as legally binding upon all members, the Council for political reasons is barely capable of agreeing on such a determination, which requires seven affirmative votes, including those of the five great powers. It might also become increasingly difficult to attain the two-thirds majority required in the Assembly. But in any case a determination by the Assembly can hardly be considered as binding upon the members in a strictly legal sense. It has at best moral and political significance. The distinction between the moral and legal force of United Nations decisions is admittedly tenuous, and the resort to it might not always be helpful. Nonetheless no member nation seems to be ready to dispense with it altogether and thus to recognize implicitly the legal authority of the world body as superior to its own.

At the same time, governments appear to be most eager to cover their acts with the authority of the United Nations and to justify their actions and omissions in terms of the Charter. The Charter has come to play the role that the *Jus Publicum Europaeum* played in the nineteenth century. It has become a matter of respectful reference. There is an increasing tendency to assume what one might call vicarious responsibility for the United Nations. The argument is advanced that if the United Nations proves incapable of maintaining international peace and security, it falls to particular members to do so in its place. The Truman Doctrine of 1947, the Tripartite Declaration of 1950 regarding the Arab-Israeli armistice borders, the Joint Resolution on the Defense of Formosa passed by Congress in 1955, and the Eisenhower Doctrine of 1957 suggest the extent to which we ourselves are ready to assume such vicarious responsibility. Admittedly, in contemplating actions under these doctrines and resolutions we hope they will eventually be approved by the United Nations, explicitly or implicitly. But it is nonetheless significant that the United States, which can claim to be second to none in devotion to the ideals of the United Nations, is finding it ever more necessary in its interpretation of the Charter to go to the very limits of what United Nations law presumably permits.

The same tendency is apparent in the interpretation, or rather reinterpretation, of Article 51 of the Charter, which recognizes self-defense as an inherent right of all members of the organization. Comparatively speaking, the formulation of the right of self-defense in that article is less flexible than the formulation in Article 2 of the principles governing the conduct of the United Nations and of its members. According to the wording of Article 51, the exercise of the right of self-defense was to be permissible only "if an armed attack occurs against a Member of the United Nations." It seemed to preclude the legitimacy of any preventive action against armed attack that was merely imminent but had not yet actually begun. However, by practically accepting in 1947 the First Report of the Atomic Energy Commission, the Security Council itself recognized implicitly that so strict an interpretation was not justified in view of the conditions of nuclear warfare.[3] Moreover, there is a distinct trend among United Nations members today to claim that the term "armed attack" must be interpreted also to cover indirect aggression, in the form, for instance, of foreign support for domestic subversion. As the discussions on the definition of aggression indicate, some

---

[3] The report contains the following recommendation: "In consideration of the problem of violation of the terms of the treaty or convention on atomic matters it should also be borne in mind that a violation might be of so grave a character as to give rise to the inherent right of self-defense recognized in Article 51 of the Charter of the United Nations." See United Nations, *Repertory of Practice of United Nations Organs*, II (1955), 435.

members—especially those who have grievances against economically more advanced nations, or think they have—are even inclined to consider economic exploitation as a form of indirect aggression and therefore as a legitimate title for the exercise of self-defense. In other words, in spite of Article 51, self-defense tends again, as was the case in former times, to be held legitimate in practically any case in which a nation feels wronged by the policy of another nation.

In point of fact, international lawyers have posed the question whether and to what extent the United Nations still has the legitimate authority to control its members' exercise of their inherent right of self-defense. It is not surprising that such authority should be questioned. Is it not a time-honored maxim of political philosophy that society may legitimately claim to restrict the right of its members to judge for themselves and to assert their own cause only to the extent of its willingness and ability to afford them protection? It was on this general ground that members of the League of Nations began to deny the validity of the Covenant in the second half of the thirties, after the failure of League sanctions in the Italo-Abyssinian War. No member of the United Nations, including the Soviet Union, has gone so far as yet. But the tendency among all United Nations members to take advantage of the flexibility of the law of the Charter is unmistakable. Indeed, it is natural enough in view of the undeniable fact that the United Nations cannot be relied upon to protect nations against the perils of international politics, which are infinitely greater today than they have ever been before.

Certain practical conclusions should be drawn from the constitutional and political development of the United Nations. They have been most clearly and convincingly stated by Mr. Dag Hammarskjold, the present Secretary-General of the United Nations, in the "observations" on the Suez crisis with which he introduced his "Annual Report on the Work of the Organization," submitted to the General Assembly in 1957. The United Nations, Mr. Hammarskjold warns, should not persevere in its tendency to claim "a world authority enforcing the law upon the nations." It possesses neither the legal powers nor the physical power to give effect to that claim. The members should rather look upon the organization as "an instrument for negotiation among, and to some extent for, governments." In other words, the United Nations is essentially a diplomatic body and not a government. United Nations procedures, accordingly, should not be conducted upon the pattern of parliamentary procedures but be inspired instead by the spirit of traditional diplomacy. Debate and vote are not intended to supply nations with additional means for displaying and satisfying their pugnacious instincts, but to guide "the development in constructive and peaceful directions" and thus assure the reconciliation of their divergent interests. In sum, the United Nations should not try to act as a legislator but should act as a moderator.

But Mr. Hammarskjold also makes clear that his suggestion that the United Nations serve primarily as a mediator, standing between the parties to a conflict rather than claiming to be their superior, is not meant to imply that it should disregard the rights and wrongs in the conflicts it tries to resolve.

In fact, the notion that a mediator has to pretend moral indifference was already rejected by the classical writers on international law at a time when the mediator, as a rule, was an individual state. It would indeed be preposterous to impose moral indifference upon a collective mediator like the United Nations. True, Emmerich de Vattel, who taught the fathers of the American Republic the principles of international law, begins his discussion of mediation by emphasizing that "the mediator ought to observe an exact impartiality; he should soften reproaches, calm resentments, and draw minds towards each other." But he then continues: "His duty is to favor what is right, and to cause to be restored what belongs to each; but he ought not scrupulously to insist on rigorous justice. He is a moderator, and not a judge; his business is to procure peace; and to bring him who has right on his side, if it be necessary, to relax something with a view to so great a blessing."

It is undoubtedly more difficult today than it was in the eighteenth century to act in the gentle spirit of Vattel's words. But, all the same, is it not worth trying?

5

COLLECTIVE DEFENSE:
THE MILITARY COMMITMENT

James E. King, Jr.

THE GROWTH OF the United States network of collective defense arrangements has occurred in surges, propelled by contemporary political events. Until 1947 we continued to avoid "entangling alliances" with individual countries; we based our hopes for the future on the agreement of the victors in World War II to maintain "peace and security" through the machinery of the United Nations. The rapid pace of transition from peace to Cold War, which became apparent in that year, produced the Truman Doctrine of March 1947, an ambiguous offer of unilateral support to "free peoples who are resisting attempted subjugation by armed minorities or by outside pressure." [1] The offer was made good at first only in the cases of Greece and Turkey. But our deep concern for the security of those parts of Europe not yet under Russian domination increased until we committed ourselves, in the North Atlantic Treaty of April 1949, to the proposition that a

---

[1] For an excellent discussion of the origins of the Truman Doctrine see Joseph M. Jones, *The Fifteen Weeks* (New York, 1955). The text of President Truman's address to a joint session of Congress on aid to Greece and Turkey is given in an appendix, pp. 269-74, also *Department of State Bulletin,* March 23, 1947, pp. 534-37.

military attack upon the countries of Western Europe was tanta-
mount to an attack upon our homeland, and we therefore joined
"the first peacetime military alliance entered into by the United
States since the adoption of the constitution." [2]

Along the way, in September 1947, we concluded the Inter-
American Treaty of Reciprocal Assistance with our sister republics
in the Western Hemisphere. The Rio Treaty, while not commonly regarded as a military alliance, accomplished two purposes.
It transformed the historic Monroe Doctrine into a collective
arrangement, thus giving permanent effect to joint defensive
agreements made during the war. It provided for the settlement
of inter-American disputes, including armed conflict, without resort to the United Nations—or at least before such resort—thus
giving formal and collective expression to the United States policy
of the Good Neighbor.

The Rio and North Atlantic treaties completed the first phase
of a process of development that was carrying the United States
toward the revolutionary policy of national security based upon
collective defense. The second surge in this process came in 1951,
when the United States decided to push through a treaty of peace
and reconciliation with Japan despite opposition from behind the
Iron Curtain. The Japanese Treaty, signed in San Francisco on
September 8, 1951—but more particularly the United States-
Japanese Security Treaty, signed at the same time—aroused the
fears of some of the victims of Japanese aggression in World
War II by anticipating the rearmament of Japan. In order to calm
these fears, and in application of the policy of containing Communist expansion, the United States consented to formalize the
heavily precedented but hitherto informal commitment to their
defense by entering into the Philippine-American Defense Pact,
of August 30, and the Security Treaty between Australia, New
Zealand, and the United States—known as the ANZUS treaty—
of September 1, 1951. After the conclusion of the Korean
Armistice in the summer of 1953, the pattern established in the
case of the Japanese Treaty was repeated in a treaty of mutual

---

[2] Harry S. Truman, *Memoirs,* Vol. II: *Years of Trial and Hope,* (Garden
City, New York, 1952) p. 241.

defense with the Republic of Korea (October 1, 1953). These treaties of 1951 and 1953 may be regarded, from the point of view of the United States, as constituting formal recognition of its responsibility for the peace and security of the Far East assumed during World War II and its aftermath. To the world at large, they were evidence that the United States had moved into a large section of the power vacuum left by the defeat of Japan.

The four Pacific treaties of 1951-1953 did not produce a closed system of collective defense in that area. This was accomplished, albeit most imperfectly, by the Southeast Asia Collective Defense Treaty, signed at Manila, September 8, 1954, which linked the security interests of the signatories of the Philippine and ANZUS treaties with those of Britain and France and of the two south Asian countries, Pakistan and Thailand. Although the three states of South Viet Nam, Laos and Cambodia were excluded from membership in the Southeast Asia Treaty Organization (SEATO) by the terms of the armistice agreement of July 20 that ended the Indochinese civil war, these states were specifically included in the area covered by the treaty itself. The Republic of China, however, was as definitely excluded because Britain and France both had recognized the mainland regime of the People's Democratic Republic of China. Consequently, the United States felt it necessary, under pressure from the government of Chiang Kai-shek, to conclude a mutual defense treaty with the Republic of China, on December 1, 1954. This Formosa treaty completes the list of formal United States collective defense commitments.

There remains, however, the Middle East. The United States did not become a member of the Baghdad Pact of 1955 between the United Kingdom, Turkey, Iraq, Iran, and Pakistan, but agreed from the beginning to participate in the meetings of two Baghdad Pact committees—the Economics Committee and the Committee to Fight Subversion—and in June 1957 began participating in the work of the Military Committee. Linked to NATO by Britain and Turkey and to SEATO by Pakistan, the Baghdad Pact Middle Eastern Treaty Organization, or METO, was meant to close a gap in the encircling containment of the Communist bloc of nations. In the interest of maintaining good relations with the Arab states of the Middle East, all of which except Iraq regarded the Baghdad

Pact as an effort to disrupt Arab unity, if not to perpetuate British influence in the area, the United States still has not become a member. It has, however, enlarged its support of the pact, as its efforts to reconcile the aspirations of Arab nationalism with its own determination to limit the penetration of Russian influence into the Middle East have met with indifferent success. Moreover, the Middle East Resolution, or Eisenhower Doctrine, of March 1957— by which the United States sought to repair the damage wrought by the fiasco of the British and French invasion of Egypt in the Suez war of October-November 1956 and their ignominious withdrawal under combined pressure from the United States, the Soviet Union, and the British Commonwealth—has been described by the Secretary of State as having "as much effectiveness as membership in the Baghdad Pact organization."[3]

The Middle East Resolution declares that the United States "regards as vital to the national interest and world peace the preservation of the independence and integrity of the nations of the Middle East," and that the President may "use armed force to assist any nation or group of nations requesting assistance against armed aggression from any country controlled by international communism."[4] The area of the "Middle East" is not defined, but the political setting in which the Eisenhower Doctrine was evolved makes it evident that the United States was, in effect, extending a unilateral guarantee to each Baghdad Pact power, as well as to any other Middle Eastern government that might request help. Moreover, the landing of United States troops in Lebanon in July 1958, upon the request of the government of that country, which was engaged in fighting a rebellion of its own subjects, has established the precedent that United States military support under the Middle East Resolution may be forthcoming in the event of threatened ("indirect") as well as actual aggression. It suggests, in addition, that the relation of the suspected aggressor to "international communism" may be no more explicit than the willingness of the Arab nationalist leader, Gamal Abdel Nasser, President of the United

---

[3] John Foster Dulles, quoted in *The New York Times,* January 31, 1958.

[4] Joint Resolution of Congress, signed by President Eisenhower March 9, 1957. For complete text see *Department of State Bulletin,* March 25, 1957, p. 481.

Arab Republic of Egypt, Syria, and the Yemen, to purchase arms and to accept military and technical aid from the Soviet Union. Finally, it was announced at a meeting of the Baghdad Pact Council in London, July 28, 1958, at which Iraq was not represented (owing to the *coup d'état* in Baghdad on the fourteenth of that month), but which was attended by the United States Secretary of State, that the United States planned to co-operate fully with the Baghdad powers "for their security and defense" and would promptly enter into agreements "designed to give effect to this co-operation."[5]

Although the wording of treaties is less important than the spirit in which they are written, it is of interest and of some importance to note the different verbal formulae by which the mutual obligations are expressed in the various treaties. The Rio and North Atlantic treaties, which reflect United States national security interests long established—in the first case by the Monroe Doctrine, and in the second by participation in two world wars—use the most explicit form of commitment. Article III of the Rio Treaty says: ". . . an armed attack against an American State shall be considered as an attack against all American States." Article V of the North Atlantic Treaty uses essentially the same formula: "The Parties agree that an armed attack against one or more of them in Europe or North America shall be considered an attack against them all." The later treaties have employed a more reserved formula, reflecting in part the inferior status of the areas they represent in the universe of United States national interests, and in part the misgivings of senators who felt that the North Atlantic Treaty had gone too far toward suggesting that the United States might find itself at war without courtesy of Congress. In all of these, except the Japanese Security Treaty, each party recognizes that an armed attack in the area defined "would be dangerous to its own peace and safety and declares that it would meet (or would act to meet) the common danger in accordance with its constitutional processes." When the Japanese treaty was signed, Japan had no armed forces with which to act to meet the common danger. The security treaty

---

[5] E. W. Kenworthy, "Senators Not Forewarned of U.S. Baghdad Pact Role," *The New York Times,* July 30, 1958. Also *The London Times,* July 29, 1958.

therefore authorizes the United States to dispose forces in and about Japan to be "utilized to contribute to the maintenance of international peace and security in the Far East and to the security of Japan against armed attack from without." For the same reason, it provides that "at the express request of the Japanese government" these United States forces may be used "to put down large-scale internal riots and disturbances in Japan, caused through instigation or intervention of any outside power or powers."

The Japanese Security Treaty is not, however, the only collective defense arrangement that authorizes the United States to station its troops on the territory of the other party. The same authorization is a feature of the bilateral treaties with the Republic of Korea and with the Republic of China. This provision may not unfairly be taken as an indication of the basic lack of mutuality in the guarantees afforded. These three bilateral treaties, in other words, are United States security guarantees, more unmistakably so than the four multilateral treaties or even the Philippine treaty.

In addition to their operational articles, all these postwar (World War II) treaties pledge the parties to peaceful settlement of international differences. All provide for peacetime collaboration in one form or another "separately and jointly by self-help and mutual aid" to prepare for the contingency of an attack. All likewise acknowledge the superiority of the United Nations Charter and justify themselves by referring to the inherent right of individual and collective self-defense recognized by Article 51 of the Charter. Thus, all provide (a) that action taken to resist aggression will be reported promptly to the Security Council and (b) that this action will be suspended should the Security Council effectively assume responsibility. The multilateral treaties provide for an executive agency, called the "organization" in the Inter-American Treaty and the "Council" in the North Atlantic, ANZUS, and SEATO treaties. The Rio Treaty, however, is unique in its provision for action by a two-thirds vote (except that "no State shall be required to use armed force without its consent."). In the other treaties the rule of unanimity may be assumed since the question of voting is not mentioned. Only the Southeast Asia security treaty explicitly recognizes threats "in any way other than by armed attack or . . . any fact or situation which might endanger the peace of the area" and provides that the parties will immediately consult in such cases "in order to agree on measures which should be taken for common defense." In a minute to this treaty the United States specified that the only "armed attack" it would regard as endangering its "peace and safety" and thereby requiring action "to meet the common danger" must be "communist aggression." Any other armed attack it would treat as a threat of the second order just mentioned, calling for immediate consultation on measures to be taken rather than action "to meet the common danger."

The scope of this network of United States commitments is impressive. The United States has bilateral or multilateral security arrangements by treaty with forty-two separate nations. Including the United States, the Rio Treaty has twenty-one signatories; the North Atlantic Treaty, fifteen (as of 1955 with the addition of the Federal Republic of Germany); the Manila Treaty, eight—and to these must be added Japan, Korea, and Formosa. Moreover, the Manila Treaty extends its guarantees to an area, and thus to a number of states that are not members of the treaty, provided they are willing to accept help, leaving the ultimate scope of even our treaty obligations indeterminate. Add the undefined limits of "the Middle East"—the nations of which are invited to request assistance against "international communism" by the Eisenhower Doctrine—and the sweeping inclusiveness of the Truman Doctrine, which gave rise to sharp criticism when it was pronounced in 1947, turns out to have been a reasonably accurate forecast of later collective defense commitments. Indeed, the limits of this policy of mutual assistance and defense have been authoritatively defined only once. That was when the people of Hungary rose in revolt against their Russian overlords in October 1956, and the United States Secretary of State let it be known that "we do not look upon these nations [i.e., the Russian satellites of Eastern Europe] as potential military allies."[6] Later, President Eisenhower was to explain that military intervention was unthinkable so close to the borders of the U.S.S.R. because the Russians would almost certainly respond by starting World War III.

The policy of containment through collective defense evolved

---

[6] *The New York Times,* October 28, 1956.

only gradually, and a satisfactory explanation of the growing network of commitments would have to treat each "doctrine" or treaty separately; nevertheless there is apparent a general rationale behind collective defense. It may be summarized in four major principles. First: the United States cannot expect to maintain its power position, and thereby preserve the kind of world in which it will feel safe, without either the help of allies or a reorganization of our national life in rough approximation of the Communist pattern so that we may be able to devote a larger portion of our national wealth to military and other instruments of national power, thus increasing our available strength at the expense of other values. Second: the non-Communist world cannot defend itself against Communist infiltration and subversion without our moral and material support, including military support. Third: the expansion of "international communism" by overt aggression is an imminent and dangerous threat to our security whenever local conditions in the non-Communist world permit aggression at minor risk to the major centers of Communist power. Fourth: our bases on allied territory enable us to increase the military effectiveness and consequently the deterrent effect of our strategic retaliatory forces; at the same time the presence of these outposts and, in appropriate circumstances, other United States forces including ground troops, increases the credibility of our deterrent by evidencing our commitment to the security and integrity of the local political unit with which we are allied.

These principles may be inferred from a general survey of collective defense in its current form. This is not of course to say that there are no official statements that, at one time or another, have expressed one or more of these principles. A famous example is the "massive retaliation" passage from Secretary John Foster Dulles' speech before the Council of Foreign Relations, Inc., in New York, January 12, 1954. "We need," he said, "allies and collective security. Our purpose is to make these relations more effective, less costly. . . . We want, for ourselves and for the other free nations, a maximum deterrent at a bearable cost." This is one way of expressing what has been called the first principle here. We shall have to return to its special application to the *nuclear* deterrence commitment that the Secretary of State was justifying. Again, three years later, when he was presenting the Middle East Resolution to the Senate Committees on Foreign Relations and the Armed Services, Secretary Dulles remarked: "Experience indicates that a nation rarely, if ever, loses its independence (1) if that nation is not exposed to open armed attack by overwhelming force; (2) if it has loyal and adequately equipped forces for at least internal security; and (3) if the economic situation does not seem hopeless." In connection with an appeal to Congress to sanction economic and military aid coupled with a security guarantee to the countries of the Middle East, this statement fairly accurately reflects our second principle, while also suggesting the third—though the threat of overt aggression is not emphasized in the Secretary's presentation because he was responding to the argument that aggression was not the problem in the Middle East and consequently that military aid and a security guarantee were not what was required.

Passages might similarly be chosen, almost at random, from all the great and minor documents of containment, beginning with President Truman's address to Congress on aid to Greece and Turkey of March 12, 1947 ("At the present moment in world history, nearly every nation must choose between alternative ways of life. The choice is too often not a free one."), moving on to Secretary of State George C. Marshall's address at the Harvard Commencement in June 1947 proposing economic aid to the free nations of Western Europe, down to President Eisenhower's latest "state of the union" or defense address. The refrain is recurrent. The United States needs the co-operation of the weaker non-Communist powers if it is to limit the growth of communism toward world dominion without excessive strain on its own institutions; these minor powers need United States support—in the form of military, economic, and technical aid, but also in strengthening assurance of political, moral, and military support—to resist the disruptive pressures of their internal forces of discontent and to stand resolute before the external intimidations of the Communist world.

It is difficult to find a satisfactory term to describe the sum total of the collective defense arrangements created over the years since 1947. The word *system,* often used, has been avoided here because the whole does not comprise a system, although it contains systematic elements.[7] Nor, for that matter, is the "whole" really a whole, for the exigencies of day-to-day foreign policy, particularly as they reflect divergences and often enough even conflicts of interest between the United States and its major allies in all quarters of the world, have made it impossible to fit all our commitments together in a consistent whole. Indeed this has been urged upon us at one time or another by first one and then another of our allies. But always it turns out that behind the suggestion lies the hope of reconciling our world view, at least in all major particulars, with that of the proponent ally, and this has been a forlorn hope because behind the differences of view—with Britain over Formosa, for example— lie real differences of national interest, or at least emotional differences that are currently irreconcilable. There has been, to be sure, an effort to create a system of regional arrangements, each internally consistent and all having in common the fact that they serve as links in a containment chain surrounding the Communist bloc of nations. The incompatibilities of the hoped-for system are, however, notorious and are made more so by each crisis in the Middle or Far East. The weakness of some of the links in the chain is equally notorious; this has given rise to the observation so often made that the containment policy would actually have been more effective had collective defense not been carried to the extreme (sometimes called "pactomania") of insisting upon regional arrangements in the absence of viable "regions" on which they might be based.

To minimize these semantic difficulties the term "network" has been chosen to describe the result of the United States policy of collective defense even though the term enjoys little sanction in common usage. The thread of containment—i.e., the United States policy of doing all it should, or at least all it can, to prevent the spread of the Communist domain—runs through all the arrangements, bilateral and multilateral, legal and doctrinal, that make up the network. There are, of course, other linkages such as the common membership of Britain and France in NATO and SEATO, of Britain and Turkey in NATO and METO, and of Britain and Pakistan in METO and SEATO. But it is not just sound drafting

---

[7] Arnold Wolfers, p. 62 above, speaks of an "alignment system" to encompass both collective defense arrangements and other looser arrangements.

that limits the areas of the regions defined in each treaty—that in one instance excludes Formosa but includes Pakistan and New Zealand in "Southeast Asia" and in another includes Turkey but excludes the remainder of the Middle East from the "North Atlantic area." These oddities of inclusion and exclusion reflect the local conditions under which united action is possible; they reflect equally the limits on common action both within and between "regions."

We are more interested here, however, in what *is* an element common to all the arrangements in the network, though with variations of weight and style, as we shall see. This common element is the United States contribution to local collective defense. Moreover, without intention to disparage the moral, the psychological, and the economic elements of support that combine with the military to make up the political totality of the United States contribution, it is the last of these elements, the military, that will be examined in greater detail.

And here the first thing that must be said about the United States military contribution to local and collective defense is what it is *in essence*. It is not military aid and advice, not the sale or gift of arms, not the supply of military training missions or places on the student roster of the Command and General Staff College; it is not even the stationing of United States troops, the location of a SAC base on the allied territory, or the Seventh Fleet just over the horizon. The essence is *the commitment*. It is the extension to an ally of the magic concession that an attack upon *his* territory is an attack upon *ours,* or at least that it will be regarded as endangering *our* peace and security. For this concession spreads over his weakness the mantle of our strength. It sanctions the risks he must take when he combines his fortunes with those of his neighbors and thereby shares their vulnerability. In unity there is strength. But in the unity of resistance to dominion in a world overcast by the duopoly of great power there is also provocation. Without the support of one of the superpowers, a union of minor powers may increase more than it diminishes the danger to security. Hence the non-Communist alternative to membership in the United States collective defense network is not membership in a "third force," but neutralism, not the creation of another power center, but the abnegation of power.

What, then, does the United States security commitment mean? This is a question to which an answer found in the language of treaties can be most misleading. Is an attack upon Latin America, or upon Western Europe, to be regarded and treated by the people of the United States precisely as though it were an attack upon the continental United States? This would not have been the meaning attached to the formula a few years ago. Such an attack would have called for a major national effort, but an effort that could easily have been distinguished from the desperation, say, of the Confederacy's defense of Petersburg and Richmond. It would have meant the promise to employ United States armed forces and an undertaking to mobilize the manpower and industry of the United States if required, as was done in two world wars. It would not have meant literally identifying Rio or Caracas, or Berlin or Paris, with New York or Chicago. Moreover, it would not have meant the abandonment of the exercise of judgment, of the application of a sense of proportion, or of the drawing of distinctions regarding the nature of the attack, its cause, and its purpose. All the more *totalitarian* conceptions of the meaning of the formula— those that require the use of our nuclear military power to overwhelm the aggressor, and to destroy the sources of his military power if that is the only way he can be overwhelmed—we owe not to the words of the treaties, nor to the historical precedents, but to the logic of nuclear deterrence. And it is open to question whether this "logic" is logical now that the prospect of total nuclear war is becoming total in both directions. It is easy enough, and in terms of power politics sensible enough, to assume the obligations of a total nuclear guarantee from a position of nuclear monopoly or unassailable predominance. But just as the totality commonly assumed to be implicit in our major collective defense commitments today would hardly have been possible, as a practical matter, for a continental power before the advent of planes and missiles and nuclear weapons, so it becomes illogical when these instruments of destruction are available to both sides.

The issue is not "total" versus "limited" war; it is certainly not "peace through deterrence" versus "appeasement." The issue concerns the nature of the collective defense commitment in practical terms. These terms encompass the weight of our national security interests and an estimate of the interests of the opposing side in each separate conflict. They include the nature and limits of the means we have available (or can make available) to uphold our commitment, together with the effort we can reasonably expect our local allies to exert on their own behalf, but also the means available to the prospective aggressor. The terms include also the relation of the commitment in question to other commitments for which we may have to reserve some of our resources, as well as the impact upon those other commitments—and, indeed, upon the network of collective defense commitments as a whole—of the course of action we elect when a particular commitment must be honored. All these considerations must be assembled and balanced, one against the other and each against all, before statements are justified such as those so often made: for example, that while we might conceivably respond to local or otherwise limited aggression in the Middle East with such conventional (nonnuclear) forces as we can bring to bear, we cannot possibly pretend to oppose the conventional masses of Red China without using at least "tactical" nuclear weapons—i.e., nuclear weapons of low yield in explosive power, confined to the "battlefield"—and any kind of war that is not "total" in every respect is unthinkable on the NATO front, or indeed, in any conflict in which the armed forces of the United States and the U.S.S.R. are openly engaged.

All such dogmatic assertions are attractive in their simplicity and in their apparent necessity in terms of the logic of nuclear deterrence. But if, as we have suggested, the logic of nuclear deterrence is obsolete, these inferences from it are anachronistic. In the light of the military realities of nuclear parity between the United States and the leading Communist power, they are no more and no less valid than other dogmatic propositions emotionally inspired by what Sir Winston Churchill named "the balance of terror." "There is no alternative to peace." "There will never be another war because any war in the nuclear era will destroy civilization and no statesman would ever deliberately make such a choice." "Because nuclear weapons exist they will be used in any future war." "No nuclear power will ever concede defeat while the destructive force of nuclear weapons lies unused in its arsenals." "In any war in which the United States is engaged we must use whatever force is necessary to win." "No power will deliberately initiate the use of nuclear weapons except in a last-ditch effort to survive, and no winner will dare press an advantage against a nuclear power far enough to compel the latter to initiate the use of nuclear weapons." "War has become so destructive that military power is irrelevant to the relations of states. Henceforth decisions between competing national interests will be made in terms of the political, psychological, and economic components of the conflict." There is truth in some, perhaps in all, such assertions, but far less than sufficient truth to constitute them Holy Writ. There is also untruth in them, and fatalism, and wishful thinking.

Our planning for the era of rocket missiles, intercontinental and trans-sonic jet bombers, electronic warfare, and "tactical" and thermonuclear warheads, cannot rest upon certainties; uncertainty is inescapable. At best, knowledge in the military sciences and arts is a matter of comparative probabilities, and the probabilities are often quite difficult to estimate. Some future technical and tactical developments are more probable than others, often a great deal more probable than the really cataclysmic ones that tease the morbid imagination. Some military capabilities and some strategies offer higher probability of success than others; so, likewise, do some adaptations of strategy and tactics to available and foreseeable weapons. Allowance must always be made for an erroneous estimate of the probabilities, but it is as unwise to concentrate effort and resources on the most "dangerous" but less probable contingencies as it is completely to ignore the less probable, and even the unforeseen.

We are familiar with the charge that the military profession customarily anticipates the next war by perfecting its preparation for the last one. The avalanche of technological developments in the military field, however, has produced another infatuation equally devastating in its consequences. This is the tendency to make military gadgetry an end in itself, which too often takes the form of judging the tools of war only in terms of their maximum destructiveness. As long as the capacity of weapons to kill and to destroy was limited, and the destruction of war came mainly from its disruptive effect upon society—including its tendency to spread lawlessness, famine, and disease—each increase in the destructiveness of weapons was a significant quantum of addition to the equations of force in the relations of peoples. But with the advent of nuclear weapons, and even more so with the advent of thermonuclear weapons—if not, indeed, earlier with the advent of long-range aircraft—the destructive force available in the world seems clearly to have become excessive in relation to the human aims that normally have meaning.

The ultimate of war's destructiveness is the occasional extermination of a victim people. Given time and determination, this could be achieved with stones and clubs as well as with "modern" weapons. Short of this, but still "total," is the extirpation of a rival power: *delenda est Cartago.* Either conception of the purpose of war makes a fetish of "security," makes the maximum accumulation of power an end in itself, or substitutes "fury" for reason. But in the historical context in which such purposes have been realized, the risk of self-immolation of the people bent on the annihilation or extirpation of an enemy was low. No doubt this self-destruction did occasionally come to pass, owing to the socially Pyrrhic consequences of disorder, famine, and plague brought on by long-lasting conflict. But in general the outcome of war could be counted on to be an either-or outcome, with the losses on one side significantly outweighing the losses on the other. And, in fact, in historic times the decision to push war to the ultimate of annihilation or extirpation was usually not made unless there was a winner with enough energy left to complete the process.

The first half of the twentieth century has witnessed a fundamental change in these historic conditions and choices. Now it is highly probable that any people will destroy themselves who in error or fury refrain from imposing limits upon the excessive force of military destruction at their disposal—if they and their enemy both are advanced in the technology of war. This is, to be sure, not a certainty. There are a number of improbable developments that are foreseeable, in addition to all the unforeseeable developments, that might, in fact, reduce the present high probability of mutual destruction in such a conflict. But it is an optimist indeed who does not see the trend running in the contrary direction—toward reduction rather than increase in a "winner's" chance of survival.

When the destructiveness of military weapons is low, or in any circumstance in which the means available to honor a military commitment are limited, it is reasonable to think of that commitment in terms of the maximum force that can be mobilized from existing resources and spared from other requirements. But when the destructiveness of the weapons is excessive, in the sense defined, the problem is not to maximize but to measure their employment in support of a commitment. This may well mean a shift of emphasis from destructiveness as such to the nature of the weapons and their suitability to the requirements of the particular case. And this shift may be dictated not only because destruction alone may prove inappropriate, but also because it may prove insufficient in the form available. Destructiveness will prove inappropriate if it cannot be employed with sufficient discrimination so that it is visited only on the enemy and not also on an ally or on a people whose friendship we desire to win or keep, or if the enemy's destructive response may be counted on to have the same results. Destructiveness will also be inappropriate if used in such a way as to cause us to overreach the scope of the commitment and thereby expand the conflict, risking, as an ultimate limit, our own destruction. Weapons designed to maximize destructiveness (either in terms of the size of the package, or in terms of cost, or in terms of the number of men necessary to employ them) may also prove unsuitable, inadequate, and therefore insufficient, if the conditions of the conflict preclude their use in a manner that exploits their destructiveness.

For these reasons our widespread collective defense commitments reinforce the need for military forces in sufficient variety and strength—in the various arms and in terms of various types of weapons and methods of employment—to give us a balance of military resources corresponding to the expected needs. The great "unbalancer" of our forces has been the "theory of the deterrent," or "massive retaliation" as it is known familiarly to the world press. Several references have already been made to this theory and to the strategy of nuclear deterrence based upon it. We must now examine it more closely.

Four historical facts are essential to an understanding of the strategy of nuclear deterrence. All relate to the circumstances in which it was evolved and therefore presumably bear a causal relationship to the strategy itself. First, it should be remembered that the "doctrine" of massive retaliation, which was the first systematic statement of the theory of nuclear deterrence, was formulated in connection with the Indochina crisis of 1953-1954. In other words, it was a strategy evolved to meet the requirements of collective defense. The second and third facts provide the political background: a new administration pledged (a) to the proposition that the Korean war had been wrongly and wastefully fought by the preceding administration; and (b) to a program of defense economy. The fourth historical fact is that the United States military forces were just then entering upon the period in which our nuclear predominance had real meaning.

In the passage from his address of January 12, 1954, a part of which was quoted earlier, Secretary Dulles went on to say:

> Local defense will always be important. But there is no local defense which alone will contain the mighty landpower of the Communist world. Local defenses must be reinforced by the further deterrent of massive retaliatory power. A potential aggressor must know that he cannot always prescribe battle conditions that suit him. Otherwise, for example, a potential aggressor, who is glutted with manpower, might be tempted to attack in places where his superiority was decisive.
> The way to deter aggression is for the free community to be willing and able to respond vigorously at places and with means of its own choosing.

The general theme of the statement was economic. With obvious reference to the way the Korean war had been fought, the Secretary said: "We do not need self-imposed policies that sap our strength."[8]

In later statements, and particularly in an article published in *Foreign Affairs* in April 1954, Secretary Dulles spelled out in detail what he meant by "the further deterrent of massive retaliatory power." This was that the possession of nuclear weapons gave the United States the capacity to "punish" aggression, quickly and economically, not in the sense that the aggressor must be utterly

---

[8] "The Evolution of Foreign Policy," address before the Council on Foreign Relations, Inc., New York, January 12, 1954. For complete text see *Department of State Bulletin,* January 25, 1954, pp. 107-110.

destroyed, but in the sense that he would "lose from his aggression more than he could win." In brief, the aggressor must be assumed to have chosen the object of his aggression in the belief that its attainment would be worth the costs and risks of attaining it. We could, however, deprive him of this expectation by convincing him that no matter what the worth of the objective might be to him, we would, by the use of nuclear destructive power, make him pay *more* than it was worth. And if we did convince him, he would be deterred from making the attack.[9]

At this point a fifth historical fact needs to be recalled. This strategy of nuclear deterrence was formulated to meet the expansionist pressures of Communist China, a power that while "glutted with manpower" had *no* nuclear weapons. Moreover, the greater power with which the Chinese People's Republic was allied, though it did have nuclear weapons, was as yet far inferior to the United States in respect to their possession and use.

The major difference between 1954 and 1950, in terms of United States military strength—not in terms of United States domestic politics—was the following. In 1950 the United States possessed only the beginnings of its nuclear force and almost certainly could not have prevented the Red Army from occupying Western Europe had its use of its limited nuclear stocks against the Chinese precipitated a world war. By 1954 the growing power of the Strategic Air Command, the mounting stockpiles of nuclear weapons, and the coming stocks of thermonuclear bombs, had given the United States the certain capacity to destroy the Soviet Union, as well as Red China, with very little risk of effective reprisal. But it was almost equally certain that this happy state of affairs was not going to last for long. This is why it is difficult to treat the strategy of nuclear deterrence, in the original form, with respect. It is difficult to escape the conclusion that the thinking it expressed reflected an improvident decision to build the national defense policy upon sand.

Mr. Dulles, whom it is by no means unreasonable to quote because he has best articulated the thinking of all the architects of the

---

[9] John Foster Dulles, "Policy for Security and Peace," *Foreign Affairs*, 32, No. 3 (April 1954), 353-64.

national defense policies of this period, later tried to adapt his "theory of the deterrent" to the rising nuclear power of the U.S.S.R. This effort appeared, again in *Foreign Affairs,* in October 1957, in an article entitled: "Challenge and Response in United States Foreign Policy."[10] In this article he explicitly acknowledged the arrival of the U.S.S.R. at maturity as a nuclear power: "Today," he said, "a general war between the great military Powers could destroy almost all human life, certainly in the northern latitudes. Our working hypothesis must be that what is necessary is possible. We assume that the forces which man has created, man can by wisdom, resourcefulness and discipline harness and control." But along the way to this somber diagnosis and this suggestion of a hopeful prescription, he took comfort in the existence of the so-called "small" or "tactical" nuclear weapons. For, without assuming their possession to be an exclusive privilege of the "free world," he concluded that their use could be a tremendous advantage, first: because they would enable the United States and its allies to defeat (and therefore to deter) an attack by the massive conventional armies of the Communist bloc, and second: because the Russians would be reluctant to initiate *nuclear* aggression, the only kind they could rationally initiate, and would consequently be deterred again: "Thus the tables may be turned, in the sense that instead of those who are non-aggressive having to rely upon all-out nuclear retaliatory power for their protection, would-be aggressors would be unable to count on a successful conventional aggression, but must themselves weigh the consequences of invoking nuclear war."

This argument appears not to have been very convincing to our allies, particularly in NATO, who were much more disturbed by the implication, inherent in Mr. Dulles' interest in "tactical" nuclear weapons, that the United States might be contemplating a nuclear war "limited" to their territories, reserving massive thermonuclear retaliation as the ultimate response only in case of a Russian attack upon North America.

Mr. Dulles' article was followed shortly by the launching of the Russian earth satellites and talk of a "missile gap"—which reflected the fear that our strategic retaliation forces might actually become inferior to the Russian. Since then—the fall of 1957—official in-

---

[10] *Foreign Affairs,* 36, No. 1 (October 1957), 25-43.

terest in the problems of local defense and limited war has increased within the United States government. But even more eloquent proof of the changed climate is the fact that, during the Middle East crisis of 1958, when United States marines and airborne troops were landed in Lebanon, and during the Quemoy crisis that erupted a little later, most of the "deterrence" talking was done by the other side.

The change-over, in fact, began earlier. It was during the Suez war in 1956 that the Russians first began uttering threats of nuclear retaliation specifically aimed at the Western allies, rather than contenting themselves—as they had done for several years—with the observation that it was capitalism, and not communism, that would be destroyed in a nuclear war. The new and more pointed threats presumably reflected growing confidence in their intermediate range missiles, with which they may believe they could annihilate the population of Western Europe and, even more to the point, destroy the overseas bases upon which the United States still depends for the bulk of its strategic striking power.

When the Chinese Communists opened artillery fire on Quemoy Island in August 1958, after a tacit cease-fire that had endured for over two years, the United States response was not only minimal *action* (as had also been true in 1955), it was also minimal *declaration* (which had certainly not been true when the Formosa Straits Declaration was being proposed, debated, and passed by Congress in 1955). Indeed, in this renewal of the Far East crisis it was rare for the word "deterrence" even to be used, and nothing was said about nuclear retaliation, "massive" or otherwise, beyond a few fugitive utterances from irritated generals who were promptly cautioned to control their tongues. Instead, it was the Soviet Union that assumed the role of the deterrer, warning "the inspirers and organizers of the new military adventure in the Far East"—in words reminiscent of Mr. Dulles' "in places and with means of its own choosing"—not to expect "that the counter-blow will be limited to the offshore islands and the Straits of Formosa. They will receive a devastating blow that will put an end to imperialist aggression in the Far East."[11] It was Nikita Khrushchev who announced,

---

[11] *The Washington Post,* September 5, 1958, quoting from *Pravda* of the same date.

using the terms of the Rio and North Atlantic treaties, that "an attack on the People's Republic of China . . . is an attack on the Soviet Union." Moreover, he observed that the ships of the United States Seventh Fleet in the Formosa Straits "are fit, in fact, for nothing but courtesy visits and gun salutes and can serve as targets for the right kinds of rockets."[12]

The wheel of fortune has now come full circle, and the Russians imagine themselves possessed of the prize of nuclear deterrence. But the wheel is a notorious swindle, leading the Russians, in their turn, to improvidence, or at least overconfidence, based upon their latest technological successes. For them now, as for the United States earlier, this may well prove a highly unsatisfactory basis upon which to build national defense and a national security policy. Their verbal exaggerations quite aside, however, the undisputed facts of Russia's arrival at maturity as a nuclear power require that we take a critical look at our policy of collective defense. Up to this point, there has been no examination of the military forces we have, and have had, to support our commitments because it seemed pointless to deal in numbers and in deployments, of which the significance depends entirely upon the strategy they are expected to implement, before cutting away the underbrush surrounding that strategy.

We are now, it appears, at the heart of the problem. Our policy, still designed to contain communism within its present boundaries, rests upon the belief that we can achieve our purposes with minimum economic strain upon the United States by developing effective local defenses, tying them into regional self-defense arrangements, and committing our power to support these collective forces in the event of Communist aggression. But there is some evidence of a shift from faith in *deterrence,* interpreted as a posture virtually guaranteeing that the other side cannot win, to reliance on *defense,* a more modest posture meant to assure the prospective aggressor that we and our allies can put up a respectable fight in support of our interests and anticipating that he will, in fact, be "deterred," at least most of the time, by his estimate of the price of overcoming

---

[12] Nikita Khrushchev to Dwight D. Eisenhower, letter of September 7, 1958, published in *The New York Times,* September 9, 1958.

the expected resistance. At a news conference on United States defense planning, November 14, 1958, the Secretary of Defense, Mr. Neil H. McElroy, was reported as saying that there would be further reductions in United States forces, pursuant to the standing search for defense economy, and that greater reliance would be placed on strengthened local forces in non-Communist areas, "since such forces are better suited than United States forces to meet instantaneously the 'probings' of the Communists." There was no consoling mention of "sea and air forces . . . equipped with new and powerful weapons of precision which can utterly destroy military targets without endangering unrelated civilian centers," as Mr. Dulles stated the virtues of nuclear retaliation in 1955. Instead, the Secretary of Defense foresaw "an enhanced role for the Navy to keep the sea lanes free should Marine or Army units need to be moved quickly."[13]

The evolution of United States thinking on collective defense has so far been reviewed mainly in theoretical terms. After a brief survey of the network of collective defense commitments, we considered first why collective defense was chosen as an essential element of United States national security policy and then asked what the United States commitment to the defense of its allies means, specifically when both the prospective aggressor and the primary defender have an abundance of destructive nuclear military power. The nuclear era did not burst upon the world full grown, however, but came to maturity by stages over somewhat more than a decade, during most of which time the United States enjoyed a substantial lead in nuclear power; we therefore found it necessary to trace the historical evolution of United States strategic thinking as regards collective defense. This required an examination of the theory of nuclear deterrence, including its origins in response to various technical and political stimuli and the changes to which it has been subject owing to the emergence of the U.S.S.R. as a nuclear power. It now seems desirable, even at the cost of some repetition, to go back over the same historical course to record in broad outline what happened to United States military forces

---

[13] Jack Raymond, press conference report, *The New York Times*, November 14, 1958.

and to United States military assistance to its allies, under the impact both of the historical influences that help to account for the evolution of strategic concepts, and of those concepts themselves. "Local defense will always be important," Mr. Dulles has said, "but there is no local defense which alone will contain the mighty landpower of the Communist world." What, then, have we in fact done to stimulate local defense efforts, and what provision have we made for United States military forces which might be used to enable the local defenses to contain the Communist world? The examination will conclude with a tentative evaluation of the dual effort, and with some suggestions for the future.

The hasty demobilization of 1945 and 1946 left United States armed services in a situation that can fairly be described as a shambles, from which they were only slowly recovering when they were catapulted into a new emergency rearmament effort by the Korean war. The armed forces, which numbered over 12 million men on V-E Day in 1945, had dropped to less than 1.4 million by the spring of 1948. The Air Force, first given separate existence by the National Security Act of 1947, had at the time only 38 combat groups of planes. The Army's first postwar personnel ceiling was 670,000, but by 1948 actual strength had fallen to 541,000 because of the inadequacy of volunteer enlistments. The Navy fared better than the other services, but its strength by early 1948 was under 500,000, including the Marines. The defense budget submitted in 1947 for the fiscal year 1948-1949 called for $11,256,000 for all services. Meanwhile, it was becoming evident that the Russian armed forces had been subjected to no such reduction. On the contrary, they retained a total strength of approximately 4 millions, including ground forces in excess of 175 divisions, of which 20 to 30 divisions were located in East Germany and the satellite areas.

The security considerations that prompted the formulation of the policy of containment during the period 1946-1949 also inspired a re-examination of the United States' own defenses. The first postwar increases were proposed by President Truman in March 1947, when he called for the passage of universal military training (and a temporary extension of the wartime draft to fill the gap until universal military training could become effective), and a $3-billion addition to the defense budget. At the same time he recommended an Air Force of 55 groups, together with minimum strengths for all the services. Congress that year extended the draft but postponed consideration of universal military training, raised the service minima above the levels recommended by the Department of Defense, and voted the budget of $14 billion. Also, listening to the Air Force, which had appealed over the heads of the administration, Congress authorized 70 groups. These increases enabled Secretary of Defense James Forrestal to plan 25 Army divisions, a Navy of two fleets with 562,000 men, and the 70-group Air Force. This program continued in existence, with minor variations, down to June 1950. Meantime, economic aid to Europe had begun in 1948 and the first appropriation, of $1.3 billion, for European "mutual defense assistance" was voted in September 1949.

The Korean war affected all these programs, immediately raising the defense appropriations for 1950-1951 from $15.5 to $28.1 billion, with plans to double the armed forces—to over 3 million— by mid-1951, and increasing Mutual Defense Assistance from the $1.2 billion planned to over $5.2 billion. The trend continued upward, and was expected to reach a peak in the fiscal year July 1, 1952—June 30, 1953, at $51.2 billion for defense and $10.5 billion for foreign aid, leveling off somewhat lower in later years. In fact, Congress voted $7.3 billion for foreign aid—called "mutual security" for the first time—in the fiscal year beginning July 1, 1952. Meanwhile, the Truman administration's defense program for 1952-1953, which was expected to determine the level of post-Korean war armaments—not to create "an active force adequate to carry on a full-scale war" but to put "ourselves in a position to mobilize rapidly if we have to"—reflected the decline in military activity in Korea.[14] Nevertheless, it called for total military strength of 3.5 million, with an Army of 21 ready divisions, an Air Force of 143 wings, a Navy of 408 major combatant vessels in active fleets (with 16 carrier groups), and a Marine Corps of 3 divisions.

This was the defense program at which the Eisenhower administration took its "new look" during 1953 and 1954. It was during

---

[14] The quotation is from President Truman's State of the Union Message, January 9, 1952.

these same years that collective defense came to the fore as a major security policy, and "massive retaliation" or nuclear deterrence emerged as the basic national strategy. Congress had already cut Mr. Truman's proposed budget for the fiscal year 1953-1954 from $51.2 to $46.6 billion, and had reduced his Mutual Defense Assistance proposals by nearly 25 percent (from $7.9 billion to a little over $6 billion). On April 3, 1953, President Eisenhower announced a further reduction of $8.5 billion in the defense budget. He later made other reductions, and Congress eventually voted $34.4 billion for defense (and somewhat under $4.8 for mutual security). In the later Truman defense budgets the share going to the Air Force had increased greatly, owing to the tremendous expansion program for SAC and the increasing cost of planes. President Eisenhower's first cuts were in aircraft construction, resulting in a revision of plans from the scheduled 143 wings down to 120. Reductions in the other services were to come later; the Army was perhaps most substantially affected, as major combat forces fell during the five-year period 1953–1958 from 21 to 15 divisions. During 1958 and the first half of 1959 a further cut was made to reduce the Army to 870,000 men and 13 divisions. By June 1959 the over-all strength of the services was scheduled to decline to 2,525,000, with a defense budget of about $40 billion, however, which reflected the rising cost of military equipment. Meanwhile, mutual security appropriations likewise declined, to $2.8 billion for 1954 and to $2.7 billion for 1955 and 1956, but rose for the fiscal year 1957 to $3.7 billion, which was to be representative of the new level during the next several years.

Paralleling the reductions in the strength of the United States Army, the new administration instituted a policy of disengaging our ground forces from their forward positions in the Pacific, beginning in December 1953, six months after the Korean Armistice, when President Eisenhower announced that two of the seven Army divisions then in Korea would be withdrawn to the United States. By 1958 there remained only four divisions in the Pacific (two Army divisions in Korea, and one in reserve in Hawaii, and a Marine division in Okinawa). Meantime, United States ground forces in Europe, though they never reached the total of six divisions promised to NATO in 1950, have remained at the five-division level since 1952.

As the record shows, the Truman administration was able to do very little about the force requirements of collective defense, beyond extending military aid to Western Europe and increasing our troops in West Germany, until the Korean war. The record also suggests, however, that prior to 1953 there was little systematic thinking regarding the United States armed forces required for collective defense. The Korean war itself, though fought by the United States within the collective security system of the United Nations, was also an expression of the policy of collective defense. For this reason, and also because it was the only experience available to serve as a planning guide, the Korean war might have been expected to exert a profound influence upon thinking about the military needs of the collective defense network. And indeed it did, but after January 20, 1953, that experience became more an example to be avoided than one from which constructive lessons of profound importance were to be learned.

The Chief of Staff of the United States Army, General Maxwell D. Taylor, has said on several occasions that South Korea was the one place along the vast Asian crescent of the Communist bloc where the United States, in 1950, had even a chance of effectively opposing military aggression. This was because of the presence of United States forces on occupation duty in Japan; the presence of the United States military advisory teams with the South Korean forces; and the existence of supply lines, bases, and airfields in and around Japan and Korea. By 1953 it was at least possible to believe that United States military capability was no longer so limited. The growth of our air power and of our naval air arm, and their armament with nuclear weapons, could be said—and were said—to have changed the circumstances most desirably. Mr. Dulles, then, could embark upon his moves to perfect the network of collective defense commitments while assuring the American people that neither we nor our allies need be prepared to face "the mighty landpower of the Communist world" on the ground again, as we did in Korea. Rather, as he said in March 1955 with reference to SEATO:

For military defense we shall rely largely upon mobile allied power which can strike an aggressor wherever the occasion may demand. That capacity will, we believe, deter aggression. We shall not need to build up large static forces at all points and the United States contribution will be primarily in terms of sea and air power.[15]

Whether this policy stood the test of time successfully is the subject of debate. We are told that in the spring of 1954, when the United States was trying desperately to keep the French in the fight against the Communist-supported Viet Minh rebels in North Viet Nam, a proposal was made within the administration to use mobile air power in a nuclear strike against the rebels, only to be turned down by the Joint Chiefs of Staff on the ground that it would be ineffective.[16]

Mr. Dulles himself, according to the interview that appeared in *Life* Magazine in January 1956, eventually recommended that the United States should join in a *ground* offensive against the Viet Minh "just as the United Nations stepped in against the North Korean aggression in 1950," using our nuclear air power to destroy "staging bases in south China" in retaliation if the Chinese Communists then intervened openly on the Viet Minh side.[17] This proposal was not accepted by our British allies, but the fact that it was made (and Mr. Dulles has never denied it) seems to indicate a fallacy in the comforting assurance that "we do not need self-imposed policies [requiring us to use ground forces in support of our collective defense commitments] that will sap our strength." It must be added, however, that the Secretary of State claims success for his nuclear deterrence from the fact that the Chinese Communists never did intervene openly in North Viet Nam as they did in Korea (but neither did the United States), despite massive United States assistance to the French. It is presumably because of this conviction that he could subsequently make the statement quoted earlier—and other similar statements—regarding the mean-

---

[15] Radio and television address, March 8, 1955, upon his return from a two-weeks visit to Southeast Asia.

[16] Chalmers M. Roberts, "The Day We Didn't Go to War," *The Reporter,* 11, No. 14 (September 14, 1954), 31-35.

[17] James Shepley, "How Dulles Averted War," *Life,* 40 (January 16, 1956), 70-80.

ing of the United States contribution to the collective defense of the signatories of the Manila Treaty of September 1954. Against the claim, and the conviction, stands the fact that the French were defeated in North Viet Nam, and another satellite was added to the Communist bloc.

It should be noted that this test of the strategy of nuclear deterrence occurred at a time when the United States unquestionably had a decisive advantage in nuclear weapons and air power. Four years later, as we have already seen, when there was once again a crisis in the Far East—this time resulting from Chinese Communist aggressive action against the Chinese Nationalists on Quemoy Island —nothing was said on the United States side about nuclear deterrence, presumably because the United States nuclear advantage was open to serious question. By then, in other words, we were facing the future, with defense commitments to scores of nations, covering substantial parts of two hemispheres and six continents; with forces in steady process of reduction from the levels reached in the Korean rearmament; and with little faith remaining in the magic of nuclear deterrence. An abiding hope that the risks of military action in the nuclear era might in themselves "deter" the Communists from military aggression—particularly as their political, economic, and propaganda offensives have not lacked success —could lead to the conclusion that there is really little we can do or need to do to put usable muscle into our guarantees. But if that hope proves false, as have other sanguine predictions regarding developments behind the Iron Curtain that might favor the West, we must assuredly anticipate the day when our lack of prevision will be disclosed, with unfortunate consequences for our standing in the world. We cannot play the role of a superpower if our military power does not exist in forms in which we can and will use it.

It may be inferred from the statement of the United States Secretary of Defense, which was quoted earlier, that the diminishing utility of the nuclear deterrent, together with mounting defense costs, mean that "greater reliance" will be placed upon "strengthened local forces in the non-Communist areas." It is impossible to review the Mutual Defense Assistance program in detail, but it is said that from 1950 to 1957 nearly $20 billion in military aid has been extended to our allies; over half of this, however, went to the

NATO area. During this period the United States Army was help-ing to train over 200 divisions of allied ground forces, the element of military strength our allies were, on the whole, best able to support. Aside from the NATO forces in Western Europe, where United States organization and training assistance was perhaps less substantial than material and foreign exchange support, the bulk of this effort has been concentrated in five countries. South Korea, with an army of perhaps 600,000, now actually possesses the second largest army in the non-Communist world. Turkey's army, with about 400,000 men, is the fourth largest. The other three are Greece, which was the first country to benefit from United States military aid; the Republic of China on the island of Formosa; and the latest beneficiary, the Republic of South Viet Nam. These five countries are in the front lines of the non-Communist world, and United States policy has made them into citadels of containment. In the case of three of them—South Korea, Formosa, and South Viet Nam—the military forces with which they have been provided cannot possibly be supported by the domestic economies. Conse-quently, these three are more than beneficiaries of United States aid backed by the United States security guarantee; they are *de facto* dependencies of the United States.

The military aid record looks impressive, and one may be in-clined to wonder what more can be done "to strengthen local forces" than is already being done. It is claimed that the nearly $20 billion of United States aid, 1950-1957, has been "matched by allied expenditures of about $122 billion," resulting in allied strength in 1958 of "almost 5,000,000 ground troops, 2,500 com-bat vessels and 32,000 planes." (The 1950 figures for comparison are given, respectively, as 3.6 million, 1,200, and 2,500.) In addi-tion to this numerical increase there has of course been a substan-tial improvement in quality, both of men and of equipment; for example, allied jet aircraft have increased from under 600 in 1950 to about 14,000 in 1957.[18]

The record is less impressive in detail than a general view sug-gests. In a number of instances military aid has been extended for

---

[18] "The Mutual Security Program, Fiscal Year 1958," A Summary Presentation, February 1958. Pamphlet released by the Departments of State and Defense and the International Co-operation Administration.

"political" reasons little related to collective defense. Moreover, the supposedly political justification in these cases sometimes raises questions regarding the political wisdom displayed. A particularly striking example of this is the delivery of a handful of jet fighters to Saudi Arabia, presumably in order to feed the vanity of the ruling monarch and make him less likely to press the question of our continued use of the Dhahran airbase in that country. Similarly open to question is the extension of military aid to the military clique in control of Thailand. But the most disputable military aid program of all is probably that to Pakistan, for, despite the high quality of the Pakistani armed forces, it may honestly be doubted that by supporting them we have added as much to the firmness of the non-Communist world as we have subtracted by offending and distracting India. A similar and in fact related question, although it involves far more complex political considerations, concerns our support of the Baghdad Pact in order to close the Middle East "gap" in the "free world perimeter."

Even at its best the military aid program gives rise to justified concern. There is a tendency, understandable though often unsuitable, for United States military aid missions to endeavor to create local forces in the image of United States forces. In part this results from the fact that these forces are supplied with surplus United States equipment, and with equipment from current production designed to meet United States standards when the surplus is exhausted. But the result might be the same even without the influence of this complex equipment, simply because of the standards of military organization, equipment, training, and operations with which the United States military aid teams are indoctrinated—standards evolved to match the productive capacity of an advanced industrial society. Even when a conscious effort is made to overcome these influences, the habit of the mass rules against the imagination of the few. The general consequence is to saddle even the "best" of our allies with a military apparatus that is exorbitantly expensive and perhaps no better suited to the terrain and personnel resources of the recipient country than to its economic capacity.

These strictures, of course, do not apply to military aid to the advanced countries of Western Europe, though even within the NATO area they are not entirely inapplicable to Turkey. It is mainly the military dependencies of Asia, however, that give cause for concern. If the Communists were really as clever as they are often given credit for being, they would relieve the external pressure on South Korea, South Viet Nam, and Formosa and devote their energies to boring from within, castigating the Rhee, Diem, and Chiang governments as "tools" of the United States. The charge would be a most difficult one to meet. For if any one of these governments tried to reduce its dependence upon the United States, it would shortly find itself in difficulties with its own military, upon whom it is dependent for its very existence. On the other hand, if it simply resisted the charge, without the saving justification of external military pressure, it would risk uniting all dissident elements within the country under the banner of anti-imperialist nationalism. As long as the external military pressure remains, there is probably little that the United States can do or needs to do except pay the bills. But forward planning against the time when the Communists might change their tactics would be wise. It is difficult without access to all the facts to know what form that planning might take, but a less costly military establishment, combining a smaller standing army with some kind of militia adapted to local terrain and social institutions, might prove to be an acceptable solution. The standing army would need to be large enough to sustain the authority of the central government. If the stigma of foreign support and domination were removed, it might also serve, if given responsibility for supplying and training the local militia, as an integrating force within the country.

Throughout the underdeveloped world, the military elements of society occupy a key position. The underdeveloped world does not, of course, really differ in this respect from the rest of the world, except that the institutions that establish civilian control of the military in more advanced countries are weak in these African and Asian countries lately arrived at independence. In any country a deep internal crisis will bring the military to the forefront, as happened in 1958 in France. But in a country such as Pakistan, or the Sudan, it takes rather less to produce such a crisis. Military aid, consequently, has an obvious *mission—exemplaire* if not *civilisatrice*. By giving the officer groups with which it deals not only professional competence, but in addition a sense of pride in a national society built as far as possible on the Western model, the military aid missions can, and do, add substantially to the domestic solidity of these new countries. The case of Indonesia, despite the political unrest there during recent years, may well be an outstanding example of what the United States military can do, largely by advice and example, with limited formal aid and no collective defense agreement, to strengthen the forces of anti-communism. In addition, in underdeveloped countries, the army may well concentrate its major national assault on the problem of illiteracy, so that its enlisted members, when they have completed their period of training, may add substantially to that small portion of the country's labor force qualified to acquire modern skills.

Our brief look at the military aid programs justifies no final conclusions regarding their strengths and weaknesses, but does suggest that a purely quantitative measure of their effectiveness would give a quite false impression. It may be difficult to imagine, for example, the kind of war in which the 200 divisions our Army is training overseas would all be employed simultaneously. It would be misleading, certainly, to think of them as freely available for employment at the point of need in a particular local collective defense effort. As the network of defense commitments has not been tied into a system, we could not expect to move forces between the various treaty areas. But it is also quite unlikely that there could be much movement within the separate areas. The element of military flexibility, so essential to counter the advantage the Communist world enjoys by virtue of its interior lines of communication, must be supplied by the United States, with some assistance in the appropriate cases from Britain, Australia, and New Zealand, and perhaps the Philippines. The local defense picture is not, of course, all black because of this rigidity. The increased numbers and improved quality of local defense forces do impose greater requirements upon an ambitious aggressor, and consequently do increase the deterrent effect of the collective defense network as a whole, and this may be counted a net gain wherever the accretion of strength is not offset by local or intra-area weakness created by the same programs.

We have seen that the experience of 1953-1955 in the Indochinese and Formosan crises, plus the experience of 1958 in the

Middle and Far East, has undermined the concept—evolved in the moment of our nuclear ascendancy, 1953-1954—that the United States can add the essential element of flexibility to collective defense simply by means of its nuclear air power. Evidence that the lesson has been read correctly in the Department of Defense may be seen in the nature of the responsibilities assigned to the XVIIIth Airborne Corps by the Department of the Army and to the XIXth Air Force by the Department of the Air Force. The former has been constituted the headquarters, Strategic Army Corps (STRAC), and has been charged with seeing that the four divisions of the Army strategic reserve (probably to be reduced to three by the summer of 1959) are trained and ready for prompt movement, by air and sea, to any point of urgent need. The latter has been given the mission of creating tactical task forces specially tailored to meet the needs of particular crises, by bringing together existing Air Force components. One such force was dispatched to Turkey during the Lebanese crisis in the summer of 1958; another was sent to Formosa later in the same year. The Navy, which for many years has employed the task force concept, is at least as well equipped as either the Army or the Air Force to make use of existing resources to go to the support of our allies at the point of attack. Also its attack carrier groups, provided they are not equipped exclusively for "strategic" conflict, and its Marine landing forces, are particularly suitable for such employment.

In terms of the theoretical "total" versus "limited" war debate of the last few years, these are the provisions the services have made for "limited" war. In practical terms, they suggest what the armed services can do organizationally to meet the requirements of each particular crisis as it arises. The United States can land a battalion (or less) of Marines—as well as hundreds of thermonuclear bombs. The very existence of this range of capabilities, as evidence of what we are prepared to do, and the employment that has been made of some elements of the range, as evidence of our willingness in fact to translate our preparedness into action, may be expected to discourage military adventures by the Communists. The military capabilities represented at the lower end of the range are, however, quite restricted, and seem grossly out of balance with those capabilities for destructive nuclear war that we have developed with our eyes on the Soviet menace to North America—and to Western Europe.

Despite natural reluctance to create another higher command, it seems desirable that the provisions for tactical task forces that have been made by the separate Service Departments should be rounded out by the creation of a joint (interservice) command for tactical operations. Such a command would ensure the necessary interservice planning in the detail required for prompt employment, particularly of larger task forces that require a combination of air and sea lift. More important, perhaps, it would establish a more effective claimant for the personnel and equipment needs of this type of employment when funds are being allocated. The argument is easily made that the Department of Defense, the Joint Chiefs of Staff, and the three Service Departments are all seized of this problem. But, in defense as elsewhere, what's everybody's business tends to be nobody's. No one argues against the Strategic Air Command that all elements of the Defense Department are concerned with "the deterrent," nor against the North American Air Defense Command that all are concerned with the defense of the North American continent. If the international scene, and particularly United States collective defense commitments, create military requirements that are *sui generis*—a proposition for which a very good case can be made—then it seems appropriate to provide a special joint planning command, reporting directly to the Joint Chiefs, as SAC and NORAD do, to ensure the best possible effort to meet these requirements.

The creation of such headquarters would not, of course, automatically remove the limits on our tactical forces, which are in large part limits of resources: men, equipment, and transport. We can move a small body of men by air very quickly almost anywhere. During the Lebanese crisis we moved roughly a battalion a day by a combined sea and air lift, until there were 17,000 United States fighting men in Lebanon. But this move was made after considerable advance notice and without opposition; it was more important as evidence of the risk we were willing to take than as proof of the military power we could exert in actual hostilities. Against active opposition—for example, to counter an actual attack on the frontiers of one of our allies—our so-called "limited war" forces are actually so limited that we run great risk of being confronted with the difficult choice between falling back on nuclear retaliation or admitting our incapacity for effective action. And while we are in this situation, we must expect that the "threat," when it comes, is very likely to be one for which our nuclear force is either an insufficient or an excessive response, as appears to have been the case in Indochina in 1954.

There are two possible solutions to this shortfall of available tactical force. One is to create additional strength; the other is to make better use of the strength we have. Let us first consider how we could better employ the force we have—in addition, that is, to the organizational arrangements already made by the Services and to the joint command suggested above.

One possible method of improvement might be to proceed further with the disengagement of United States forces—from fixed overseas commitments, which began when the Eisenhower administration reduced our ground troops in Korea from eight divisions to two. Both engaged and disengaged forces serve a "deterrent" purpose. As long as nuclear retaliation was our basic national strategy, there was probably a general deterrent advantage in having our forces engaged at certain critical points. We were drawing lines all over the world which we told the other side it must not cross, and placing a few Americans on those lines to be killed no doubt helped to prove we meant what we said. Also the strength of our allies was at a low ebb, so that concrete evidence of our commitment to their defense was in some cases essential. In addition, our ability to move our forces promptly was quite limited, so that it was well to have some of them where they might be needed—in case we found we could not rely completely upon nuclear retaliation. The new strategic situation, with nuclear power on the other side comparable to our own, together with the evidence already noted that the United States is no longer even pretending that the threat of nuclear retaliation is our sole or even primary deterrent suggest that we may soon no longer be able to afford to engage so large a portion of our forces unless we can afford substantially greater forces. In general terms, disengaged central reserves, provided they can be moved promptly enough to the point of need, constitute the most effective deployment for forces as limited as ours now are relative to their possible employments.

The realization of this possibility, of course, depends upon whether the change can be reconciled with our commitments to Korea and to NATO. Certainly it could not take place in a hurry, nor should the possibility even be raised until the time is right politically. In Korea, in fact, little can be done in the way of further disengagement, unless it should be decided that no United States troops are required in Korea at all. The two understrength divisions there now are probably the minimum required as long as a token engagement is considered necessary. But maximizing the flexibility of our tactical forces is not incompatible with maintaining token engagements—which, in fact, it might well be to our advantage to have elsewhere in the collective defense network. By the same token, however, the principle that the bulk of local defenses must be supplied locally should apply in Western Europe as elsewhere.[19]

The pressing and difficult problems of NATO's defenses cannot be examined in detail here. This much, however, can be said: there appears to be no solution that does not require a greater defense effort on the part of our European partners, and along with it greater reliance on their own resources.[20] Moreover, what has been said above about the nature of the United States collective defense commitment applies in principle to NATO as well as to SEATO.

It is true that Western Europe's defense is more vital to our security than is that of Southeast Asia. But something is gravely amiss if the five divisions we keep in Europe excuse our European allies from making an adequate defense effort because they believe their security is guaranteed by our determination to administer thermonuclear retaliation against the Russians if our troops are attacked. And if they do not believe this, then the number of American troops at present assigned to the NATO forces ought not to be required to indicate what we *will* do in the event of an attack. We are, it is to be hoped, determined to defend Western Europe, and would probably expend our military efforts to the limit to prevent its conquest and incorporation in the Communist

---

[19] On obstacles in the way of greater European effort, see Arnold Wolfers, "Europe and the NATO Shield," *International Organization,* XII, No. 4 (Autumn 1958), pp. 425-39.

[20] See the chapter "On NATO Strategy," by Roger Hilsman, pp. 146-83.

world, even though we had little hope of surviving the debacle our-selves. But conquest is by no means the only threat against which the nations of Western Europe require defense.

It is difficult to believe that the logic of nuclear deterrence, which has been so widely discredited in other parts of the world where the destructive effects of nuclear retaliation might well be confined to the immediate area of conflict, applies without qualifi-cation to the defense of Western Europe, where nuclear retaliation means, at the least, exposing our allies and the friendly peoples of the satellite countries to risk of annihilation and, only a little beyond that, the thermonuclear involvement of the North American continent. It would be absurd for us, and for our allies, to assume the worst about any Communist "aggression" against Western Europe before exploring every other possibility, because the deci-sion we may have to make, once we assume the worst, may be, if we chose to retaliate "massively," the last decision the United States of America will ever make, or, alternatively, may result in an uncalled-for surrender. Indeed, the tragedy of the present situation in Western Europe is that the weakness of existing forces means that we are as gravely threatened by the possibility that we may needlessly be faced with that ultimate decision as we are by the consequences of an attack.

Again it is flexibility that is required. NATO needs forces that will discourage aggressive action, but these "deterrent" forces must be adaptable to the full range of crisis situations that may arise when deterrence fails—as it may through accident or through the agency of some third party (e.g., East German rebels) as well as by Communist "miscalculation" of NATO strength and intentions. The theory of nuclear deterrence required threats of *maximum* ac-tion ("maximum" enough to "punish"). When both sides possess unlimited resources for nuclear destruction ("unlimited" because the upper limits lie somewhere beyond the utter destruction and annihilation of the enemy), the ultimate consequences of any single military decision are more significant than the immediate conse-quences. The most elementary requirement, then, is the need for time to judge the danger and to adjust the response. And the one fatal mistake is to make decisions that foreclose later decisions.

The Western European defense requirement is for forces of all kinds, armed with conventional and with nuclear weapons, which can be fed into a crisis situation in whatever strength is required. There is now no lack of NATO force to "contain" (if that is the word for it) an all-out nuclear attack, assuming that such an attack would invoke a United States strategic counterstroke. There is also no lack of NATO force to compel the Russians to *make* a nuclear attack rather than a purely conventional one. But if the Russians do not desire to make a nuclear attack, it is also difficult to believe that it is in Western Europe's interest to compel them to do so. Yet the mere capability of compelling the Russians to use nuclear weapons may not be a very effective deterrent, despite Mr. Dulles' hopes, particularly if we consider the chance that accidents and third parties might intervene. What NATO notably lacks is a sufficiency of force at the lower end of the spectrum of military destruction to deal with crisis situations that can be contained with conventional weapons.

The additional NATO strength in conventional forces must come from the European NATO countries themselves. Even so, it may seem paradoxical to be considering, at the same time, the possibility of withdrawing some of the United States forces committed to NATO. Two indisputable facts can be advanced in defense of this possibility: first, the changed circumstances in Western Europe since NATO was first conceived and set up, and second, the vastly increased United States collective defense commitments elsewhere. Our European NATO partners are no longer in the state of weakness and instability that endangered their security when we went to their assistance in 1949. On the contrary, their economic recovery has been accomplished, and their governments are strong. In addition, substantial progress has been made toward the closer integration of their economies, and at least for some of them, there seems a real hope of eventual political union. It is not at all unreasonable that they should assume larger responsibility for their own defense, particularly in view of the fact that they alone can supply what, at the moment, is most needed.

This does not mean that the United States should sever its relations with NATO, nor anything like it. In fact, in keeping with the practice we have followed to date of combining both the engagement and the disengagement of our forces in an effort to find the most "deterrent" combination, it is certainly desirable that we should keep some of our troops with NATO forces. But it ought not to be necessary to keep more than a third of our Army combat units tied down in Western Europe. A smaller force, of say two or three divisions, ought to suffice to prove our commitment to NATO defense. In addition, once we had properly organized our strategic reserves, it would be desirable to run periodic exercises, involving the actual movement of parts of this reserve to possible points of need, including Western Europe. These exercises would be invaluable as training—if we are indeed to depend upon the prompt reinforcement of our allies for the integrity of our collective defense commitments—and also as proof to the world of what we could do. They would be expensive, but the expense would be justified if the exercises reduced the total requirement for forces, or if they increased the effectiveness of the forces we had. Moreover, the expense would be reduced if the exercises did not in all cases originate in the United States, which suggests the desirability of strengthening the area reserves we now maintain in the Pacific (one understrength Marine division on Okinawa and one Army division in Hawaii).

Increasing our disengaged reserves, even at the cost of reducing the forces we have assigned to NATO, and possibly spreading our token engaged forces to a few other exposed fronts—these are possible ways of making better use of the forces we have left after five years of steady reductions. They are not meant to suggest, however, that the total strength of United States defense forces is adequate. No final solution to the problem of manpower economy can be given here. Indeed it is doubtful if a perfect solution is ever possible. There must always be a choice of evils. It does seem an odd choice, however, when all other indications point to growing recognition of the shortcomings of nuclear deterrence, that we should be continuing to dismantle the forces we acquired in the Korean war rearmament. Citation of the disengagement of our ground forces from the Pacific to indicate one thing that might be done in the future was not meant to suggest that a partial European disengagement should be carried out for the same purpose that animated the Pacific disengagement. For while our Army divisions in Korea were being decreased from seven to two, our total strength in divisions was decreased from nineteen to fourteen. Consequently, the five divisions were disengaged only to be dissipated. The last two Army Chiefs of Staff, with all the facts before them, have protested the sacrifice of Army strength to help pay the costs of the strategic deterrent, and have appealed for a force of twenty divisions as the minimum required to discharge their many responsibilities.

In any realistic discussion of the forces required to honor our commitments to collective defense, the Army inevitably assumes the center of the stage. This is for the simple reason that if we are to support the development of local defense forces, and if we are to counter local attacks locally, we must do it on the ground—as Mr. Dulles proposed in 1954. It is no accident that the Army has had major responsibility for the administration of our foreign military aid programs. But the Army also has a vast number of other responsibilities not directly contributory to strength in reserves for tactical employment around the world. If the Army is to fulfill its responsibilities in connection with collective defense more adequately than is possible with a reserve of three or four half-ready divisions, it must have more men and more funds. We saw during the Lebanese affair that both the Marines and the Army were using equipment obsolescent by the standards of that supplied by the Russians to the Syrian armed forces. We should certainly continue to try to get a larger combat force out of the Army's present personnel authorization, though this is a solution that occurs to everyone who first looks at the problem of ground strength, and the possibilities have been rather thoroughly worked over by now. But whatever personnel base we start with, there seems to be no escaping higher costs per man, for new and better equipment and for more and better transport.

We should also be considering the advantages of overseas supply bases in areas where we do not now have them, such as in the Middle East and on or off the shores of South and Southeast Asia. These bases could be prestocked with the supplies we expect our ground and tactical air forces to require if we have to employ them in those areas. These supply bases could greatly simplify the problem of moving our forces rapidly into position, because the movement of personnel is vastly easier than the movement of their equipment. Also we should be considering the prospects of improving our ability to move troops by air by acquiring and developing the airbases required for long-range movement in "strategic" transports. And finally, we should be taking a long look at the various means of transport. These include both the long-range air transports and the shorter-range "tactical" transports that may be needed to relay our forces from the forward strategic airbases to the battle areas. They include also special-purpose ships of various kinds, including the "roll-on, roll-off" type that can land a unit in a condition to go directly into battle. Of these latter the Military Transport Service now has one, already considered obsolete.

All these suggestions for more adequate provision for the flexible strength needed to support our collective defense commitments raise the question of funds. It may be true, as some have argued, that the mounting cost of military hardware is such that we have no choice but to rely ever more heavily on nuclear weapons simply because they pack "more bang for a buck." The same argument, of course, suggests that we should concentrate more and more on the bigger bangs, because they are more economical than the smaller ones. But, considering the price we shall pay in other ways, we surely do not want to yield to this argument until all other possibilities have been explored. It may be futile to suggest here, in view of the alarms and confusions current in that area of defense, that one possibility deserving of more exploration than it has received to date is that some measure of "sufficiency" may be found for our strategic military forces, so that the tactical forces will not always have to survive on the leavings from the budget table. There is also, of course, the possibility that the capacity of our economy to support national defense has been underrated and that the relation between the general productivity of our economy and the level of our defense expenditures has been misunderstood.

What is important to keep in mind while these possibilities and many others are being explored is what it is we can buy with additional funds if they can be found, and what we shall pay for not finding them. It may well be that the real measure of what constitutes a great power in the nuclear age is the ability to dispose of *usable* military force—which is after all only another way of saying that it is a measure of the ability to retain great power. A tremendous national effort is required to pass the threshold of nuclear maturity. Two powers have made the journey, a third is on the way, and doubtless others will follow—failing those international controls on nuclear weapons that all claim to desire but none will agree to. But as nations achieve this high estate—two now, more later—significant distinctions between them in terms of the *total* military effort they can make, the amount of destruction they can accomplish, the number of lives they can snuff out, seem to fall away, leaving all equal in this ultimate sense of power. Yet, as the troubled record of our time forcefully demonstrates, national power does not for this reason lose its utility. Nor do the nonmilitary components of national power (if there are any such that cannot be traced ultimately to military roots) completely displace the military. On the contrary, in a world in which all governments and all peoples proclaim themselves lovers of peace, military action, actual and anticipated, supplies the headlines of the world's press. And we, who surely are not least in our devotion to peace, find ourselves compelled to deploy our forces, to use our military strength, more frequently—or at least more openly—than the other side in the great competition between "ways of life" in which we are engaged.

What we can buy, then, and what we will buy if our thinking is straight, is military power we can use, not just for threats that may be idle or fatal depending upon the import of the issues over which they are made, but power to be employed in proportion to the import of the conflict. Only in this way can we also buy that precious commodity, freedom to choose. For it is freedom of choice among the available actions that we sacrifice when we precommit ourselves to military decisions. In this analysis the freedom to choose conventional means of defense has been emphasized, in part because it is that particular freedom that has been most endangered by our defense policies of the past few years, but in part also because it is really difficult to foresee the circumstances in which our determined ability to employ military force in support of our interests cannot be amply demonstrated without resort to the excessive destructiveness of nuclear weapons. Nor is the argument very convincing that is so fervently advanced by some writers, namely that the atomic nucleus is inherently pro-United States, pro-West, or pro-Free World. But nothing in this examination is meant to suggest that the non-Communist world does not require "tactical" nuclear weapons in its arsenals, to limit the Communist option to employ them and to respond appropriately if the other side chooses nuclear war. Nor is there the least intention to suggest that a major continuing effort to uphold our strategic nuclear power can be avoided. The "balance of terror" is anything but static. We may indeed perish if we do not find ways to maintain it. But we may perish anyway, though possibly more slowly, if we continue to allow the effort to maintain the strategic balance so to preoccupy and exhaust us that we lack the time, the energy, and the resources to safeguard our priceless freedom to choose.

6

ON NATO STRATEGY

Roger Hilsman

WHEN NATO was first established, in 1949, it was not intended to be the integrated coalition army it now is, with the combined headquarters, common supply lines, and detailed war plans that make it unique in the history of peacetime alliances.[1] Its functions were those of the traditional alliance: to ensure maximum, pooled strength in the event of war and to deter a potential enemy by putting him on notice that if he upset the balance he would have to face not one enemy, but the combined strength of several. Article 5 of the treaty states that the "Parties agree that an armed attack against one or more of them in Europe or North America shall be considered an attack against them all; and consequently they agree that if such an armed attack occurs, each of them, . . . will assist the Party or Parties so attacked by taking forthwith, individually and in concert with the other Parties, such action as it deems necessary, including the use of armed force, . . ." In Congressional hearings and in public statements, the responsible American officials described the treaty as being designed both to strengthen European confidence and determination and to prevent the Soviets

---

[1] Perspectives differ from a point of vision high in the policy apparatus, but Mr. Hilsman decided to let his earlier description of the landscape stand unamended.

146

from making Hitler's mistake of assuming that he could commit aggression piecemeal, without interference from the United States.[2]

I

As long as NATO remained purely a traditional alliance, it had little that could be called a military strategy. But a change was not long in coming. It was the United States Congress that provided the initial impetus by insisting on fully developed war plans as a condition for further military aid. Their purpose was to ensure that aid would not be diverted to purely national purposes, unrelated to the needs of collective defense; but the result was an expansion of the military liaison committees of the Brussels Pact into something resembling a planning staff and to greater participation by the American observer group.

Other events that had a more direct effect on the transformation of NATO were the Soviet success in developing nuclear weapons and, following soon after, the Communist attack on South Korea. Immediately after discovering, in 1949, that the Soviets had exploded an atomic weapon, the United States plunged into a reappraisal of its military and foreign policies. One result of this reappraisal was the decision to accelerate the attempt to build an H-bomb; the second was NSC 68, a paper approved by the National Security Council pointing toward rearmament at a pace that required, in effect, partial mobilization.

But one may doubt whether the provisions of NSC 68 would have been carried out if it had not been for the attack on South Korea. If the atomic explosion in the Soviet Union brought a change in our evaluation of Soviet capabilities, to borrow the classic terms of military intelligence, the war in Korea brought a change in our evaluation of their intentions. It seemed certain that the Soviets had known and approved of the attack on South Korea and very likely that it had been launched at their direction. Thus the attack

[2] See *Hearings Before the Committee on Foreign Relations, United States Senate, 81st Congress, 1st Session, The North Atlantic Treaty*, (Washington, D. C., 1949). The text of the treaty is contained in *American Foreign Policy, 1950-1955*, Department of State, Washington, D. C., Vol. I, p. 812.

seemed to mean that the Soviets, having broken our monopoly of the atomic bomb, had decided that the time had come to test both our defenses and our will.

The assumption in the West was not so much that the Soviets had established a timetable for conquest as that they were now willing to adventure. Correctly or incorrectly—and it may well have been incorrectly—the West assumed that this willingness to adventure applied not only to Asia, where the attack had actually occurred, but also to Europe. It was always possible, indeed, that one of the motives for the attack was a Soviet hope that it would draw our troops from other parts of the perimeter of defense and so leave Europe weakened or even defenseless.[3]

The West began to put its European defenses on a war footing. Prior to 1950, NATO had neither a commander nor a true headquarters; what troops it disposed of were still scattered about in Germany on occupation duty. It had only a tenth of the tactical airfields needed to support those troops, and many of the airfields it did have were forward of the forces they were to support. Its most important supply lines ran, not across France perpendicular to the front, but from Hamburg and Bremerhaven across Germany parallel to the front and within easy reach of Soviet tanks. The first step was to increase the number of troops on the line. After the Senate had debated and passed its resolution in 1951, the United States undertook to send four additional divisions to Europe, and at the same time agreements were signed to provide bases for American air forces in allied territory. By the end of 1952, there were the equivalent of six American divisions in Europe as well as American bomber and fighter bases in North Africa, France, Germany, and the United Kingdom.

The second step was to provide an effective command and logistical structure. It was also in 1951 that Supreme Headquarters Allied Powers, Europe (SHAPE) was established and General Eisenhower appointed Supreme Commander. His first task was to

---

[3] See, for example, the testimony of General Omar Bradley, Chairman of the Joint Chiefs of Staff, at the MacArthur hearings. *Military Situation in the Far East, Hearings before the Committees on Armed Services and Foreign Relations, United States Senate, 82nd Congress, 1st Session* (Washington, D. C., 1951), pp. 731-32.

make the command operational; and by 1952 well over 100 air-fields for tactical support aircraft had been built, new supply lines established across France, pipelines and communications nets installed, supply bases established and stocked with food and ammunition—in sum, a good beginning had been made in all the complex preparations that stand behind an army ready to fight. NATO had completed its transformation from a traditional alliance, with little more than a mere commitment to stand together, to its new form, an integrated coalition army.[4]

II

Having arrived at this new form, NATO found itself confronted with an entirely new situation. The original strategic problem facing NATO was a familiar one. The two areas to be defended were the old western front—from Basle to the mouth of the Rhine-Ijssel—and the Brenner-Trieste area. Western staff officers had been all but weaned on the problem: they knew the different routes of approach so well they could have recited by heart the numbers of troops that could have been brought through them. The assumption was that a major war would resemble World War II, modified mainly by the existence of atomic bombs in only limited quantities. The necessary strength was therefore calculated on the basis of established rules of thumb—so many troops for each mile of front to be covered in the main approaches; so many more to screen the intervening areas; and so many more to provide a reserve of roughly one third of the total.

With such a force, NATO could have hoped to hold off an enemy two or even three times as numerous. The issue would then have turned on skill, luck, and the other intangibles of war. With a substantially weaker force, however—say, 50 divisions—one approach or another would have had to be left uncovered or the reserve so weakened that it could not have intervened effectively. A force that is adequate to the terrain it must defend, with its

---

[4] There was some co-ordination of plans between Britain and France in the period prior to World War I, but this was primitive as compared to what has taken place in NATO.

flanks anchored on natural obstacles, may hope for success even if it cannot match the enemy man for man. But neither skill nor luck is likely to save a numerically inferior force that is also inadequate to the demands of the terrain.

It was this force goal that was approved at the Lisbon Conference in 1952, the actual figure chosen being 96 divisions. But this decision had no sooner been taken than the strategic situation began to change, and radically. The sources of the change were two. The first was "nuclear plenty," the development of a wide range of nuclear weapons on both sides of the Iron Curtain and a substantial increase in the numbers available. After the Soviet Union exploded an atomic weapon in 1949, it rapidly developed a strategic air force comparable to our own. Soon both sides had built an H-bomb and begun to produce a range of battlefield atomic weapons suitable for supporting troops on the ground.

The second source of change in the strategic situation was the increasing reliance the West itself put on nuclear weapons and the policy of deterring war by threatening nuclear reprisal. The factors motivating this policy were understandable. First, the cost of the new weapons piled on top of the cost of maintaining conventional forces added up to a fabulous total. Second, almost everyone in America recoiled from the bloodletting in the "limited" Korean war. Third, the Communist bloc did not follow the attack on Korea with other aggressions, which led us to believe that our defense effort had been successful in deterring aggression and that international relations had achieved a measure of stability. All this contributed to an increasing discontent with existing strategy and a search for a way to provide military security at some less formidable cost. At the same time, the awesome destructiveness of nuclear weapons seemed to offer a way of substituting firepower for armies. The result was Secretary Dulles' doctrine of "massive retaliation," indicating that we would meet aggression by retaliating "by means and at places of our choosing," thus permitting "a selection of military means instead of a multiplicity of means."[5] This statement of policy was understood to mean that the United

---

[5] John Foster Dulles, "The Evolution of Foreign Policy," *Department of State Bulletin,* January 25, 1954, p. 108.

States would rely on the threat of nuclear air power to deter aggression of any kind and that the policy would permit the United States to cut down on ground and naval forces.

In the public debate that followed, there were two basic criticisms that seemed to lead Secretary Dulles to modify his policy. The first was that the consequences of meeting any aggression whatsoever—even a conventional, clearly limited attack—with nuclear weapons would entail an unacceptable risk of general war. The second was that by denying ourselves a range of means we would put a straitjacket on future policy. But in spite of Mr. Dulles' careful qualification that the United States would not automatically make little wars into big ones the "new look" decision to emphasize nuclear air power at the expense of ground and naval power still stood. In 1952, for example, the United States had 20 divisions; in 1958, it had 15, and a further reduction to 14 was planned for 1959. Britain, where the "new look" idea of concentrating on nuclear weapons had actually had its beginnings, was not long in following suit. The British White Paper of 1957 announced a decision to reduce British forces from 690,000 men to 375,000 by 1962 and to equip the remaining forces with "atomic rocket artillery." British forces stationed in Germany, the British Army of the Rhine, were cut from 77,000 men to 64,000 immediately, with further reductions to follow.

As these developments unfolded, the military commanders of NATO became increasingly concerned to make it clear that in the event of war nuclear weapons would have to be used at the outset. Their fear was that war might find them with neither troops nor atomic weapons, or that out of political considerations they might be ordered to resist without using nuclear weapons, only to be given permission after the battle had been lost. If nuclear weapons were to substitute for manpower, NATO's war plans had to be altered. Accordingly, in December 1954, anticipating the cuts to come, the North Atlantic Council granted the military permission to base their planning on nuclear weapons.[6]

Thus the strategic situation facing NATO changed completely,

---

[6] For the text of the communiqué, issued at Paris on December 18, 1954, by the North Atlantic Council, see *Department of State Bulletin,* January 3, 1955, p. 10.

and to this new situation there has still been no solution. Nuclear weapons of a range of types are present in substantial numbers on both sides of the line, and Western preparations have not allowed for any wars but nuclear ones. NATO forces along the line in Germany number no more than 16 to 18 combat-ready divisions, the actual figure depending on how one defines "combat-ready." The Soviet Union, on the other hand, has 22 divisions in Eastern Germany, which might be increased, without attracting attention, to about 30 with Eastern German troops or other divisions stationed nearby. Farther back, in the homeland, the Soviets have the remainder of their regular army of 175 divisions as well as other divisions manned by reservists.

In the face of this new strategic situation, Europeans have begun to translate $E = MC^2$ into local terms, and they find themselves wondering how NATO could defend them without bringing down devastation so widespread as to amount to annihilation. The only protection that the coalition army could offer seems to imply the very destruction that defense forces are intended to guard against. In an all-out war, Europe would be doubly devastated—by long-range bombers and missiles from the air and by battlefield nuclear weapons on the ground. Europeans could at best hope that their territory would not be occupied, and this might be a questionable benefit in view of what they would suffer, not only from Soviet bombs but from the backlash of our own. In General Gavin's words: "Current planning estimates run on the order of several hundred million deaths that would be either way depending upon which way the wind blew. If the wind blew to the southeast they would be mostly in the U.S.S.R., although they would extend into the Japanese and perhaps down into the Philippine area. If the wind blew the other way they would extend well back up into Western Europe."[7]

In the event of a limited aggression the dilemma would be even sharper. The official policy of "massive retaliation" was an attempt to deter the Soviet Union and its satellites by threatening interven-

---

[7] See testimony of Lt. General James M. Gavin, *Hearings before the Subcommittee on the Air Force of the Committee on Armed Services, United States Senate, 84th Congress, 2nd Session* (Washington, D. C., 1956), pp. 860-61.

tion of the American Strategic Air Command and all-out war in the event of any aggression whatsoever. Here again, the Europeans fear destruction. But they also wonder whether the United States would actually come to their defense at all if an attack were very clearly limited or were launched in ambiguous circumstances. For the Soviet Union would undoubtedly strike back, with death and destruction for many millions of Americans.

Yet the alternative of resisting without relying on a nuclear reprisal seems equally unattractive. With its present force of only 16 to 18 divisions, NATO could probably cope with a limited conventional war of only the smallest dimensions—perhaps no more than mount a police action against a satellite aggression. In any fight that involved the Soviet forces in Eastern Germany, it would have little hope of holding the enemy without at least using battlefield atomic weapons.[8] But for the Europeans, this might be as bad as all-out war. In Exercise *Carte Blanche,* a NATO maneuver designed, as the name implies, to study the effects of a battle in which tactical nuclear weapons were used without restriction, 335 simulated atomic bombs were used by the maneuvering forces in 48 hours. It was estimated that over one and a half million Germans would have been killed and some three and a half million wounded. In Exercise Sagebrush, conducted by United States forces in the Louisiana maneuver area, 275 simulated nuclear weapons with yields of from 2 to 40 kilotons were dropped, and the umpires concluded that the resulting destruction and fall-out would have been so high as to make it difficult for the civilian population of the region to survive.[9] The Europeans did not fail to note the implications of these figures, and they are also aware that there is only a grim chance of holding the Soviet forces even if NATO does use battlefield atomic weapons. The Soviets would undoubtedly

---

[8] "Battlefield" atomic weapons are not necessarily small or low-yield weapons. By the term "battlefield" is meant only that the weapons are used in the theater of war and not on the Soviet and American homelands. On this point see Bernard Brodie, "Nuclear Weapons: Strategic or Tactical?" *Foreign Affairs,* January 1954.

[9] This conclusion, however, may be questioned, both as to the extent of fall-out from weapons of this kind and as to the implication that casualties could not be reduced through civil defense measures.

use them, too, and there is no reason to believe that either our weapons or our troops can be made so superior in quality as to give us a decisive advantage.[10]

III

Thus NATO's dilemma is a strategic one, and the question it pushes forward so insistently is whether the NATO coalition army can continue to serve useful military and political purposes. Is there a strategy that will enable NATO to meet the entire range of possible aggressions and that will also offer Europe a hope of surviving?[11]

---

[10] It is on the argument that the West is technically superior that Henry Kissinger ultimately rests his case for relying on tactical nuclear weapons in limited wars, although a fairer statement would probably be that he argues not so much that there is an advantage to the West in using nuclear weapons as that it is only through nuclear weapons that we can overcome the disadvantage placed on us by Soviet superiority in forces in being. See his *Nuclear Weapons and Foreign Policy* (New York, 1957). For a discussion of the possibility that our technological advantage may actually lie not in nuclear war but in conventional, see below and my "Coalitions and Alliances," in William W. Kaufmann (ed.), *Military Policy and National Security* (Princeton, 1956).

[11] For discussions of limited war and the strategic and political implications of the nuclear revolution in military strategy, see the following: Bernard Brodie, "Nuclear Weapons: Strategic or Tactical?" *Foreign Affairs,* January 1954; "Strategy Hits a Dead End," *Harpers Magazine,* October 1955; "Unlimited Weapons and Limited War," *The Reporter,* November 18, 1954; "Some Notes on the Evolution of Air Doctrine," *World Politics,* April 1955; "More About Limited War," *World Politics,* October 1957; and "The Anatomy of Deterrence," *World Politics,* January 1959; chapters by Wm. W. Kaufmann, Klaus Knorr, and Roger Hilsman in *Military Policy and National Security;* Henry A. Kissinger, *Nuclear Weapons and Foreign Policy;* Wm. W. Kaufmann's review, "The Crisis in Military Affairs," *World Politics,* July 1958; Robert E. Osgood, *Limited War* (Chicago, 1957); Paul Nitze, "Atoms, Strategy, and Policy," *Foreign Affairs,* January 1956; Malcolm Hoag, "NATO: Deterrent or Shield," *Foreign Affairs,* January 1958; Arnold Wolfers, "Europe and the NATO Shield," *International Organization,* 1958; "Could a War in Europe Be Limited?" *Yale Review,* Winter 1956; James E. King, Jr., "Nuclear Plenty and Limited War," *Foreign Affairs,* January 1957; Klaus Knorr, "The Crisis in U.S. Defense," special section of the *New Leader,* December 30, 1957; Sir Anthony Buzzard, "Massive Retaliation and Graduated Deterrence," *World Politics,* January 1956; Royal Institute of International Affairs Pamphlet, *On Limiting Atomic*

There seem to be three possibilities. The first would constitute not a military strategy but a political arrangement that would either make NATO's strategic problem more susceptible of solution or eliminate it entirely—i.e., some form of negotiated settlement with the Soviets about the status of Europe or a withdrawal on the part of Europeans themselves from the great-power struggle. The second would be to help the European members of NATO acquire enough independent strength either to stand alone or to meet certain kinds of threats more effectively. The third would be to strengthen the NATO army—as its Commander, General Norstad, has proposed —so that it would no longer be so dependent on nuclear weapons in defending Europe against less-than-total aggressions.

The first possibility, as suggested above, is not a military strategy but a political arrangement. Recent Soviet statements seem to indicate that it might soon be possible to negotiate some sort of agreement about the status of Europe. And even if the great powers did not arrive at such an agreement, the Europeans might themselves decide on a policy of neutrality, choosing both the role and limited political objectives usually associated with only very small powers. The result would be the neutrality of Europe and its partial demilitarization, a possibility that seems outlandish at first glance but one that the Europeans might conceivably come to view as not only wise but even inevitable. Certainly there is truth in the general proposition that there are conditions in which a whole region may sit outside the Cold War arena with no greater risk of being the victim of aggression than if it participates as a member of one of the great blocs. The question is whether these conditions now exist in Europe or are likely to emerge as a result of impending developments.

One scheme that cannot be ignored is George Kennan's proposal for "disengagement," a negotiated neutralization of Europe agreed to by both the United States and the Soviet Union.[12] What Kennan

War; Washington Center of Foreign Policy Research, *East-West Negotiations,* 1958.

[12] George F. Kennan, *Russia, the Atom, and the West* (New York, 1958). For a fuller treatment of "disengagement," see my "Some Requirements for East-West Settlement," *Social Science,* October 1958, which this discussion parallels.

proposed was, first, a mutual withdrawal of Soviet and American troops; second, a reunification of Germany; and, third, the demilitarization of Europe as a whole. Although Kennan and the other advocates of disengagement are not so naive, the appeal of this proposal lies in its suggestion that the Cold War can be settled and the satellites liberated in a single stroke.[13] There seems to be no disagreement on the general proposition that Soviet troops are essential to the maintenance of Soviet control over the satellites and that if those troops are ever withdrawn in circumstances that make the withdrawal seem genuine, political changes are bound to follow. In some of the Eastern European countries these changes would undoubtedly be on the model of recent events in Poland— a gradual liberalization carried out with one eye cocked for Soviet reactions and the end result a Communist state still basically friendly to the Soviet Union. This pattern of only partial change would seem especially likely in countries in which the fear of a new German Reich parallels fear of the Soviets. But just as surely as political change in some of the liberated countries would be moderate, in others it would be violent. Once the Soviet troops were gone, the people might not remain content with a mere liberalization of the Communist regime and might rise to sweep it away entirely.

Seen in this light, disengagement is basically an aggressive policy. Certainly Khrushchev would so regard it. In his Minsk speech in January of 1958, Khrushchev referred to Eisenhower's request that the agenda for a summit meeting include the questions of the Eastern European countries and the reunification of Germany. Khrushchev then said: "What then do Messrs. Eisenhower and Dulles want? Evidently they wish to meet us and have a talk about the liquidation of the people's democratic regime in the people's democracies. They evidently wish that we should give up socialist building and that we should restore the capitalist order." For a summit conference to yield positive results, he said, "the status quo should be recognized; that there are two systems of states in the world, the capitalist and the socialist. . . . If the status quo is not

---

[13] See Dean Acheson, "The Illusions of Disengagement," *Foreign Affairs*, April 1958.

recognized, if the socialist states are ignored, their sovereign rights violated, and their domestic affairs interfered in, then it is, of course, absolutely impossible to come to terms." Such a policy, says Khrushchev, is a "policy of war."

Behind the hope that disengagement would settle everything lies the assumption that Soviet foreign policy is motivated principally by fear. This may well be true, but the significant question is not whether the fear exists but whether it can be erased by some dramatic change in Western foreign policy. The Soviet Union is and thinks of itself as a revolutionary force aimed precisely at upsetting the old order and remaking the world in its own image. It seems reasonable to suppose that the Soviets know that upsetting the world order is the logic of revolutionary movements; that they know that they intend to remake the world if they can; and that they therefore expect the West to oppose them and thus to be a threat to them. It would probably be an absurdity to the Soviets, knowing themselves and their own goals, if the West did not oppose them. As a result, it seems idle to believe that we might remove their fears by an act of foreign policy no matter how dramatic. Indeed, the more dramatic and radical the act, the more it would be likely to alarm them.[14] Unilateral disarmament, for example, would undoubtedly be viewed as a trick of some kind, all the more alarming because its "true" goal was so well hidden. The point is simply that the basic Soviet attitudes, both their ambitions and their fears, do not seem to be the kind that can be changed by negotiation. For the Soviets, accepting a general and final settlement would mean giving up their ultimate goals and the driving force of their society. Peaceful coexistence, in the sense that Christians and Mohammedans or Catholics and Protestants finally came to accept it, means that neither side can continue to entertain ideas of one world ideologically united. For the Soviets, peaceful coexistence in this sense would mean finding some new goal around which they could orient both their movement and their state. And no reappraisal could be more agonizing; indeed so fundamental a reorientation would be in itself a form of self-destruction.

---

[14] Of the many works on the Soviet Union on which I have relied, I am most indebted to those by the following: Nathan Leites, Frederick Barghoorn, Raymond L. Garthoff, and Robert C. Tucker.

Ironically, in fact, far from settling the Cold War, disengagement might well create an even more unstable situation in Europe. Some have argued that the Soviets would not agree to withdraw their troops if they intended immediately to return. This may be quite correct, but could the Soviets discipline themselves into standing by while a Communist regime was overthrown and the security system they have built out of the fruits of their victory in World War II was destroyed? It seems unlikely. Even the United States, after all, found it impossible to accept the political and diplomatic consequences that would have flowed from the loss of South Korea, and rushed to meet the Communist attack despite its earlier decision that Korea was a strategic liability not worth including within the perimeter of defense. It seems obvious that a Soviet intervention following a mutual withdrawal would create a level of tension that intervention before it, as in Hungary, would never do.

However, as Kennan and the other advocates of disengagement point out, there are several sets of possible circumstances in which a mutual withdrawal might be both stable and desirable to both sides. The Rapacki plan, the Soviet decision to turn Berlin over to the East Germans, and Khrushchev's hints that he might be willing to withdraw his troops from Eastern Germany all indicate that the Soviet Union's attitude toward Germany may be in the process of changing. Certainly the Soviets have reason to be uneasy about the course of events in the Germanies, although it is also possible that the change in Khrushchev's attitude is due not so much to the course of events in Germany as to his growing confidence that he can soon accomplish with the threat of missiles what he now must do with troops. For the West, on the other hand, there are considerable benefits in even a partial withdrawal of Soviet troops and perhaps even more in the reunification of Germany. Indeed, the benefits may be great enough to justify our agreeing to German neutrality, with certain safeguards. Such an arrangement would not solve NATO's strategic dilemma, but it might make it more susceptible of solution.

The possibility must also be considered that the Europeans might decide that conditions had so changed as to make it both possible and desirable for them to adopt neutrality as their policy. If this decision were rational, at least three conditions would have to be met as long as the rivalry continues between East and West. First, the neutral country or region could not be a center of potential power that could threaten the Soviet Union or that would provide sufficient additional power if incorporated into the Soviet bloc to shift the world balance. Second, it could not be so located geographically as to provide either side with an essential base or as to be the inevitable battlefield, given the existing level of military technology. Third, there must exist in the particular nations a willingness to withdraw from world political affairs, either accepting the inconsequential role of a very small power or at least pursuing the kind of "active neutralism" India follows, which itself requires a special geographic and political situation. Finland, Sweden, Austria, Afghanistan, and India all meet these prerequisites, and it is not really surprising that the Soviet Union has not violated their neutrality. The Soviet goal of a world system in its own image does not require physical occupation of every country in the world, but only the elimination of all rival centers of power. Once the competing power centers were eliminated, all else would follow naturally. If the Soviets defeated and occupied the United States, for example, they would have no need to occupy South America or even to insist that all South American countries adopt the Communist form of government. The world political system would be on the Soviet model; and, secure from threat to that system, the Soviets would have no need to shoulder the burdens of enforcing conformity in what would be inconsequential detail. It follows that if a country neither contributed to a rival power center nor was an element in the struggle between the big two, it might well come to regard neutrality as a feasible policy for it to pursue.

At present, it seems clear that Europe meets none of these conditions. Taken as a whole, the European economy—with its productive plant, resources, and highly skilled population—is a center of potential power rivaling the big two. If integrated and organized as a single political entity, it would itself constitute a potential threat to the Soviet Union. On the other hand, a defenseless Europe would be a great temptation: its incorporation into the Soviet system would shift the world balance of power radically. At the present level of military technology, Europe also remains a strategic area. The limitations in range of present aircraft and operational missiles make it essential for us to have SAC bases in North Africa and the United Kingdom, if not on the European continent proper; and it is not entirely certain that in an all-out war fighting would cease after each side had expended its strategic bombers and missiles. Europeans, finally, though shaken by the decline in Europe's relative power and by horror at the devastation that an atomic war would wreak, are not yet so neutralist as to permit their countries to abdicate their places in world affairs. France and Western Germany in particular seem determined to continue having a voice.

But it is also true that all this might change. The doubts that have arisen because of Europe's declining power and the threat of atomic destruction may be only the first step. The increasing burdens of the arms race are a powerful incentive to neutralism. Then, too, if the European countries fall too far behind, their views would unavoidably carry less and less weight in allied councils. This would contribute still more to their feelings of helplessness and the tendency to resign themselves to what might seem inevitable anyway. The principal reservation here concerns the division of Germany. A movement toward neutrality in Western Europe, since it would not require a Soviet withdrawal from all of Eastern Europe, might change the Soviet attitude toward reunification and present a new Western German government with an opportunity to negotiate. But as long as Germany is divided it seems improbable that its people would be content with the silent and passive role a policy of neutrality would require.

As regards strategic position, the coming of the Polaris and intercontinental missiles will probably alter the significance of Europe's geographical position sharply. If it should then appear that the intercontinental battle of missiles will indeed be decisive without a land battle of any consequence, and if radar warning is accomplished by earth satellites or by some other means not requiring installations in Europe, then from the European point of view still another prerequisite for neutrality would have been met.[15]

---

[15] For a discussion of the possibility that an all-out war might entail a substantial land battle, see my "Strategic Doctrines for Nuclear War," in *Military Policy and National Security,* already cited. It is interesting that the Soviet Union has apparently hedged against this possibility. See

The factor that seems least likely of all to change radically is Europe's potential power. Although it seems unlikely that the Europeans themselves will in the foreseeable future be able to integrate Europe and so organize its great potential, Europe's attraction remains strong for the Soviets, who undoubtedly could organize its potential power. In addition, Europe, with its long history as the center of Western power and dominance, is a political symbol of great potency. The only reservation to a conclusion that Europe will retain its importance as a power center would appear to lie in the overwhelming destructiveness of nuclear weapons. If it turns out that a finite number of these weapons and their carriers is sufficient to accomplish the certain and complete destruction of either side, and if this level of armaments is well within the capabilities of both the Soviet and American economies, then an additional increment of economic potential may no longer have any significance to the balance of world power. Changes so radical as to lead the Europeans to adopt neutrality as a policy seem remote, but they are not inconceivable.

IV

The second possibility is a policy designed to make the European members of NATO not only strong, but independently so, which might permit some alteration in the role of NATO, including a decentralization of the responsibility for meeting certain of the threats confronting it. Since Europe seems unwilling or unable to integrate, the United States, in order to make Europe independently strong, would as a practical matter have to help at least the larger members of NATO to acquire nuclear weapons and missiles.

Assuming that the European members of NATO had both battlefield missiles and a reliable type of intermediate range ballistic missile (IRBM), what kinds of threats could they reasonably be expected to meet? Even when they had nuclear arms, the European countries would presumably have to maintain conventional ground forces at least as large as those they now maintain. This would

---

Raymond L. Garthoff, *Soviet Strategy in the Nuclear Age* (New York, 1958); and Peregrine Worsthorne, "Our Bomb and Theirs; How the Russians See It," *Encounter,* July 1958.

mean that they could be expected to meet aggression from one of the Eastern European satellites, and to meet it in exactly the same terms in which the attack was mounted. Western Germany, for example, with the conventional forces it is already building could be expected to meet a conventional assault from either Eastern Germany or Czechoslovakia, or even from a combination of the two. With atomic arms, it could also be expected to meet an atomic assault launched by the satellites alone.

But it is doubtful whether a single country could by itself stand up to an attack by the Soviet Union, even a conventional attack. In a conventional attack, the 22 Soviet divisions in Eastern Germany could probably defeat the 12-division force Western Germany is now building, and even if Germany succeeded in fielding a larger force, the Soviets could more than match it by bringing up divisions from their almost unlimited reserves. And atomic weapons would be of little help. If Western Germany initiated the use of battlefield atomic weapons, the Soviet Union would undoubtedly respond in kind. It would be West German territory that would suffer, and the superior Soviet manpower would probably be decisive in a limited atomic war as it would in conventional war.

It also seems doubtful whether Western Germany could meet a clearly limited challenge by threatening nuclear reprisal on the Soviet homeland. Suppose, for example, that the Soviets charged Western Germany with fomenting a revolt in Eastern Germany from a base in Bavaria and seized the area in a punitive action confined solely to conventional forces. Even with a very large supply of nuclear weapons and intermediate range missiles at its disposal, Germany could not hope to hurt the Soviet Union as badly as the Soviets could hurt Germany. In the second place, in this case in which the threat is just as clearly limited for the Germans as it is for the rest of NATO, the German government will face the same dilemma confronting NATO as a whole. If the Western Germans retaliated by attacking cities in the Soviet Union, their action would undoubtedly bring down a counterretaliation on Bonn and the Ruhr. The force used, and the consequences of using it, would be grossly inappropriate to the need. The conclusion would seem to be that nuclear weapons would not help the Europeans very much in meeting a limited attack by the Soviet

Union, even if the Soviets confined their attack to conventional weapons. For limited wars, and perhaps especially for those in which only conventional weapons are used, the Europeans will probably continue to need American help.[16]

To summarize: if we were to share nuclear weapons and missiles with our NATO allies, they could meet limited nuclear attacks by the Soviet satellites and could also fight more effectively alongside American troops in an all-out war, assuming there is a role for ground forces in all-out war. On the other hand, nuclear weapons of their own would probably not enable the European members of NATO to cope by themselves with a clearly limited Soviet aggression whether conventional or nuclear—an attack that does not threaten the particular country with either annihilation or conquest.

But suppose the Soviet attack does imply annihilation or conquest? As suggested above, one of the most persistently stubborn questions facing the West is how to respond to a Soviet attack limited so far as NATO as a whole is concerned but total for the particular member against whom the attack is directed. How can the West meet the threat of missile blackmail against France, for example, or against Western Germany? If the United States threatened massive retaliation, France or Western Germany might well be encouraged to resist, and the Soviets might back down. But, as suggested earlier, it would be difficult to make this threat credible to the Soviet Union, especially if the further development of missiles makes the United States less dependent on bases overseas. The question is bound to be raised whether an American president would carry out the threat, knowing that his action would bring death to many millions of Americans and devastation to the continental United States, from which it might never recover. And the mere existence of the question casts doubt on the credibility of our threat, which is the essence of its effectiveness as a deterrent.[17] The Soviets will also see opportunities for posing the challenge in ambiguous terms calculated to divide the West on the moral and

---

[16] This same point is made by George W. Rathjens, Jr. See his "Notes on the Military Problems of Europe," *World Politics,* January 1958.

[17] For a discussion of the role of credibility in deterrence, see William W. Kaufmann, "The Requirements of Deterrence," in *Military Policy and National Security,* already cited.

legal justifications for retaliation—in the midst of a revolt in Eastern Germany, for example, and after the Soviets have built up a case charging Western Germany with intervention. The tactics of long-range attack are enormously complex; but there seems to be a reasonable probability, if both sides take certain measures to protect the means of reprisal, that the nation initiating a nuclear strike will suffer awesome damage.[18] At the same time, the greatest chance of escaping with a level of damage from which recovery is possible lies in being the first to strike. This means that it is very dangerous to use nuclear reprisal as a deterrent for anything less than all-out war. For using the threat of retaliation as a means of deterring less-than-total provocations gives the enemy an opportunity to launch a first strike himself. For all these reasons, it will be difficult to keep the Soviets convinced that the United States will actually find it reasonable to launch a thermonuclear reprisal for anything short of an attack threatening its own survival.

Thus it seems probable that over time the only threats of nuclear reprisal the Soviet Union will find consistently credible are those that come from the nations whose own survival is at stake.[19] For example, if in some future crisis the Soviet Union threatens an attack that is clearly designed to reunite the two Germanies as a Soviet satellite but is just as clearly designed to be limited to that purpose, the only nation that may be able to convince the Soviet Union that it will meet this peculiar challenge that is total for Western Germany but limited for the rest of NATO is probably Western Germany itself. And the threat of nuclear reprisal seems to be the only way that even Western Germany can meet it.

What the country attempting to deter the Soviet Union has at stake is thus the first element determining whether its threat of nuclear reprisal will be credible to the Soviets. The second element would be the effectiveness of the retaliatory forces the country actu-

---

[18] The measures to protect the means of reprisal would include "hardening" for SAC bases, that is, providing underground hangars for the airplanes with extremely thick concrete roofs. So far the United States does not seem to have taken these measures. See Bernard Brodie, "The Anatomy of Deterrence," loc. cit.

[19] On this point, see also Raymond Aron, "NATO and the Bomb," Western World, June 1957.

ally had at its disposal. Could Western Germany, for example, be equipped with and could it maintain a retaliatory force large enough to be a credible threat to the Soviet Union? Certainly it would be difficult to equip each of the European allies with a manned bomber force large enough for that purpose or for them to maintain it.[20] It would also seem unlikely that the purpose could be met with a force of liquid-fueled missiles, which are difficult to maintain, require a dangerously long time to launch, and are very vulnerable. It is solid-fueled missiles of the Polaris type that seem most promising, but only the inside specialist who has access to classified technical data can say whether a particular weapon has the necessary characteristics. The outsider can comment only on the political and broad strategic consequences that might be expected if a weapon with certain presumed characteristics is introduced or, in this case, shared with our allies. The Polaris apparently has neither the accuracy nor the yield to make it suitable as a deterrent for our allies, but here I am assuming a kind of idealized Polaris—a missile that can be launched from "hard," underground installations, that has the required accuracy in relation to size of warhead, and that is capable of carrying the necessary electronic equipment to penetrate sophisticated defenses. I am also assuming that this idealized missile can be supported by the radar and communications networks needed to detect an attack and to make and communicate a decision to retaliate,[21] although it is important to stress that there is as yet no warning system, even on the drawing boards, that cannot be circumvented by electronic and other means.

Assuming weapons with these essential characteristics, there still remains the question of whether they would constitute a deterrent to the Soviets. There is no doubt that in a thermonuclear exchange between the Soviet Union and a country like Western Germany it would be Western Germany that would suffer most. Its territory is

---

[20] The United Kingdom, however, has built such a force in its V-bomber force, which numbers 200 planes, presumably armed with thermonuclear weapons.

[21] For an excellent discussion of the characteristics of particular missiles and of the conditions to be met in developing an adequate retaliatory force, see Albert Wohlstetter, "The Delicate Balance of Terror," *Foreign Affairs,* January 1959.

relatively so small, its people and industry so concentrated, that one must assume that even if the Germans build deep shelters, their casualties would be enormous, perhaps on the order of 50 per cent of their population or more, and that the bulk of their industry would be destroyed. On the other hand, Germany could hope to destroy at most only a few of the Soviet Union's largest cities— perhaps five or ten. These contain only a small proportion of either the Soviet population or its productive plant, and their destruction would hardly constitute a crippling blow. In the first few weeks after Hitler's attack in World War II, for example, the Soviet Union lost a much higher proportion of both its population and its plant by occupation—40 per cent of its population and 60 per cent of its coal, iron, and aluminum output[22]—but fought on, eventually to win. But even five or ten cities would be a high price to pay for a limited victory—one, as in our example, that destroyed Western Germany but left the United States unharmed. On balance, the capacity to destroy five to ten Soviet cities would seem to be an effective deterrent against this particular level of missile intimidation.

There may also be another kind of threat against which a modest but independent nuclear strength would be an effective deterrent. At present, an assault that is obviously directed toward the conquest of the whole of Europe is probably the one kind of aggression other than an attack on the continental United States itself that would be most likely to trigger an American reprisal on the Soviet homeland. We will continue for some time to be dependent on SAC bases in North Africa and the United Kingdom, if not Europe proper, and both sides must also assume that at present the incorporation of Western Europe into the Soviet bloc would radically shift the balance of world power, as we have said. The advantages of being the first to strike with nuclear weapons are so great that the Soviet Union could not afford to risk the kind of attack that threatens American survival in this way without combining that attack with a strike on the American means of reprisal. Similarly, these same advantages of a first strike would be a compelling argument to the United States in the face of an attack that

---

[22] See Raymond L. Garthoff, *op. cit.*

would not only shift the balance but would be regarded by much of the world as a justifiable provocation. For all these reasons, it would seem that the Soviet Union is unlikely to launch a massive conventional assault on the whole of Europe except in combination with a strike on the continental United States, at least for the moment.

On the other hand, when the United States is no longer dependent on overseas bases, the Soviets might feel that an attack on the whole of Europe would be less certain to bring down American reprisal. They might be very wrong in this conclusion: the psychological stake the United States has in Europe's survival is very high, and America could hardly survive as the kind of society it is except in a wider world of which Europe is an essential part. But the Soviets may not see this, and the question is one of making the threat of reprisal credible to the Soviets. Here again, it might be an independent nuclear strength in Europe that would turn the trick. Although the Soviets might doubt that the United States would respond with a nuclear reprisal, they could not be so sure about the Europeans and would again have to consider whether the price was not too high for a limited gain.

An independent nuclear strength in Europe, in sum, may go a long way in helping to meet the threat of missile intimidation against a single country and in deterring the Soviets from an assault on the whole of Europe. But the case need not be put solely in terms of a showdown. In the first place, a relationship of dependency in an alliance is a source of resentment and instability, and it is important that all the NATO members retain the dignity of a substantial role in their own defense. In the second place, there is a whole range of crises less stark than a Soviet missile threat in which events may well turn on the self-confidence and steady nerves of the NATO countries on the forward line. The danger, in other words, lies almost as much in the political discounting of a Soviet attack as in the attack itself. If the European members of NATO are completely dependent on the United States to counter a Soviet threat against themselves at all levels, any doubt about the willingness of the United States to come to their defense with means appropriate to the particular level of threat will leave them peculiarly vulnerable. In some circumstances, they will begin to think they have no alternative to submitting. The point is simply that a measure of independent strength in each of the NATO allies is likely to contribute to the cohesiveness of the alliance in several sets of circumstances ranging downward from the ultimate threat, even though that strength may not be completely adequate for meeting the ultimate threat itself.

The possibility of meeting missile and other forms of Soviet blackmail is a persuasive argument for nuclear sharing. But there are also disadvantages. The cost of developing and maintaining a missile force appropriate to these purposes for each of the NATO allies would undoubtedly be high. There is not only the initial cost of the missiles, but also the cost of their emplacements (which would probably have to be underground) and of the electronic warning and control systems needed to operate them. Just how high this cost would be is a technical question that only those on the inside can answer.

There are also other kinds of cost. There is no question that increasing the number of countries armed with nuclear weapons will add to the risks that some local outbreak of violence will spiral into all-out war. Still, the danger is not really so crude and direct as it is sometimes pictured. For example, it will not be as easy as it may seem for a small nation to use atomic weapons to trick the big two into destroying each other. If Argentina sets off an atomic bomb in New York's Grand Central Station, no one is going to be fooled into triggering retaliation against the Soviet Union. Of one thing we can be sure: if the Soviets ever do decide to launch a thermonuclear strike on the continental United States, there will be no trouble whatsoever in recognizing it for what it is. If the Soviets ever do decide to strike, they could risk nothing less than a full-scale, co-ordinated attack. Thus there will not be one bomb, but hundreds—coming as nearly simultaneously as the Soviets can manage it, and from as many different directions. The danger in the spread of nuclear weapons is more the greater power the leaders of the irresponsible smaller nations—the petty dictators and uncompromising nationalists—would have to do more effectively what they can already do in part. These leaders already have the power to start wars that might drag in the big two and so start a spiral into a world struggle. With atomic weapons at their disposal, they might be more than ever tempted to adventure, and the wars they fight will be incomparably more destructive. But the greatest difference would seem to lie in the fact that the line between conventional and nuclear weapons would have already been passed before the great powers got drawn into the fighting and in the difficulties this would create in confining it.

Another cost is the obverse of the advantage in the possibility that nuclear weapons might enable a country like France or Western Germany to stand up to a Soviet missile threat. If one of these countries had enough nuclear strength to threaten reprisal for an attack on itself, it could conceivably so manipulate events as to commit the United States to a war it did not want. Here again, the problem is not so crude as it is sometimes pictured. Even with a substantial force of missiles and nuclear warheads, Western Germany will not be so powerful that it can have much hope of accomplishing the reunification of Germany by force. There is certainly danger here; of that there can be no doubt. But our experience with both Chiang Kai-shek and Synghman Rhee indicates that it is a danger we can manage if we are determined to manage it. The greater danger would seem to lie in circumstances in which it is the Soviet Union that is making the aggressive moves, and our ally is, perhaps, entirely too self-confident and determined. If through accident or miscalculation events did come to a showdown, could the Soviet Union afford to suffer a nuclear blow and the consequent weakening of her strength without making sure that the United States—the principal enemy—suffered an equal reduction of strength? If not, sharing nuclear weapons with our European allies will also mean sharing the power of deciding the great question of war and peace. And this is a possible effect of nuclear sharing the United States would wish to ponder long and carefully.

On the other hand, there is some question whether the United States actually has the power to stop the spread of nuclear weapons. Nuclear technology is apparently progressing very rapidly, becoming simpler and more economical every day. Reading between the lines of the scientific periodicals, one suspects that this may be particularly true of thermonuclear weapons. France will soon become a nuclear power. Sweden has announced that it has the technical capacity to be one and unless the prospects of a world-wide disarmament agreement improve, domestic opposition to a decision either to manufacture or purchase the weapons is not likely to prevail. And Switzerland, which already has a short-range missile, will not be far behind. There is a large gap between having a few first-generation atomic bombs and having a full thermonuclear capacity with the long-range missiles and electronic control and warning systems that make a nuclear power in the full sense, but the trend is there even if it takes two or three decades to reach its culmination. Barring an international agreement for a test ban and a limitation on production and trade in nuclear weapons, we are faced with a trend that is apparently going to pick up speed rather rapidly. In such circumstances wise statesmanship may consist not in trying to hold back the tide but in anticipating and channeling it to positive purposes. It is worth considering whether it might not be better to approach the nuclear age gradually, building up precedents, experience, a sense of responsibility, and, possibly, some wider political organization. There are obvious risks in a policy of attempting to pick and choose the members of the atomic club, but there may be even greater ones in attempting to hold things exactly as they are only to have fifteen or twenty nations suddenly acquire the weapons overnight.

V

The final possibility is for an increase in the NATO army, as proposed by General Lauris Norstad. General Norstad has called for a force of 30 divisions, armed with both conventional and nuclear weapons. These divisions are to be a standing force, ready and on the forward line at all times.[23] Behind them would presumably be a certain number of divisions manned principally by reservists, though not so many as was envisioned in the Lisbon force goals. The Norstad proposal calls for a total force about 25 per cent smaller than the 96 divisions approved at Lisbon. In addition, in

---

[23] General Lauris Norstad, "NATO—Deterrent and Shield," address to the American Council on NATO, New York, January 29, 1957; text in *NATO Letter,* v, No. 2 (February 1957), 27-30; address at Cincinnati, November 12, 1957, text in *NATO Letter,* v, No. 12 (December 1957), 26-28; and "Interview with General Lauris Norstad," *NATO Letter,* IV, No. 12 (December 1956), 34-37.

the Norstad proposal a higher percentage of the total would be standing forces, and the reserve divisions could be mobilized on shorter notice.

As Norstad describes them, the purposes this force of 30 divisions is to serve are three. The first is to hold the frontier in an all-out war while the nuclear retaliatory force does its work—which would take, it is apparently assumed, no more than three or four weeks at the most.

The second purpose of the 30-division force, according to Norstad, is to give NATO the means of dealing firmly with a probing action to achieve a political advantage or with a swift movement designed, for example, to seize a bit of Western Germany and so face the West with a *fait accompli*. With 30 NATO divisions on the line, the Soviets could accomplish this only by using a substantial force, which would raise the question of nuclear reprisal. Thus the 30 divisions act as a deterrent against minor aggressions and blackmail by probing actions and at the same time provide enough resistance to clarify the meaning of an attack. They would give the NATO commanders and governments the time needed to assess the situation and to decide upon the appropriate response.

The third purpose is a partial answer to the need for an intermediate response between nuclear reprisal on the one hand and a skirmish to confine a border incident on the other. In Norstad's words:

> Should we fail to maintain reasonable shield strength on the NATO frontier, then massive retaliation could be our only response to an aggression, regardless of its nature. There is real danger that inability to deal decisively with limited or local attacks could lead to our piecemeal defeat or bring on a general war. If, on the other hand, we have means to meet less-than-ultimate threats with a decisive, but less-than-ultimate response, the very possession of this ability would discourage the threat, and would thereby provide us with essential political and military manoeuverability.[24]

Norstad has denied that he means by this that a limited war in Europe is possible.[25] But this denial can probably be explained by

---

[24] General Lauris Norstad, *NATO Letter,* v, No. 12 (December 1957).
[25] *New York Times,* July 21, 1958.

the fact that his public pronouncements on NATO strategy must be addressed not only to the Western but also to the Soviet audience. While he puts forward his reasons for supporting a goal of 30 divisions, he cannot forget that he has only 16 to 18 divisions on hand. This is not sufficient strength to fight a limited war involving the Soviets, and he must be careful to put them on notice that at the moment even a limited action may bring down nuclear reprisal. Norstad clearly recognizes and fears the fact that in the face of a limited attack designed to present the West with a *fait accompli* we would have only the choice between acquiescing to the seizure and invoking nuclear reprisal. It also seems clear that he fears that in the event of a limited attack the disadvantages in a nuclear retaliation might throw the decision against its use. He must argue for a force that will enable him to meet a limited attack with a limited response, but he cannot forget his other audience and so must leave the matter in some doubt—enough, it is hoped, to operate as a deterrent.[26]

The thinking behind this proposal obviously takes account of the greater mobility and firepower of present-day divisions as compared with those of World War II. But it also seems to be based on two other propositions. The first is that a Soviet assault on the whole of Europe—even if it were limited in geography to Europe and in weapons to conventional types—would still require the West to call down nuclear reprisal on the Soviet homeland. The second proposition is that a war involving strategic nuclear weapons would be very short.

The first of these propositions might be open to argument. If the allies had a standing force of 30 divisions, the 22 Soviet divisions in Eastern Germany would require substantial reinforcement before they could launch a successful attack. But moving a division with its equipment and supplies calls for an impressive volume of road or rail transport, and the more troops moved forward, the more transport is required to support them. Indeed, the logistics problem is such that it is doubtful whether the Soviets could bring up any

---

[26] For a discussion of the divergencies between NATO's declaratory and operational policies, see Robert E. Osgood, "NATO's Strategic Troubles," Center for the Study of Foreign and Military Policy, University of Chicago, Chicago, Illinois. Mimeographed, 1958.

more than 30 or 40 divisions in a 30-day period. Although the Soviets might be able to bring in a few divisions—say, half a dozen —without attracting attention, any further movement of troops could hardly go unnoticed. If the Soviets attempted this reinforcement before initiating hostilities, the allies would probably have about three weeks' warning in which they, too, could mobilize and even bring troops from the central reserve in the United States. If the Soviets attacked first and then began their build-up, the allied situation might be even better, depending on how the initial battle went. In either case, the NATO nations would have time to bring up their own reinforcements. Thus there is some reason to believe that a 30-division force on the line might be able to cope with a massive conventional assault without calling down reprisal. What would make it possible would be first of all more plentiful means of transport for the reinforcements and a modest number of divisions manned by reservists to be mobilized after D-day in addition to the standing army divisions that are already planned. With these measures the total force available on the central front might reach 70 to 75 divisions by D + 30.

It is sometimes suggested that although there is some doubt about holding the Soviets in a conventional war with a force of this kind, General Norstad could defend Europe without calling for an attack on the Soviet homeland if he met the attacking force on the ground with battlefield atomic weapons. The proposition is that even though the Soviets would then use battlefield nuclear weapons, too, the advantage would be with NATO.

The question is whether nuclear weapons do indeed permit the substitution of firepower for manpower when both sides are using them. If there is a case for relying on battlefield nuclear weapons, it must offer the possibility of holding off a force that is actually superior in numbers, as the 96-division force of Lisbon could have held off a much larger force at the time it was proposed. What would happen in a limited nuclear war if the Soviets reinforced their present 22 divisions from their great reserves? There is no doubt that atomic weapons are bringing about a revolution in tactics, in the way a division will fight as well as in its size and composition. Current thinking emphasizes firepower and mobility, much smaller divisions, and a higher level of mechanization. It is thought that division fronts will be about twice what they were in World War II, but that they will be as much as four times greater in depth. About the same proportion of reserves is assumed to be necessary, but a much greater number of replacements for casualties. And these replacements will probably have to be not by individual soldiers but by whole battle groups (a new unit larger than the old battalion but smaller than the old regiment), since in atomic warfare a hit will probably wipe out the unit as a whole. If this thinking is correct, atomic weapons would not reduce the requirements for manpower, but may actually increase them, as General Ridgway has contended.[27]

There is nothing to indicate, in other words, that a good, big atomic army would not be able to defeat a good, little atomic army. What may be even more significant for the defense of Europe, however, is the suggestion implied in these tactics that it may no longer be possible to fight a battle successfully with a static defense of terrain, the tactics which made it possible to plan on the 96 divisions of the Lisbon force goals holding off a force of several times that size. Although atomic weapons seem to favor the defense in that a force massing for an attack would make a vulnerable target, they may favor the attacking force even more if the defense is a static one. This indicates that the defense, too, must be mobile—in all probability a further development of the mobile defense tactics used in Korea at the time of the fighting around Pusan. Here the "line" was defined by outposts and active patrolling, and an attack was met not so much by a static defense as by a counterattack from reserves that were larger than usual and more mobile. With these tactics a highly mechanized, better-trained and better-equipped force can undoubtedly hold off a force that is numerically superior but not so well equipped and trained. Even when the forces are equal in equipment and training, a defense using these tactics could probably hold off a force superior in numbers for a time. But given the blanket destructiveness of nuclear weapons, the time is likely to be rather short, and then superior numbers seem certain to carry the day.

It may well be, in sum, that the West's superior technology might

---

[27] General Matthew B. Ridgway, *Soldier* (New York, 1956), p. 296.

bestow greater advantages in a conventional war than in a nuclear one. In nuclear war the destructiveness of the weapon is overwhelming. But in conventional war, flexible and sustained power—moving men and materials and concentrating and shifting fires in mass—depends upon an ability to orchestrate a vast intricacy of tools, gadgets, skills, and administrative techniques. If there is an advantage to be gained from our more highly skilled population, it would seem to be here. Although Soviet troops are undoubtedly better trained than Chinese or North Koreans, it is worth pondering the fact that at one time during the Korean war, twelve United Nations and South Korean divisions were on the offensive against what was the equivalent, even when differences in size are considered, of several times as many enemy divisions.

There is also a possibility of using nuclear bombs and missiles to interdict lines of communication and so prevent the Soviets from bringing up their reserves. In an all-out war, of course, interdiction might play an important role. But the argument here is that the possibility of preventing reinforcement would justify raising the level of conventional war to nuclear. The point is that using nuclear weapons to bomb the supply lines running across Poland and Eastern Germany would still not raise the war to the ultimate level because Soviet territory itself would remain inviolate. Here again, the Soviets would undoubtedly retaliate by bombing our supply lines across France, with all the additional destruction this would bring to Europe. Then, too, if the Soviets began their build-up as a "normal rotation of troops" before launching an attack, it would pose a nice question for the West—whether and when to initiate hostilities itself. But the most formidable doubt is whether interdiction would be effective enough to justify changing the level of the war. Successful interdiction requires extremely accurate and up-to-date intelligence and high-precision strikes. It is much more than a one-shot affair; it requires repeated attacks and sustained pressure throughout the campaign. It seems doubtful whether our intelligence, our manned aircraft, which would have a reconnaissance if not a bombing role, or our present missile systems are up to these requirements. And even when all the factors are favorable for interdiction, a determined and ingenious enemy can find ways of dribbling through a build-up of almost any given size if he has enough time, as we learned in Korea.

By way of summary, then, it seems unlikely, on the one hand, that Norstad's 30-division force would do any better with battle-field atomic weapons than with conventional. On the other hand, against the purely conventional attack, its chances seem fairly good, although one's final judgment may be mixed. But a 30-division force may still make sense on other grounds. Although we cannot be certain that in an all-out war the devastation of the Soviet and American homelands would not be followed by a land battle in which the vastly greater number of Soviet divisions would be decisive, there is a strong probability that such a war would be a short one in which 30 divisions could protect Europe from occupation. This may be a questionable benefit after the devastation of an all-out exchange of H-bombs, but a larger force could not stop the bombs and missiles either.

A 30-division force could also deal with a probing action, as General Norstad says, and prevent a swift movement designed to present us with a *fait accompli*. Since it roughly matches the force the Soviets would be able to gather without a large-scale troop movement, the 30-division force would also seem to be completely adequate for the functions of clarifying the meaning of an outbreak of violence and giving us time to assess the situation and decide on an appropriate response.

But there is still another possible benefit. Even though the 30-division force might not be able to meet successfully a massive conventional assault on the whole of Europe launched as a co-ordinated attack at the outset of an aggression, it should have an excellent chance of enabling us to meet a limited war that grew slowly into a war for the whole of Europe, which might be the more likely contingency. The argument mentioned above—that a 30-division standing force plus a modest number of reservist divisions might cope with a massive, conventional assault after all—applies here with even greater force. If the Soviets had only their present force of 22 divisions when the fighting started and then began to reinforce it, a 30-division NATO force with skill and luck might well delay the Soviet advance until the West, too, could bring up additional forces.

Here again, it must be added, there would seem to be little advantage in initiating the use of battlefield atomic weapons. Ground atomic warfare would appear to be so fluid, so far-ranging and destructive, that it seems doubtful whether the NATO forces could hold long enough for reinforcements to be brought to bear, or that enough communications, port, and logistical facilities to land and transport reinforcements could be preserved to handle them. And it seems to make even less sense to try to use battlefield atomic weapons as a way of bailing us out if we lose in the opening conventional battle. Crippled and disorganized, we would probably be in a worse position trying to survive an exchange of nuclear weapons than if we continued to fight in conventional terms.

Most of the benefits of a 30-division force derive from the fact that it is roughly equal to the force that the Soviets now have on the forward line or could put there quietly, without large-scale troop movements. So long as the Soviets maintained this force at its present level, as they have done since just after the end of World War II, a NATO force of 30 divisions would retain its validity. But if the Soviets increased their forces on the forward line, the NATO forces would also have to be increased.

VI

Having examined the range of possibilities that might contribute to a solution of NATO's dilemma, the first comment that one must make is that they are not true alternatives. Three possibilities have been considered: first, European withdrawal from the great-power struggle through disengagement or a policy of neutrality; second, the development of independent nuclear strength in the European members of NATO and a corresponding decentralization of NATO's responsibilities for meeting certain kinds of threat; and, finally, strengthening the NATO coalition army as proposed by General Norstad. And in the process of considering these possibilities, we have distinguished five contingencies: first, all-out war in which an attack on Western Europe is combined with an attack on the United States and nuclear and thermonuclear weapons are used by both sides without restriction; second, a massive, co-ordinated assault, with either conventional or battlefield nuclear weapons, on the whole of Europe but clearly limited to Europe; third, a limited war that does not begin as an attack on the whole of Europe but grows into a war for Europe; fourth, missile or other blackmail singling out a particular member of the NATO alliance and posing a threat that is total for that country but limited for the rest of NATO; and, fifth, a probing or punitive action that is clearly limited for all concerned, both for the particular country against whom the attack is directed and for NATO as a whole.

Norstad's 30-division force has a possible utility in all-out war in that if the war is very short, 30 divisions might prevent the occupation of Europe although not its destruction. Against a co-ordinated assault on the whole of Europe, but limited to Europe, the 30-division force has some chance of holding if the attack is launched with conventional weapons, but little chance at all if the attack is nuclear. In a limited war that does not begin as a war for Europe but grows slowly into one, the 30-division force would have utility as long as the West also provided some reservist divisions and as long as the Soviets did not increase their standing force in Eastern Germany much beyond its present size of roughly 22 divisions. For missile blackmail, the 30-division force would have no utility at all except as an earnest of our determination. But for probing or punitive actions, it would be entirely appropriate, at least as long as the Soviets did not increase their forces in Eastern Germany. Thus Norstad's 30 divisions would be most helpful at the two ends of the scale, in all-out war and especially in limited, conventional war.

The second possibility, helping Europeans build a modest but independent retaliatory force of their own, would contribute nothing at all to the capacity for meeting probing or punitive actions. By itself, neither would it seem to contribute very much to our capacity for meeting an attack confined to conventional weapons—except for the possibility, dangerous to the rest of us, that a nation threatened with conquest and occupation anyway might find the courage to risk its existence in another way, by threatening nuclear reprisal and risking a counterreprisal. On the other hand, independent nuclear strength might do a great deal in helping to meet other kinds of threat. It would bring some improvement in our capacity to fight an all-out war, mainly through dispersal of our force. More important, it would make the threat of reprisal in response to an attack on Europe, whether conventional or nuclear, much more credible to the Soviets. In addition, independent nuclear strength might be the only way of meeting the fourth contingency, that of missile blackmail against a single member of the alliance.

The only true alternatives would therefore appear to be Europe's withdrawal from the great-power struggle through disengagement or a policy of neutrality, on the one hand, and, on the other, some combination of independent nuclear strength in the European members of NATO and Norstad's 30-division goal, including some reservist divisions and improved transport.

It seems doubtful whether a policy of neutrality for Europe would serve our goals any better than the present tentative and uneasy gamble. A viable "disengagement," on the other hand, is not ours alone to choose, and there are peculiar dangers in our seeking it too eagerly. But we do have the power to strengthen both the European members of NATO individually and NATO as a whole.

Actually, we may not be so far from the combination of independent nuclear strength in the Western European nations and Norstad's 30-division force as it may seem. We have moved a long way toward sharing nuclear weapons by our decision to furnish our allies with missiles of various types while we keep the nuclear warheads nearby under American control. It is not much of a step to turn the warheads over, and it may be doubtful whether we could resist the pressure to do so if an ally were under a threat to its survival. Indeed, there is also the possibility that in the face of a threat to its survival an ally might seize the warheads anyway. Even so, our present compromise on sharing weapons probably does not fulfill the requirements for independent strength. It could, in fact, turn out to be one of those compromises that brings not the best but the worst of both possible worlds, since it spreads the weapons but does not contribute to the dignity of an independent role or to increased responsibility.

There is also a possibility for improvement in NATO's division strength. If there is a settlement in Algeria, the French divisions taken away from NATO could be returned. With these, and with what will be produced by Germany as her planned rearmament goes forward, NATO might build up to as many as 25 divisions, provided always that there is a halt in the trend toward reliance on nuclear air power at the expense of ground forces, as typified by the United States' "new look" and the British policy outlined in the 1957 White Paper on Defence.[28]

Since we are already taking these steps toward sharing nuclear weapons and increasing NATO ground forces, it seems worth considering whether we ought not go further and provide the full 30 divisions and independent nuclear strength that offer a hope of breaking NATO's strategic dilemma by providing a full range of responses. Certainly the risks of continuing as we are will be high. The consequences of having no more than this grim and narrow choice, of meeting limited aggression with massive retaliation and all-out war on the one hand or with battlefield atomic weapons on the other, would seem to be an increasing tendency toward a corrosion of European will and the cohesiveness of the alliance. As the mass of the European population comes to understand still better the nature of the strategic choice facing NATO, the pressures on European governments will undoubtedly increase. In some future crisis, when the Soviet Union attempts to blackmail or intimidate the Western Europeans by threatening to use either its massive ground strength or its missiles, as it did at the time of the Suez crisis, some of the European governments will probably face insistent demands to seek from the Soviets whatever separate deal they can.

All these difficulties seem likely to be magnified by the coming of missiles. When the submarine-based Polaris and ICBM's are common, Europe's importance for the defense of the continental United States is likely to diminish sharply, as we have said. One can expect, if not a revival of isolationist sentiment in the United States, at least weakened support for maintaining American ground forces in Europe and even greater obstacles to be overcome in a decision to order nuclear reprisal in the case of limited or ambiguous aggression against a European member of NATO. In the circumstances, European doubts about whether the United States

---

[28] In the United States, at least, the trend seems to be continuing. See the statement by Secretary of Defense Neil H. McElroy, the *New York Times,* November 14, 1958.

would actually come to their defense can also be expected to grow and in some future crisis to feed the pressures for a separate deal. The Soviets can be expected to make the most of the situation, pursuing a waiting game for the moment and when the crisis is upon us playing upon the doubts, the fears, and disunities, making ominous threats and, emboldened by our dilemma, backing them up with concrete moves to mobilize and concentrate military force at the points of weakness.

But we ought to be clear that even the combination of Norstad's 30-division force and independent nuclear strength will not be entirely satisfactory as a solution to NATO's dilemma. In the first place, there are the very grave risks in the wider spread of nuclear weapons. In the second place, although the combination of independent nuclear strength and a ready force of 30 divisions might serve rather well in meeting the threat of missile blackmail and most of the possible range of limited aggressions, it does not guarantee that we can avoid widespread destruction to Europe in all contingencies. The response to either a missile attack on a single member of the alliance or a massive, co-ordinated assault on the whole of Europe would, as we have said, probably still require nuclear reprisal. The fact that the only alternative for the Western countries in these cases would be submission to conquest may make their threat of reprisal more credible, but we have not avoided the risk of widespread devastation, which was the other horn of the NATO dilemma. And the Soviets always have the option of making their aggression nuclear in the first place. The question is whether there is any way at all of avoiding the risk of devastation, as long as nuclear weapons still exist.

Regarding this question of whether nuclear weapons will be used in future wars, there are two schools of thought that claim to be based on hardheaded realism. One holds that the damnable things are here, that they cannot be "undiscovered," and that it is inevitable that they will be used. The argument is that even in a war that starts out as limited, at least a war that involves the big two, the stakes would be too high for either side to accept defeat or even the possibility of defeat without using all the strength at its command. If either side began through attrition to lose its capacity for all-out attack, or if it saw a strategic position that it needed to launch that attack under threat, it would feel impelled to use its full strength while it still could. The argument is reinforced by the difficulty of maintaining both a nuclear and conventional posture simultaneously. It is difficult enough to do so when there are none of the pressures of battle; once the shooting started, maintaining both postures simultaneously might be very nearly impossible. Even more important, we may have already gone so far toward nuclear war that we can no longer turn back. We have, for example, tended to replace artillery with missiles as they have become available, and missiles may justify their expense only by the vastly increased effectiveness of their nuclear warheads.

The other view is that just as the power of nuclear weapons is unprecedented, so is the attitude of nations toward them. Since the consequences of nuclear war are incalculable, no nation will use nuclear weapons except as what it feels is a last resort, and at the same time all nations will undoubtedly be meticulous in trying not to put an enemy into a situation of last resort. In the future, as the story goes, nations in war will approach each other with the same ceremonious caution as porcupines in love.

The fact that we have relied so heavily on nuclear weapons in our military preparations does not necessarily negate the point. Indeed, it would not be the first time we have made a decision in a period of calm only to reverse ourselves when faced with the political and military realities of the event. We placed Korea outside the perimeter of defense, but when it was attacked we neither abided by the decision nor initiated the use of atomic weapons, but scraped together what forces we could to meet the attack in the terms in which it was posed.

The truth is probably that both views are correct, depending on the circumstances. It seems very likely that a limited war in Europe may become nuclear for any one of several reasons, not all of which lie within our own control. But it may also be true that in most circumstances the wiser course would be to avoid using nuclear weapons—or that we may have to avoid using them, because the consequences would bring even greater disaster.

It is the function of military strategy to serve political goals. If our political goal is to maintain the present balance of world power, a policy of preserving an existing world, then we seek a defensive strategy, designed to protect the present order and to deter those who are the enemies of that order. It has always been the aim of defensive strategy to demonstrate by a strong military posture that an enemy could not win and that he could be kept from winning at less than prohibitive cost to the defender. Our dilemma is that modern weapons have cast doubt on the second condition, that the enemy can be kept from winning at less than prohibitive cost to the defender.

But for this dilemma there seems to be no solution. The risk of devastation is ever-present, for Americans as well as Europeans. We may by the nature of the military preparations we undertake reduce the chances of atomic war, but we can never eliminate them entirely. The irony is that whatever influence we can exert on events to minimize the risk of nuclear devastation will in a measure depend upon the willingness, both of Americans and Europeans, to face and accept that risk.

7

ALLIANCES IN
THEORY AND PRACTICE[1]

Hans J. Morgenthau

I

IN HIS *Farewell Address* George Washington advised the nation "to steer clear of permanent alliances . . . [and to] safely trust to temporary alliances for extraordinary emergencies." The nation heeded this advice until World War II, following by and large the same policy that Great Britain had pursued for four centuries. Yet since the end of World War II both the United States and Great Britain, far from trying "to steer clear of permanent alliances," have eagerly entered into them. The United States, in particular, in declarations preceding the establishment of the Southeast Asia Treaty Organization (SEATO) in September 1954 and in the Eisenhower Doctrine of January 1957, extended an open-ended invitation to all uncommitted nations of Asia and the Middle East respectively to become allies of the United States. What has made the United States and Great Britain turn their backs to a tradition that had been the very cornerstone of their foreign policies? The United States and Great Britain abandoned this tradition not because they were oblivious to it, but because the conditions under which they

---

[1] A part of this chapter was presented to the Annual Meeting of the American Political Science Association in 1957 and published in the Winter 1958 issue of *Confluence*, 6, No. 4, 311-34.

have had to defend and promote their interests *vis-à-vis* other nations since the end of World War II are radically different from those that have prevailed throughout modern history. These conditions are identical with the operations of the balance of power, and it is the new balance of power emerging from World War II that has compelled the United States and Great Britain to seek rather than avoid permanent alliances with each other and with other nations.

Alliances are a necessary function of the balance of power operating within a multiple-state system. Nations A and B, competing with each other, have three choices in order to maintain and improve their relative power positions. They can increase their own power, they can add to their own power the power of other nations, or they can withhold the power of other nations from the adversary. When they make the first choice, they embark upon an armaments race. When they choose the second and third alternatives, they pursue a policy of alliances.

Whether or not a nation shall pursue a policy of alliances is, then, not a matter of principle but of expediency. A nation will shun alliances if it believes that it is strong enough to hold its own unaided or that the burden of the commitments resulting from the alliance is likely to outweigh the advantages to be expected. It is for one or the other or both of these reasons that, throughout the better part of their history, Great Britain and the United States have refrained from entering into peacetime alliances with other nations.

Yet Great Britain and the United States have also refrained from concluding an alliance with each other even though, from the proclamation of the Monroe Doctrine in 1823 to the attack on Pearl Harbor in 1941, they have acted, at least in relation to the other European nations, as if they were allied. Their relationship during that period provides another instance of a situation in which nations dispense with an alliance. It occurs when their interests so obviously call for concerted policies and actions that an explicit formulation of these interests, policies, and actions in the form of a treaty of alliance appears to be redundant.

Both Great Britain and the United States have had with regard to the continent of Europe one interest in common: the preservation of the European balance of power. In consequence of this identity of interests, they have found themselves by virtual necessity in the camp opposed to the nation that happened to threaten that balance. And when Great Britain went to war in 1914 and 1939 in order to protect the European balance of power, the United States first supported Great Britain with a conspicuous lack of that impartiality befitting a neutral and then joined her on the battlefield. Had the United States in 1914 and 1939 been tied to Great Britain by a formal treaty of alliance, it might have declared war earlier, but its general policies and concrete actions would not have been materially different than they actually were.

Not every community of interests, calling for common policies and actions, also calls for legal codification in an explicit alliance. Yet, on the other hand, an alliance requires of necessity a community of interests for its foundation. Thucydides said that "identity of interest is the surest of bonds whether between states or individuals," and in the nineteenth century Lord Salisbury put the same thought in the negative by stating that "the only bond of union that endures" among nations is "the absence of clashing interests." Under what conditions, then, does an existing community of interests require the explicit formulation of an alliance? What is it that an alliance adds to the existing community of interests?

An alliance adds precision, especially in the form of limitation, to an existing community of interests and to the general policies and concrete measures serving them.[2] The interests nations have in common are not typically so precise and limited as to geographic region, objective, and appropriate policies as has been the American and British interest in the preservation of the European balance of power. Nor are they so incapable of precision and limitation as concerns the prospective common enemy. For while a typical alliance is directed against a specific nation or group of nations, the enemy of the Anglo-American community of interests could in the nature of things not be specified beforehand, since whoever threatens the European balance of power is the enemy. As Jefferson

---

[2] Glancing through the treaties of alliance of the seventeenth and eighteenth centuries, one is struck by the meticulous precision with which obligations to furnish troops, equipment, logistic support, food, money, and the like were defined.

shifted his sympathies back and forth between Napoleon and Great Britain according to who seemed to threaten the balance of power at the time, so during the century following the Napoleonic Wars Great Britain and the United States had to decide in the light of circumstances ever liable to change who posed at the moment the greatest threat to the balance of power. This blanket character of the enemy, determined not individually but by the function he performs, brings to mind a similar characteristic of collective security, which is directed against the abstractly designed aggressor, whoever he may be.

The typical interests that unite two nations against a third are both more definite as concerns the determination of the enemy and less precise as concerns the objectives to be sought and the policies to be pursued. In the last decades of the nineteenth century, France was opposed to Germany, and Russia was opposed to Austria, while Austria was allied with Germany against France and Russia. How could the interests of France and Russia be brought upon a common denominator, determining policy and guiding action? How could, in other words, the *casus foederis* be defined so that both friend and foe would know what to expect in certain contingencies affecting their respective interests? It was for the treaty of alliance of 1894 to perform these functions. Had the objectives and policies of the Franco-Russian alliance of 1894 been as clear as are the objectives and policies of Anglo-American co-operation in Europe, no alliance treaty would have been necessary. Had the enemy been as indeterminate as it was in the latter case, no alliance treaty would have been feasible.

The aftermath of World War II has radically changed the relationship between the United States and Great Britain, on the one hand, and the nations of Western Europe, on the other. A similar change has occurred in the relations between the United States and certain nations of Asia. The common enemy is now clearly and permanently identified, yet the general policies and concrete actions aimed at the common enemy are in need of being made precise by legal formulation. Thus it has come about that the United States and Great Britain, instead of intervening sporadically in Europe and Asia in order to restore the balance of power in the face of an ever-changing source of disturbance, are now permanently committed by way of alliances to oppose the threat to the balance of power emanating from the Soviet Union and, in so far as the United States is concerned, from Communist China.

When the common interests are inchoate in terms of policy and action, a treaty of alliance is required to make them explicit and operative. These interests, as well as the alliances expressing them and the policies serving them, can be distinguished in five different ways: according to their intrinsic nature and relationship, the distribution of benefits and power, their coverage in relation to the total interests of the nations concerned, their coverage in terms of time, and their effectiveness in terms of common policies and actions. In consequence, we can distinguish alliances serving identical, complementary, and ideological interests and policies. We can further distinguish mutual and one-sided, general and limited, temporary and permanent, operative and inoperative alliances.[3]

The present Anglo-American alliance within NATO provides the classic example of an alliance serving identical interests; the objective of one partner, the preservation of the balance of power in Europe, is also the objective of the other. The alliance between the United States and Pakistan is one of many contemporary instances of an alliance serving complementary interests. For the United States it serves the primary purpose of expanding the scope of the policy of containment; for Pakistan it serves primarily the purpose of increasing her political, military, and economic potential *vis-à-vis* her neighbors.

The pure type of an ideological alliance is presented by the Treaty of the Holy Alliance of 1815 and the Atlantic Charter of 1941. Both documents laid down general moral principles to which the signatories pledged their adherence, and general objectives whose realization they pledged themselves to seek. The Treaty of the Arab League of 1945 provides a contemporary example of an alliance expressing, since the war against Israel of 1948, primarily ideological solidarity.

Much more typical is the addition of ideological commitments to

---

[3] Sanskrit has sixteen words for different types of alliances.

material ones in one and the same treaty of alliance.[4] Thus the Three Emperors League of 1873 provided for military assistance among Austria, Germany, and Russia in case of attack on any of them and at the same time emphasized the solidarity of the three monarchies against republican subversion. In our times, the ideological commitment against Communist subversion, inserted in treaties of alliance, performs a similar function. The ideological factor also manifests itself in the official interpretation of an alliance, based upon material interests, in terms of an ideological solidarity transcending the limitations of material interests. The conception of the Anglo-American alliance, common before the British invasion of Egypt in 1956, as all-inclusive and world-embracing, based upon common culture, political institutions, and ideals, is a case in point.

As concerns the political effect of this ideological factor upon an alliance, three possibilities must be distinguished. A purely ideological alliance, unrelated to material interests, cannot but be stillborn; it is unable to determine policies and guide actions and misleads by giving the appearance of political solidarity where there is none. The ideological factor, when it is superimposed upon an actual community of interests, can lend strength to the alliance by marshaling moral convictions and emotional preferences to its support. It can also weaken it by obscuring the nature and limits of the common interests that the alliance was supposed to make precise and by raising expectations, bound to be disappointed, for the extent of concerted policies and actions. For both these possibilities, the Anglo-American alliance can again serve as an example.

The distribution of benefits within an alliance should ideally be one of complete mutuality; here the services performed by the parties for each other are commensurate with the benefits received. This ideal is most likely to be approximated in an alliance concluded among equals in power and serving identical interests; here the equal resources of all, responding to equal incentives, serve one single interest. The other extreme in the distribution of benefits is one-sidedness, a *societas leonina* in which one party receives the

---

[4] It ought to be pointed out that both the Holy Alliance and the Atlantic Charter actually supplement material commitments contained in separate legal instruments.

lion's share of benefits while the other bears the main bulk of burdens. In so far as the object of such an alliance is the preservation of the territorial and political integrity of the receiving party, such an alliance is indistinguishable from a treaty of guarantee. Complementary interests lend themselves most easily to this kind of disproportion, since they are by definition different in substance and their comparative assessment is likely to be distorted by subjective interpretation. A marked superiority in power is bound to add weight to such interpretations.

The distribution of benefits is thus likely to reflect the distribution of power within an alliance, as does the determination of policies. A great power has a good chance to have its way with a weak ally as concerns benefits and policies, and it is for this reason that Machiavelli warned weak nations against making alliances with strong ones except by necessity.[5] The relationship between the United States and South Korea exemplifies this situation.

However, this correlation between benefits, policies, and power is by no means inevitable. A weak nation may be able to exploit its relations with a strong ally by committing the latter to the support of its vital interests, which may mean nothing to the latter or may even run counter to its interests. In return, the weak nation may offer the strong ally its support, which typically is much less important to the latter than the latter's support is to the former. Historically, the relationship between Germany and Austria-Hungary before World War I was of this kind; the present relations of the United States with Pakistan and the regime of Chiang Kai-shek belong to the same type.

However, it is possible that a weak nation possesses an asset that is of such great value for its strong ally as to be irreplaceable. Here the unique benefit the former is able to grant or withhold may give it within the alliance a status completely out of keeping with the actual distribution of material power. The relationships between the United States and Iceland with regard to bases and between Great Britain and Iraq with regard to oil come to mind.

The misinterpretation of the Anglo-American alliance, mentioned before, is also a case in point for the confusion between limited and

---

[5] *The Prince,* Chap. 21.

general alliances. In the age of total war, wartime alliances tend to be general in that they comprise the total interests of the contracting parties both with regard to the waging of the war and the peace settlement. On the other hand, peacetime alliances tend to be limited to a fraction of the total interests and objectives of the signatories; otherwise they could not be distinguished from confederations. A nation will conclude a multitude of alliances with different nations that may overlap and contradict each other on specific points.

A typical alliance attempts to transform a small fraction of the total interests of the contracting parties into common policies and measures. Some of these interests are irrelevant to the purposes of the alliance, others support them, others diverge from them, and still others are incompatible with them. Thus a typical alliance is imbedded in a dynamic field of diverse interests and purposes. Whether and for how long it will be operative depends upon the strength of the interests underlying it as over against the strength of the other interests of the nations concerned. The value and the chances of an alliance, however limited in scope, must be considered within the context of the over-all policies within which it is expected to operate.

General alliances are typically of temporary duration and most prevalent in wartime. For the overriding common interest in winning the war and securing through the peace settlement the interests for which the war was waged is bound to yield, once victory is won and the peace treaties are signed, to the traditionally separate and frequently incompatible interests of the individual nations. On the other hand, there exists a correlation between the permanency of an alliance and the limited character of the interests it serves; for only such a specific, limited interest is likely to last long enough to provide the foundation for a durable alliance.[6] The alliance between Great Britain and Portugal, concluded in 1703, has survived the

---

[6] This correlation, however, cannot be reversed. Especially in the seventeenth and eighteenth centuries, limited alliances were frequently concluded *ad hoc,* that is, to counter an attack, to engage in one, or to embark upon a particular expedition. With the passing of the specific occasion in view of which the alliance was concluded, the alliance itself lost its object and came to an end.

centuries because Portugal's interest in the protection of her ports by the British fleet and the British interest in the control of the Atlantic approaches to Portugal have endured. Yet it can be stated as a general historical observation that while alliance treaties have frequently assumed permanent validity by being concluded "in perpetuity" or for periods of ten or twenty years, they could not have been more durable than the generally precarious and fleeting configurations of common interests that they were intended to serve. As a rule, they have been short-lived.

The dependence of alliances upon the underlying community of interests also accounts for the distinction between operative and inoperative alliances. For an alliance to be operative, that is, to be able to co-ordinate the general policies and concrete measures of its members, the latter must agree not only on general objectives but on policies and measures as well. Many alliances have remained scraps of paper because no such agreement was forthcoming, and it was not forthcoming because the community of interests did not extend beyond general objectives to concrete policies and measures. The Franco-Russian alliances of 1935 and 1944 and the Anglo-Russian alliance of 1942 are cases in point. The legal validity of a treaty of alliance and its propagandistic invocation can easily deceive the observer about its actual operational value. The correct assessment of this value requires the examination of the concrete policies and measures that the contracting parties have taken in implementation of the alliance.

II

It is obvious that the alliance systems as they exist today on either side of the Iron Curtain are different from what they were during the first decade following World War II. While a decade ago they opposed each other as two monolithic blocs, they are today beset by problems that threaten their internal cohesion. While these problems do not at present threaten these alliance systems with outright dissolution, they may well do so in a not-too-distant future. But they already put into question the unity of effective action that is the very purpose of all alliances. This holds true in different degrees of the three major alliance systems existing today: the Atlantic

Alliance (NATO), the Western alliances with nations outside Europe, and the Communist alliances. They have all been subject to the same eroding forces that have in different ways affected the mutual interests and policies of the members of the different alliance systems.

The vital interest of the United States in the protection of the nations of Western Europe against Russian domination is identical with the interest of these nations in preserving their national independence. Yet this foundation of the Atlantic Alliance has undergone a change both subtle and drastic. The Atlantic Alliance is beset by a crisis that the events of November 1956 have made obvious but not created. The beginnings of that crisis antedate the autumn of 1956 by several years; for the conditions that created the Atlantic Alliance during World War II and maintained it during the first decade following it have changed.

Seen from the perspective of the nations of Western Europe, three factors sustained the Atlantic Alliance in the decade following World War II: the atomic monopoly of the United States, the economic weakness of the nations of Western Europe, and the intransigence of Stalinist policies. The conjunction of these factors confronted the nations of Western Europe with the choice between suicide and the acceptance of the political, economic, and military support of the United States. In other words, the Atlantic Alliance was for the nations of Western Europe a prerequisite of national survival.

This connection between national survival and the Atlantic Alliance is no longer as close nor as obvious as it used to be. The atomic monopoly of the United States provided the nations of Western Europe with absolute protection against Russian conquest. With the Soviet Union having become an atomic power equal to the United States, the Atlantic Alliance is no longer for the nations of Western Europe solely a protection, but has become also a liability. The atomic stalemate threatens not only the two superpowers, but also their allies, with total destruction. The nations of Western Europe do not take it for granted that the United States, being thus threatened, is willing to commit suicide on their behalf.

Paradoxical as it may seem, the drastically increased threat of Soviet power has thus drastically weakened the Atlantic Alliance.

The Soviet Union has not been slow to point out, and the man in the street in Western Europe has not been slow to understand, that if there is a chance for the nations of Western Europe to survive in an atomic war, it may lie in not being too closely identified, or perhaps not being identified at all, with the United States. Thus a latent neutralism has had a slowly corrosive influence upon the Atlantic Alliance. The rise of this neutralism in Western Europe as a popular movement is not primarily the result of Communist propaganda, or of faintness of heart, or political decadence, but of the new objective conditions under which the nations of Western Europe must live in the age of the atomic stalemate.

Second, the distribution of power within the Atlantic Alliance has greatly changed since the beginning of the fifties. The weak nations have grown stronger and the nations defeated in World War II are in the process of growing very strong indeed. In the years immediately following the Second World War, the nations of Western Europe had either to join the United States or go bankrupt economically and disintegrate socially. The economic recovery of the nations of Western Europe has eliminated their dependence upon the United States due to the Coal and Steel Community, Euratom, the Common Market, and the development of East-West trade. Thus while the nations of Western Europe are still in need of American military aid, economic aid is no longer a question of life and death as it was fifteen years ago. Today, they have, or at least have evidence that they soon will have, an alternative. They can stand on their own feet again and look beyond the wall of containment for new outlets for their energies and products.

These factors affect with particular intensity West Germany's attitude to the Atlantic Alliance. Their effect is strengthened by the political issue that has the widest, and is likely to have a lasting and ever-deepening, emotional appeal: unification. The Atlantic Alliance has been presented to West Germany, both by American and German official spokesmen, as the instrument through which unification would be achieved. While this view was from the outset open to serious doubts on theoretical grounds, the historic experience of its failure has led to a crisis of confidence that is likely to deepen as time goes on without, despite German membership in the Atlantic Alliance, bringing unification closer. The Atlantic

Alliance, far from being supported as the instrument of unification, is ever more loudly and widely blamed as the main obstacle to unification.

The Soviet Union has been eager to use these new political, military, and economic conditions under which the nations of Western Europe live for the purpose of weakening and ultimately destroying the Atlantic Alliance. What has been called the "new look" of Soviet foreign policy is essentially a new flexibility that has taken the place of the monotony of the Stalinist threats. In the face of these threats, no nation that wanted to survive as a nation had any choice; thus Stalin was really the architect of the Atlantic Alliance. The new Soviet foreign policy alternately threatens and tempts, as the occasion seems to require, but always seeks to hold before the eyes of Western Europe an acceptable or even preferable alternative to the Atlantic Alliance. In consequence, the Atlantic Alliance has lost much of its urgency and even vitality. Great Britain and France, for instance, no longer feel that they have to subordinate their separate national interests to the common defense against the Soviet Union, and they have begun, in different degrees, to pursue those interests regardless, and sometimes at the expense, of the common interests of the alliance; they have also begun to vent openly their resentment at their lack of great-power status and to allow their policies to be influenced by it. The rise of Germany to a position of political, military, and economic eminence, with all the fears and expectations this rise must cause in both Western and Eastern Europe, cannot help but add to the opportunities of the new Soviet foreign policy.

As viewed from the vantage point of the United States, the Atlantic Alliance is also in the process of undergoing a subtle change, which in the end is bound to be a drastic one. For the United States, the Atlantic Alliance is the political and military implementation of its perennial interest in the maintenance of the European balance of power. However, the military implementation of this interest is likely to change under the impact of a new technology of warfare.

As long as the main deterrent to Russian aggression remained the atomic bomb delivered by plane, the military strategy of the United States required military installations in Western Europe; and the nations of Western Europe had a corresponding interest in providing them. To the extent that intercontinental and navy-borne missiles will replace airplanes as the means of atomic attack, the interest in American military installations in Western Europe will diminish on both sides of the Atlantic. This interest will decrease still further when some of the nations of Western Europe have atomic weapons and, hence, a deterrent of their own. When this day comes, the Atlantic Alliance will take on a new complexion, probably losing some of its specific military aspects and tending to revert to an implicit community of interests similar to that which tied the United States to Great Britain from 1823 to 1941. It is to this contingency that the British Minister of Defense, Mr. Duncan Sandys, appears to have been referring when he justified in April 1957, in the House of Commons, the British emphasis on atomic armaments by asking: "When the United States has developed the five-thousand-mile intercontinental ballistic rocket can we really be sure that every American Administration will go on looking at things in the same way?"

However, the interests of the United States and the nations of Western Europe are not limited to that continent. Those of the United States and Great Britain are world-wide, and France is engaged in Africa. While the interests of the United States and of the nations of Western Europe indeed coincide in the preservation of the latter's independence, they do not necessarily coincide elsewhere. The coincidence or divergence of these non-European interests has had, as it was bound to have, a strengthening or debilitating effect upon the Atlantic Alliance itself; and the vital interest of all concerned in this alliance has, in turn, limited their freedom of action outside Europe.

The United States in particular, dealing with the colonial revolutions, which are directed primarily against Great Britain and France, has been continuously confronted with a painful and inherently insoluble dilemma. The horns of that dilemma are the interest of the United States in the continuing strength of Great Britain and France as its principal allies and the American interest in preventing the colonial revolutions from falling under the sway of communism. If the United States underwrites the colonial position of Great Britain or France, as it did in Indochina, it may, at best, strengthen temporarily its principal European allies, but it will impair its standing with the anticolonial peoples of Asia and Africa. If the United States sides unreservedly with the Afro-Asian bloc, as it did in the United Nations on the occasion of the Suez Canal crisis of the autumn of 1956, it weakens Great Britain and France and, in consequence, the Atlantic Alliance.

Faced with this dilemma, which can be solved only at the price of impairing the vital interests of the United States in one or the other respect, the United States has inevitably been reduced to straddling the fence by supporting halfheartedly on one occasion one side and on another occasion the other side, or else keeping hands off altogether. Algeria and Cyprus exemplified the dilemma and its evasion. In such situations, then, the Atlantic Alliance does not operate at all; for there are no common interests that could support its operation.

This has always been obviously true of Western policies toward Communist China. The policy of the United States has been one of implacable hostility, while Great Britain has sought accommodation. The Atlantic Alliance is here not only not operating, but the policies of its two principal members have been consistently at cross-purposes. The success of one would of necessity mean the failure of the other.

That such divergencies of interest and policy have not imposed greater stresses upon the Atlantic Alliance and have left it essentially unimpaired testifies to its inherent strength. But that strength cannot be taken for granted. The common interests underlying the Atlantic Alliance have thus far prevailed over the divergent ones only because of the conviction of the members of the alliance that they have a greater stake in their common than in their divergent interests. The paramountcy of the common interests has thus far kept the divergent ones in check. But in recent years the latter have grown stronger and the former, weaker. If this trend should continue unchecked, it would indeed put in jeopardy the very survival of the Atlantic Alliance.

Common interests are the rock on which all alliances are built. Yet upon this rock all kinds of structures may be erected, some solid and spacious, others crumbling and confining. In other words, there are good and bad alliances, some that work smoothly and are enthusiastically supported, others that are cumbersome and are grudgingly accepted as a lesser evil. While the existence of an alliance depends upon a community of interests, its quality is determined by the manner in which common interests are translated into concrete policies and day-by-day measures.

It is in this latter respect that the Atlantic Alliance must cause concern. Here, too, the crisis of November 1956 has made obvious defects that antedate that crisis. Three such defects have, continuously and to an ever-increasing degree, impaired the operation of the Atlantic Alliance: its organizational structure; the policies, domestic and international, of its leading members; and the prestige enjoyed by some of its leading statesmen.

The common interest of the members of the Atlantic Alliance in the military protection of their independence has found its organizational expression in the North Atlantic Treaty Organization. The strategic conception that underlies NATO is the assumption that the European members of the Atlantic Alliance are able to defend themselves through a co-operative effort against a military attack by the Soviet Union. But NATO has never developed a convincing philosophy of its concrete military purpose. All members of NATO are agreed upon one objective: to defend their independence without having to fight for it—that is, to deter aggression. But how is this purpose to be achieved? Is primary reliance to be placed upon atomic retaliation with the local forces of NATO performing the function of the "plate glass" or "trip wire," or is a prospective aggressor to be deterred by the inherent military strength of local forces? The members of NATO have not seen eye to eye on this fundamental question, and NATO itself, in its official proclamations and policies, has not seemed to be of one mind either.

More particularly, the declared purposes of NATO have been consistently at variance with the measures requested of its members for implementation of these purposes, and the measures requested, in turn, have been invariably at variance with the measures actually taken. If the strategic purpose of NATO is the ground defense of Western Europe against an attack by the Red Army, none of the different forces successively requested by NATO have appeared to be sufficient for that purpose, nor have the forces actually provided by the members of NATO ever even come close to fulfilling the requests. Furthermore, declared purposes, requested measures, and the measures actually taken have been subjected to a number of drastic and confusing changes that cannot be explained exclusively by the revolutionary transformations that military technology has been undergoing.

This confusion in policy, in itself conducive to political disunity and friction in day-by-day operations, has been magnified by the elaborate organizational superstructure that is intended to put the policies of NATO into practice. This superstructure, encompassing a plethora of committees in charge of co-ordinating a variety of political, military, and economic policies of the member states, must, even under the best of circumstances, make for friction and inefficiency. It magnifies these defects because it is much too ambitious in purpose and elaborate in operation for the agreed purpose of NATO to support it. In the absence of agreement on philosophy and basic policy, the elaborate organizational superstructure has been, as Generals de Gaulle and Montgomery pointed out in the fall of 1958, a source of weakness for the Atlantic Alliance.

An alliance, in its day-by-day operations, rests in good measure upon the mutual confidence in the willingness and ability of its members to co-operate effectively in achieving the common purpose. That confidence, in turn, rests upon the quality of the over-all policies pursued by the members of the alliance and upon the character and ability of its leading statesmen. In both respects, the Atlantic Alliance has shown itself to be deficient.

There can be no doubt that in both respects the prestige of the United States as the leader and backbone of the Atlantic Alliance has drastically declined. It is irrelevant for the purposes of this analysis whether this decline is rooted in objective facts or whether it is but the result of subjective preconceptions and emotions. Rightly or wrongly, the United States is no longer looked upon by its allies, as it was during the period immediately following World War II, as the leader whose strength and resolution, if not wisdom, can be relied upon to keep the Atlantic Alliance on an even course. Several factors are responsible for the crisis of confidence.

The main purpose of the Atlantic Alliance being the mutual defense of its members and the United States being its military backbone, the European members of the Atlantic Alliance have a natural interest in the military policies of the United States. They are not reassured by them. For the American emphasis upon the atomic deterrent and the concomitant neglect of conventional forces, operating within the new distribution of military power discussed above, spells for them, if the deterrent should fail, either total destruction or virtually total lack of defense. In either case, the alliance fails in its purpose.

However, it is not only effective power that allies expect from the strongest member of the alliance. They also expect a reliable foreign policy that takes the interests of the allies into account. In the lack of political confidence between the United States and its European allies the Atlantic Alliance is weakened at still another point. In foreign policy it is sometimes, but by no means always, useful to keep the enemy guessing. But to keep your allies guessing, most of the time and on matters vital to them, about what you intend to do is bound to erode the foundations of confidence upon which the alliance in its day-by-day operations must rest. The allies of the United States have noted discrepancies between the policy pronouncements of our leaders and the actual policies pursued, which appear to them to have evolved into a consistent pattern of unreliability. Liberation, the unleashing of Chiang Kai-shek, agonizing reappraisal, the "new look," intervention in Indochina, the internationalization of the Suez Canal, the protection of the rights of Israel have been proclaimed as objectives of American foreign policy. Yet, in most instances, the foreign policy of the United States appears to our allies to have been at variance with these pronouncements or, at the very least, their implementation remains in doubt.

This slow accumulation of loss of confidence reached a critical stage in the Suez Canal crisis; for here unreliability in policy appeared to be joined by indifference, if not hostility, to the vital interests of America's principal allies. For the vital interests of the United States and its allies to coincide in Europe and diverge elsewhere is one thing; for the vital interests of its principal allies elsewhere to be opposed and destroyed by the United States is quite another. To the former, the allies of the United States could reconcile themselves with relative equanimity; the latter could not help but raise for our allies the crucial question as to whether the Atlantic Alliance was worth so high a price. That they answered the question in the affirmative testifies to the vitality of the alliance. Their resentment was kindled by the actual demonstration of their inability to pursue active foreign policies of their own without the support and against the opposition of one or the other of the super-powers. Thus under the dramatic impact of the experience that saw their interests and power destroyed in a region vital to them-selves, with the approval and active participation of the United States, the Atlantic Alliance tended to transform itself for our allies from an association of like-minded nations into a burden grudgingly borne.

That like-mindedness has in the past been the result not only of a community of interests, but also of a common dedication to the ideals of freedom. When in the aftermath of World War II Com-munist totalitarianism threatened to engulf Western Europe, the United States was looked upon by its European allies as the symbol and the incarnation of that dedication. That image of the United States was tarnished by the temporary decline of freedom within its borders during the McCarthy period. Yet, while American pres-tige has been largely restored under the impact of the revival of the traditions of American freedom, there has remained a latent skepti-cism and general malaise, which cast their shadow over the Atlantic Alliance.

As far as long-range policies are concerned, the relations among nations must indeed be conceived in terms of interests. As con-cerns their day-by-day relations, we must also think in terms of personalities. We say that the United States and Great Britain have agreed on a certain policy, but tend to forget that Great Britain and the United States are abstractions and that in actuality the President and Secretary of State of the United States and the Prime Minister and Secretary for Foreign Affairs of Great Britain, speaking in the name of their respective nations, have agreed with each other. The smooth and effective operation of an alliance, then, depends in good measure upon the relations of trust and respect among its principal statesmen. There is no gainsaying the fact that the decline in such relations has become a great handicap in the day-by-day operations of the Atlantic Alliance. Regardless of the objective merits of the case, there can be no doubt that the leaders of our

European allies no longer have the same confidence in the judg-
ment and the authority of our leaders that they had in times past.
These reactions have increased the strains under which the Atlantic
Alliance operates at present.

The traditional political rhetoric on both sides of the Atlantic has
tended to gloss over all these stresses and strains and has made it
appear as though the Atlantic Alliance were something broader and
smoother and also something more diffuse than it actually is. It is
indeed built upon a rock of common interests, but the rock is of
limited dimensions and its surfaces are sometimes rough. In spite
of the great damage that the crisis of November 1956 has done to
the Atlantic Alliance, it has been useful in circumscribing more
closely its limits and demonstrating, for all to see, its still considerable strength.

III

While the Atlantic Alliance reposes upon the firm foundation of
identical interests, no such general and reassuring statement can
be made about the Western alliances with nations outside Europe.
Considering Asia and the Middle East, it can be said only of the
American alliances with Formosa, South Korea, South Viet Nam,
and Japan that they are based upon identical interests. These nations, with the exception of Japan, owe their very existence as
nations to the interests and power of the United States. Their survival as nations is inextricably tied to the interests and power of the
United States. Yet only their complete dependence upon the United
States has prevented some, if not all, of these nations from pursuing
policies at variance with those of the United States. Thus the stability of these alliances rests upon both identical interests and
extreme discrepancy of power.

Our alliance with Japan, like that with Germany, was during the
first decade following World War II based upon the dual foundation of identical interests and overwhelming American power. Yet
neither foundation can any longer be taken for granted. Three
factors have combined to restore Japan's freedom of choice. First,
Japan has again become a strong power. If the wartime memories
of Japan's imperialism were not still alive in the rest of Asia, Japan

would be a natural candidate for taking over the economic and political leadership of non-Communist Asia. Second, the atomic stalemate has had the same psychological effect on Japan as it had on Western Europe; the American alliance has become for Japan a mixed blessing if not a liability. Finally, to the degree that the aggressiveness of Stalinist and Chinese Korean war policies is replaced by a new flexibility that stresses the complementary character of Russian, Chinese, and Japanese interests, Japan may find a practical alternative to its identification with the United States.

The other Asian alliances, of which SEATO and the Baghdad Pact provide the outstanding examples, are of an entirely different type. They have three characteristics in common: complementary interests tending toward transformation into incompatible ones, a radically unequal distribution of benefits, and ideological emphasis.

These alliances, on the face of them, were conceived in terms of common action on behalf of common interests. However, in view of the remoteness of the apparent *casus foederis,* that is, Communist attack upon a member, and of the virtual impossibility, in case of such an attack, for most members to act in common, commitment to common action has receded into the background and been distilled into an anti-Communist ideological commitment. Of the Asian members, this commitment requires nothing more than membership in the alliance; it requires no common objective, policy, and action—beyond anticommunism at home and abroad. Yet of the Western members, especially the United States, it requires specific policies and actions on behalf of the Asian members.

The Asian members are interested in these alliances primarily because of the economic, military, and political support they receive from the United States. Many of them consider their membership in the alliance to constitute a special claim upon the American Treasury, American weapons, and American political support for their special national aspirations. In other words, this support is the price the United States pays for having the receiving nations as allies. However valuable it judges this membership to be, in terms of actual policies and measures, the United States bears a unilateral burden. The United States is under continuous pressure to act as an ally while the Asian allies, once they have signed the treaty of alliance, preserve virtually complete freedom of action. Their foreign policies, for instance *vis-à-vis* China, could hardly be different if they were not members of the alliance. In order to show the irrelevance of the alliance in terms of common objectives, policies, and actions, the Prime Minister of an Asian nation has indeed gone so far as to equate his country's membership in SEATO with membership in the United Nations.

In so far as all that the West wants is the maximum number of Asian allies and all that the Asian allies want is the maximum amount of Western support for their own specific national objectives, the two interests can be said to complement each other, provided these objectives are compatible with those of the other allies. In view of the Western emphasis upon the ideological character of the alliance and the concomitant neglect of concrete interests and policies, this compatibility will exist only by accident and not by design and, in view of the nature of the interests involved, is bound to be precarious. It is bound to disintegrate whenever a latent conflict of interests between two allies or an ally and another nation becomes acute. The conflicts between Pakistan and India over Kashmir, between Great Britain and Greece, and Turkey and Greece, over Cyprus, and between Iraq and Israel are cases in point. It is only because these alliances limit a commitment to common action to the very unlikely event of Communist aggression that they have survived such incompatibilities. The United States, in particular, is frequently forced into the uncomfortable position of having either to straddle the fence, as between Great Britain and Greece, or else to sacrifice its interests to its alliance, as between India and Pakistan.

Thus, by virtue of its alliance, the United States increases the armed strength of Pakistan and thereby forces India to increase its expenditures for armaments from thirty million pounds in 1955 to ninety million pounds in 1957. This diversion of scarce funds from economic development to armaments threatens India with an economic and political disaster, which the United States has a vital interest in staving off through financial aid. In consequence, the United States engages, as it were, in an armaments race with itself by proxy, its left hand supporting Pakistan by virtue of the alliance, its right hand aiding India by virtue of its vital interests.

As concerns the alliances among the nations of the Western

Hemisphere, appearances are deceptive. As long as the supremacy of the United States within the Western Hemisphere provided unchallengeable protection for the independence of the American nations, these alliances could indeed be taken for granted. For the United States, these alliances provided complete safety, since, in view of its unchallengeable supremacy within the hemisphere and of the protection of two oceans, its security could be endangered only by a non-American nation acting in concert with an American one. For the other American nations, these alliances provided complete security from great-power domination, since the United States would use its superior power only for the protection and not for the subversion of their national independence.

This identity of interests and the ability of the United States to implement it has from the proclamation of the Monroe Doctrine to this day provided the rationale and lifeblood of the American state system. The intercontinental guided missile confronts this system with a challenge never before experienced. For the supremacy of the United States within the Western Hemisphere, as unchallengeable as ever from within, is of no avail as protection against these novel weapons of tomorrow. The United States can no more protect its American allies against these weapons than it can protect itself. The American allies of the United States will then view the alliance with the same misgivings with which the European allies and Japan view it already. They may no longer regard their interests to be identical with those of the United States and may conclude that safety lies not in closeness to, but rather in distance from, the United States.

IV

The Communist alliances present three different types, which must be sharply distinguished: the alliances of the Soviet Union and China with North Korea and North Viet Nam, the alliances between the Soviet Union and the nations of Eastern Europe, and the alliances of the Soviet Union with China and the United Arab Republic.

The position of North Korea and North Viet Nam within the Communist alliances is identical in the particulars that interest us here with the position of South Korea and South Viet Nam within their alliances with the United States. It is marked by complete identity of interests and extreme disparity of power.

The alliances between the Soviet Union and the nations of Eastern Europe, codified in the Warsaw Pact of 1955, are in a class by themselves. They are not true alliances in that they do not transform a pre-existing community of interests into legal obligations. It is their distinctive quality that a community of interests is irrelevant for their existence and operation and that they are founded on nothing but unchallengeable superiority of power. Power is here not superimposed upon common interests, as in a genuine alliance, but becomes a substitute for them. Thus the nation possessing such unchallengeable power makes the other contracting party subservient to its interests, regardless, and in spite of the divergence, of the latter's interests. Such so-called treaties of alliance are in truth in the nature of treaties establishing, in the legal form of alliances, relationships that are a modern version of protectorates or suzerainty, and the nations subjected to them are correctly called satellites rather than allies.

The nature of this relationship has not been affected, although it might well be in the future, by the development of a community of interests between the Soviet Union and certain satellites, such as Poland and Czechoslovakia. That community of interests results from the emergence of Germany as the predominant power in Europe. Poland and Czechoslovakia, situated as they are between two nations of superior strength, have had to seek protection either from one neighbor against the other or from Western Europe against both. Their present relationship to the Soviet Union provides this protection. Given a change in both Russian and German policies, this protective function might well form the basis for a future genuine alliance.

While this development is purely speculative, the relations between the Soviet Union and the satellites have undergone in recent years an actual transformation similar to that which has affected the Atlantic Alliance, and for similar reasons. The emergence of an atomic stalemate between the United States and the Soviet Union has loosened the ties of the satellite relationship. As long as the military contest between East and West pitted American atomic bombs against the Red Army, the latter could be regarded as the indispensable guardian of the Russian empire within and without. With the growth of Russian atomic power, the importance of the Red Army declined. The threat of mutual atomic destruction has stimulated both the desire for self-preservation in the form of neutralism and the aspirations for national independence that had lain dormant under the yoke of the Red Army.

These latent tendencies were brought to the fore by the "new look" of Russian policy following the death of Stalin. In response to it, the spirit of national independence started to push against the lid of Russian oppression, and the Russian proconsuls yielded to the pressure. They rehabilitated most of the national leaders who had tried to combine communism and at least a measure of national independence and relaxed the authoritarian controls over the economic and intellectual life of the satellites. Yet popular reaction went beyond domestic reforms to embrace national independence, that is, the end of the satellite relationship itself. At this point, the Soviet Union called a halt, reasserting the paramountcy of its interests supported by the supremacy of its power.

The events that occurred in the fall of 1956 in Hungary and Poland have clearly demonstrated in different ways the nature of the satellite relationship in contrast to a genuine alliance. Both countries, through their revolts against Russian rule, sought essentially to reassert their distinct national interests against those of the Soviet Union. In the process they were bound to put into question, and Hungary did openly challenge, the satellite status from which derived, in terms of law and power, their subservience to the Soviet Union. Yet while the Soviet Union could afford to make political, economic, and even military concessions, it could not risk the disintegration of its predominance over Eastern Europe by allowing the satellite system itself to be challenged. It was at this point that it brought its superior power to bear upon Hungary and forestalled, through this pointed example, a similarly open challenge on the part of Poland and other satellites.

In contrast, the alliances of the Soviet Union with China and the United Arab Republic are genuine alliances, based as they are upon a community of interests upon which the preponderant power of the Soviet Union is merely superimposed. The exact nature of the community of interests between the Soviet Union and China is a matter for speculation. Russian and Chinese interests appear to be identical in so far as their common objective is the strengthening and expansion of the Communist, and the weakening and retraction of the anti-Communist, camp. They appear to be complementary in so far as the alliance serves the Chinese interest in economic and military development and the Russian interest in keeping the United States militarily engaged and politically handicapped in the Far East.

Yet it cannot serve the interests of the Soviet Union to promote the development of Chinese power to the point where it threatens to jeopardize the present predominance of Russian power. On the other hand, China has a vital interest in reaching that point and thus making itself independent from Russian good will. For the governments of both nations know that if and when modern technology has been added to Chinese superiority in man power under strong political direction, China will have become the most powerful nation on earth. It is this eventuality that the Soviet Union must dread and try to forestall and that China must welcome and try to realize. This potential conflict of vital interests overshadows the alliance between China and the Soviet Union. It allows the Soviet Union for the time being to restrain Chinese policies, and it gives China the opportunity of exploiting for its advantage the actual and potential conflicts between the Soviet Union and its satellites and among the different groups competing for power within the Soviet Union.

The alliance between the Soviet Union and the United Arab Republic serves clearly complementary interests. The United Arab Republic is enabled by the military support it receives from the Soviet Union to pursue actively its specific interests in the Middle East and North Africa. The Soviet Union, on the other hand, has no stake in these specific interests except in so far as their active pursuit serves to maintain a state of tension that keeps the Western nations engaged and handicapped in still another region and threatens them with economic distress.

V

Considering the over-all picture of the alliances as it emerges from this analysis, one is impressed by the similarity of the changes that have occurred in the structure of the European alliances on both sides of the Iron Curtain. The seemingly irreversible trend toward a two-bloc system that marked the immediate postwar era has been arrested, if not reversed. The uncommitted nations not only want to remain uncommitted but have, with a few exceptions, also shown the ability to do so. On the other hand, many of the European nations that are committed as allies of one or the other of the super-powers would like to join the ranks of the uncommitted nations but have, with the exception of Yugoslavia, been unable to do so. They have at best been able to move to the outer confines of the blocs to which they belong, but have had to stop there. In consequence, the two-bloc system is in the process of loosening but not of breaking up.

The satellites may become even more unwilling and unreliable partners of the Soviet Union than they are already. Short of out-side intervention, they cannot move out of the Soviet orbit as long as Russian interest backed by Russian power keeps them there. However, the interest of Russia in the domination of Eastern Europe has been perennial, regardless of drastic changes in the personnel, philosophy, and structure of government. The weakening of that interest cannot be foreseen short of a revolution in military technology that would make the control of outlying territory irrelevant. The power of the Soviet Union to keep the satellites under control cannot be challenged from within and is not likely to be challenged from without. Yet the alliance between the Soviet Union and China is a marriage of temporary convenience, which contains in the very terms of its existence the seeds of trouble.

The fate that may be in store for the Atlantic Alliance is similarly not its formal dissolution but rather its slow erosion to the point of becoming inoperative. The common fear of communism, either as subversion from within or aggression from without, and the common dedication to the values of Western civilization are likely to remain stronger than the disruptive tendencies of divergent and incompatible interests and thus to keep the common framework of the Atlantic Alliance intact. The demonstrated inability of even Great Britain and France to pursue positive foreign policies against the opposition of the United States adds to this outward stability of the Atlantic Alliance. The real danger lies in this common framework becoming an empty shell, drained of its vitality. History abounds with legal compacts, constitutional devices, and institutional forms that have survived, sometimes—as in the case of the Holy Roman Empire—for centuries, as ritualistic observances, or in the words of Chief Justice Marshall "a solemn mockery," without any longer being capable of directing the interests of men into the channels of common policies and actions. The Atlantic Alliance is indeed in danger of becoming just such a ritual to which nations continue to pay lip service, whose procedures they still observe, and whose institutional forms they maintain, while they plan and act as though it did not exist.

The danger that threatens the Atlantic Alliance from the unsettled German problem is, however, more serious than that. The tension between the German commitment to the Atlantic Alliance and the national goal of unification, to be achieved only with Russian consent, inevitably raises in German minds the question of whether that commitment and this objective are truly compatible and whether the former must not be sacrificed in order to achieve the latter. The logic of the argument implicit in this question can be prevented from becoming the rationale of the actual policy of Germany only by the intransigence of Russian, and the wisdom of American, policies. The danger of German defection from the Atlantic Alliance, then, raises in specific terms the general issue of the merits of our alliance policy and of our response to the structural changes that our alliances have undergone in recent times.

Our alliance policy partakes of the doctrinaire, legalistic, and mechanical character of much of American foreign policy. These perennial vices reappear here in a new setting. Instead of recognizing that there are useful, harmful, and superfluous alliances according to circumstances and discriminating among them in view of the interests to be served and the policies to be pursued, we have followed what might be called the collector's approach to alliances: the more alliances, the better. Or to put it more elaborately: the more nations sign a legal document declaring their support for our policies, the better. While once we were, on principle, against all "entangling alliances," now we are, again on principle, in favor of all alliances.

This emphasis upon the quantity of alliances and, more particularly, upon their military advantages—actual or illusory—has tended to jeopardize our political interests. Frequently, our allies have turned our interest in the alliance per se to their political advantage, without any corresponding political advantage accruing to us or, at worst, at the expense of our political interests. In consequence, the weak members of the alliance, knowing what they want to get out of it, have tended to convert the alliance into an instrument of their policies with the United States paying the political, military, and economic cost.

This tendency to see intrinsic merit in any alliance, regardless of the interests to be served, the benefits to be expected, and the liabilities to be met, has been most pronounced in Asia. SEATO, originating in an indiscriminate invitation by the United States to join, is indeed the classic example of such a misconceived alliance. Its membership was determined not by the United States in view of its interests but by the other members in view of theirs. Nor has the issue of the mutuality of benefits and liabilities been ever squarely faced. More particularly, the alliance has never been correlated to our over-all Asian interests, which—except for Formosa, South Korea, and South Viet Nam—are political rather than military.

SEATO is for the United States a useless alliance from the military point of view and a harmful one politically and economically in that it alienates the broad masses of Asians and imposes economic burdens without benefits. NATO, on the other hand, especially in view of its elaborate organizational superstructure but also in its very existence, may well prove to be a superfluous alliance— a view held by a minority within and outside the government when NATO was created in 1949. It may well be asked again, as it was then, whether the obvious identity of interests between the United States and the nations of Western Europe could not have been adequately served by a unilateral guarantee on the part of the United States, fashioned after the model of the Monroe Doctrine. While the very existence of NATO has made this question obviously academic, the rationale underlying it could still be put into practice by dismantling what is useless and harmful in NATO and strengthening what is useful, essential, and lasting. If the United States fails to reduce in time the structure of the alliances in Europe and Asia to the dimensions required by the interests that it has in common with its allies, it must be prepared to face sometime in the future a real crisis of its alliances, born of disappointment and divergent interests. While it now oscillates between unilateral action oblivious of the interests and sensibilities of its allies and excessive concern for the quantity of legal commitments, it will then have no choice but to go it alone.

These observations culminate in the conclusion that the problem of alliances must be considered in the context of the over-all character of world politics. If the task facing a nation is primarily military, not to be mastered by its isolated strength alone, a policy of alliances is the answer; and this answer is still the correct one in Europe and in certain exposed regions of Asia. In so far as the task is political, requiring a variety of means applied with subtlety, discrimination, and imagination, a policy of alliances will be useless, if not harmful; and this is indeed the situation that confronts the United States in most of the world where the issue is political allegiance and not military defense. A policy of alliances, in its doctrinaire insistence upon joining the club, in its legalistic concern with signatures and stipulations, in its mechanical counting of heads, then, serves as a substitute for political creativeness, the lack of which it may temporarily conceal. What it can neither conceal nor stave off is failure, which attends upon wrong policies as punishment follows the crime.

8

ALLIANCES WITH
FLEDGLING STATES

Charles Burton Marshall

I

IF THE laboratory method applied in foreign policy, it would
be possible to appraise accurately and conclusively the effectiveness
and import of specific undertakings. By running history over again
under controlled changes of conditions we should be able to tell
for sure how creative one policy or how misguided and delusory
another actually was, and how much better or worse or how much
of a nothing the putative alternatives were.

Did the Monroe Doctrine actually make much difference in the
long run? Was Munich a default of good sense or an exercise of
prudence by Chamberlain and Daladier, given the conditions? How
differently and more favorably to our interests might other insights
and a different approach have arranged matters at Yalta? Was the
particular wording of Dean Acheson's speech at the Press Club
actually construed as a come-on by the Communists in their designs
on Korea, or was it actually a matter of no consequence at all? It
would be interesting to have knowledge of such matters in place of
the dogmatic assertion and the thin conjecture so often substituted
for knowledge in this field.

Obviously, however, the professions of punditry and diplomatic
history are in no danger of having their props knocked out from

under them by the replacement of speculativeness with certainty in such matters. There is no way of telling for sure how different the actual would have been if it had been different. Foreign policy, like all of history, gives no opportunity for the laboratory method. One may construct alternatives by hypothesis but not verify them by experiment.

In this light, it is impossible to say anything conclusive about recent United States undertakings in the contested areas of the Middle East and South Asia.

I understand, for example, the doubts raised about the Baghdad Pact, which the United States government has sponsored and encouraged though it has not actually joined. Perhaps it did serve mainly to push Egypt's Nasser into intractability and then to provide him a fulcrum by which to exercise leverage on Moscow. Perhaps without it in existence things would not have come to a head as they did in Baghdad itself, resulting in the destruction of the regime in the very city which gave the pact its name. I do not suppose it will ever be possible to affirm or to deny these suppositions for sure.

The effects of the Eisenhower Doctrine seem equally obscure. The only Middle Eastern government that put itself on the line for the doctrine wound up by having put itself on the spot instead. Maybe things would have come to such a bad pass for the Chamoun regime in any event—doctrine or no doctrine, endorsement or no endorsement. By the same token, it is hard to evaluate the intervention in Lebanon. Critics can point out its ambiguity—its stupendous-seeming start and its squeaky finish. Defenders of Secretary Dulles' policies may counter that matters in Lebanon and its environs might conceivably be much worse than they are and that the landing of United States forces saved the difference in a subtle way. Probably no one can be sure.

The same goes for SEATO. Apologists for it may point out that it was designed to stem Communist advances into Southeast Asia and that since the whole place has not fallen yet, it obviously has achieved some success. Doubters may counter that the organization has served chiefly to divert working time and travel money away from more serious undertakings for meetings in which the participants orally exchange information that might better have been conveyed by paper. Moreover, a doubter may add, if any good is being done in the area, it is through the Colombo Plan, which has some sinew instead of just having meetings, agenda, and committees.

Gladstone's mentor warned him as a young man that in choosing a political career he was entering an unsatisfactory business and would have to learn to put up with imperfect results. The inherent unsatisfactory character of politics is nowhere more apparent than among the fledgling states of Asia and Africa. The ambiguity of United States undertakings with respect to these areas results not so much from faults of policy as from the unsatisfactoriness of the political situations of the areas dealt with.

This suggests that the political character of the parties thereto has a bearing on the evaluation of alliances. It is well to understand an alliance as a political engagement between states. One must comprehend that one state may not be as highly developed as another in political capacity, that nominal states are not all alike in the level of their achievement of statehood, and that the contractive capacity of one may vary greatly from that of another.

One does not have to assume that these obvious considerations have been overlooked in recent United States foreign policy undertakings. The matter has been given explicit expression. An official high in the councils of the United States government in the field of foreign policy has laid down a doctrinal point: "There can be no first-class and second-class alliances . . . ." As if to clinch the point, he has said that this could no more be so than that the freedom of an individual in an Asian country, for example, could be considered to be worth less than that of an individual in a European country.[1]

As a moral proposition, as a judgment exercised from the standpoint of divine impartiality, the cited view about uniform concern for freedom is probably sound. An invasion of freedom in one political society should appeal to our compassion and concern just as much as the same thing in another. Yet politically one must take into account that the institutions of freedom are not really

---

[1] Christian A. Herter quoted in *Department of State Bulletin,* July 22, 1957, p. 138.

uniform from one country to another and that an impingement on freedom of individuals in one place may have vastly more importance in what it forebodes for our policy than a similar impingement in another place. The fact that large numbers of persons are held in subjection approaching slavery on the African continent arouses our indignation as a violation of justice, but it would be sheer sentimentality to pretend that it moves us in a policy sense to the same degree as would a political development rendering an equal number of Englishmen to the same status. A sundering of a constitution and the imposition of military despotism in Pakistan concerns us, to be sure, but a like occurrence in Canada would concern us vastly more. This does not mean that we value Englishmen at a premium and Africans at a moral discount. Nor does it mean that Canadians are intrinsically more precious to us than subcontinentals. It means that the United States, world power though it may be, is not so powerful as to be uniformly involved in situations everywhere in the world.

It means also one state may be far ahead of another in political development, so that the toppling of a structure of government in one case may have far greater consequences for us than in another.

An ability to establish hierarchies of importance among external entities and situations is the most basic element of prudence in foreign policy. If, by proliferating alliances, we have suffered an impairment of this ability, then the consequences would be serious indeed. Moreover, if there could not be first-class and second-class alliances, then there obviously could only be second-class.

The point I am trying to make is, I trust, amply clear. Alliances are political arrangements for common objects and mutual benefit between allies. Allies are political entities aligned together and capable of doing each other some good. One alliance may be the equal of another as a liability—as a command on our sense of obligation, but surely they differ in their value as assets to us as the capacity of allies to do us good varies from one case to another.

II

Let us fasten our attention for the moment on the idea of the state as an association for doing good. Surely the ideal of self-determination rests on this notion. It assumes national freedom as an opportunity for a people to amount to something in the world. Surely also the idea of international co-operation assumes states as entities capable of being helpful to each other. The idea of the state as we accept it as a norm—a political entity geared up to play an historic role—grows out of a sixteenth-century Europe. One of its main characteristics is the existence of a population with the attributes of a populace—that is to say, a people conscious of political identity and of an historic role and identified with a defined territory by habit and history. Another characteristic of the state as we accept it as a norm is the existence of a government with faculties for making policy. It must be identified with the populace. It must be able to make and enforce public decisions requiring the allocation of resources to new patterns of effort. It is not enough to be able merely to provide peripheral security and to enforce custom and domestic order. These are the tasks of police strength and of administration. Government must be more than an arrangement for marshaling force and conducting an administration. It must be political.

Here, in the political quotient, seems to me to lie the distinguishing difference between colonial and national government. A colonial regime has military capacity. It may present administrative resources—often of a relatively high order. It lacks that rapport and identity that enable a regime and a people to relate themselves to each other with the pronoun "we" rather than "they." This lack is not necessarily redressed by the mere fact of juridic status as a state. This inherent colonial characteristic may endure in the unconscious habits of a people and a regime long after the achievement of nominal independence.

In my years of living in Pakistan, for example, I was struck repeatedly with this simple matter of pronouns. It emerged in the discourse not only of common citizens but also of high officials of the bureaucratic structure. In contexts where one might hope for the choice of pronoun to indicate identity between government and nation, regime and people, one would hear instead the pronoun of disjunction. This was a matter of no slight import. It revealed, in a way that no end of political orations would redress, the failure of the political process in the sequel to independence. It typified a default in those concepts whence derives the accountability of governments and the strength and stability of states.

These factors have an enormous bearing on the contractive capacity of governments. I mean not simply their capacity to sign on the dotted line of an international undertaking. I mean the political character that makes such a signature a real asset to the other party of the undertaking. This is the quality of a state as a going concern. Not all states have it in the same degree. I would no more say that there cannot be first-class and second-class alliances than I would say that all corporate contracts are of the same intrinsic relative value irrespective of the quality and deportment of the corporations making them.

We were surprised—at least some people were—when sudden events of July 1958 wiped out what had been appraised as an asset to us—the whole relationship that the United States had enjoyed with the Iraqi regime, which had contracted into the Baghdad Pact. The initial response was to put this down as an intelligence failure, to cry out the words of Shakespeare's *King John:*

> O, where hath our intelligence been drunk?
> Where hath it slept?

Far more basic and important, however, was the policy surprise. Our appraisal of the regime's signature as an asset was based on the assumption of the regime's actual capability to contract. As things turned out, this proved a false assumption.

I happened not to have been surprised. This was owing to a deep impression that had been left upon me by a conversation with a Pakistani statesman, a man of deep discernment. He once related to me experiences in Baghdad during the immediate sequel to the Suez incursion in the fall of 1956. One day the people had demonstrated in the streets. Soon afterward the King and the Prime Minister, Nuri es-Said, had recounted this phenomenon to him. As he reported it, these two were "as wide-eyed as if a throng of lions or of men from Mars had suddenly materialized in the streets. The people had been out! Amazing! The place was full of Iraqis!" My friend pondered wisely the implications of the circumstance that those in seats of power could not relate themselves to a throng in the streets. He mused on the question of authority. He asked rhetorically: Could a regime really deliver in the face of such disjunction from its people?

Here surely was an instance of what Machiavelli had in mind in commenting on the folly of "alliances made with princes who . . . bring more reputation than substantial help to those who rely on them."[2] Nothing prevented our asking the same question of ourselves, and we did not ask it—it must have been the result of the fallacy of thinking every alliance is of the first class. There is surely no patent on the item of wisdom that lack of a political base is a grievous weakness in a government.

Surely the deficiency in statehood of a great many of the entities having nominal status as states is one of the deep and serious political characteristics of our time. The American disposition is an equalitarian one. We incline to accept the equality of states not only as the juridic principle, which it properly and solely is, but also as a guideline to world politics. We tend to overlook the special advantages that enabled this country to develop so rapidly from colonial status into a prototype of the states of Europe from which we had derived the example of statehood. The American habit has been to assume parallels between the facts of our own case and the potentials of others and thus to regard every political entity in colonial subordination as a frustrated state and independence as the removal of impediments to development toward a mature and reasonably effective entity according to inherent teleological elements.

In the light of such assumptions we have gone on, in our policies, to postulate economic aid as bound to help the evolutionary process along in the states receiving it, military assistance as necessarily helpful in strengthening the executive authority and thereby conducive to stability, and alliances, where feasible, as bound to be beneficial in demonstrating and thereby helping to enhance the contractive character of the fledgling states making compact with us.

We need to make careful appraisal of the fledgling states in regard to their characteristics, which bear, I think, basically on their capacity for contractual relations. One characteristic is lack of pattern of interest groups having political focus. This relates to a characteristic disjunction between political discussion and actual

---

[2] *Discourses on the First Ten Books of Titus Livius,* 2nd bk., Chap. XI.

policy and to the emotive and generalized character of political ideas, which show a negative tendency to be against some exterior or interior adversary but not for much of anything. The tendency is to make ideology rather than a line of policy the basis of consensus. Clique control, with an accompanying tendency of the clique enjoying power to consign all rival cliques to the status of enemies of the state, prevails in place of political competition between groups presenting alternative lines of policy. All of this makes for a deficiency in contractive character—that is, in the corporateness that enables a regime to commit its people and its successors.

Every state is *sui generis,* and this is true of the fledgling states as it is of the states well established. The characteristics named above apply to them in varying degrees, but the generalization is sound enough for the purposes at hand. The problems of world politics for us are not only how to fend against the threat of Communist penetration; they include also the development of the fledgling states into states in the full sense of the term. They must become politically as well as economically and militarily viable. Indeed, it is important to understand the degree in which viability in the last two senses is contingent upon viability in the first sense. It is important also for us to understand the ways in which the effort to help along with economic and political viability, especially military viability, may militate against the political goals we should have in mind.

III

Machiavelli suggested that any state paying over money to others —"though they may be more feeble than herself"—gives sure signs of great weakness and places itself in position of being a tributary.[3] This has more truth in it than we sometimes like to see in our big-hearted way with the world. Once we make another state the beneficiary of our aid, we tend in some degree to invest prestige in it. If the receiving state has marked political weaknesses, our giving of aid tends to plight us to the correction of its weaknesses. If this

---

[3] *Ibid.,* Chap. xxx.

purpose fails, not only the recipient but also the donor feels the consequences.

These aspects take on special relevance when the government with which we enter into contractual relations is not one in the sense of our usual understanding but rather a clique, an in-group. In such instances inevitably the tendency is to commit the prestige of the United States—and by prestige we mean not simply a superficial matter of pride but that standing by which a state is able to command respect, that promise of efficacy that makes for efficacy —to the fortunes and tenure of such an in-group. The recipient group will probably be fully aware of this, even if our own government does not adequately take heed of it at the moment of making commitment. The recipient regime may be able to make use of these factors so as to make its own necessitousness a source of advantage in the relationship.[4] Moreover, commitment to an in-group in the guise of a government in the usual sense tends to foreclose the United States from interchange with rival potential in-groups, which the clique in power will be disposed to regard not simply as rivals but as enemies of the state. The resulting embarrassment to relationships when, as sometimes happens, the in-group loses its grip is obvious. A companion tendency is to subordinate intelligence and reporting functions to the view of the in-group dealt with, so that United States appreciations become derivatives of what the in-group wishes to have accepted.

Through such steps the donor of aid tends to become in some degree the client. It gets a vested interest in the position of the counterpart group and in shoring up its weaknesses against the perils of a political process.[5] This has a bearing on the simple faith we tend to give repeatedly to the strong-man figure as he rises from time to time in the politically underdeveloped countries.[6] It has

---

[4] Something akin to this has happened with respect to the problem of the Formosa Strait, where, by the accounts given out by our own leaders of policy, the subjective requirements of a necessitous regime have become paramount considerations overriding even the factors of military good sense in determining our obligations and commitments.

[5] Machiavelli was surely inadequate in seeing only the dangers of alliance with a stronger power. *The Prince,* Chap. xxi. Alliances with weakness have perils of even more subtle character.

[6] And perhaps also the politically overripe ones like France.

become a cliché of our reportage on such areas to observe their prematurity for political processes and to accept uncritically as substitute every self-vaunted strongman at face value as the solution for the problems of stability and security—overlooking the point, I think easily demonstrable by experience, that strong-man rule has been as brittle and perishable as any other kind in the areas concerned.

This brings me to a basic paradox of our world position. As a people disinclined to militarism, at least inclined to regard ourselves as so disinclined, and as a people who above all assert a position against economic determinism and should certainly stand for the primacy of politics in the life and health of the state, we seem to have projected a reverse image of ourselves to the underdeveloped areas. As a people historically and sentimentally disposed against colonialism, we have worked ourselves altogether too much into the position of appearing to stake our interests on the prolongation of colonial conditions of politics in such areas.

Of course, we have not intended to do so. Our actions in this regard have been unwitting rather than purposive. Yet the effect described is inherent in our permitting ourselves to become identified with economic and military solutions, primarily and to the exclusion of others, in the fledgling states. The purposes for which we advocate become limited to strong administration, which we deem necessary to efficacy in economic programs, and to military policy.

Lucian Pye has written on the excessiveness of our expectations first of military policy and second of economic aid.[7] He refers to "our habit of greatly oversimplifying the relationship between public policy and social behavior." In a context referring to Asia but equally applicable to other areas, he notes our addiction to "the notion that political loyalties are largely determined by people's discriminating reaction to alternative policy proposals." Pye continues:

> . . . in societies where the central problem is that of building an effective national community, we often forget that it is the

---

[7] "Communist Strategies and Asian Societies," *World Politics,* October 1958, pp. 118, 127.

dynamic process of politics and not the degree of rationality in public policies or the particular values expressed by such policies that gives coherence to a people . . . .

He does not dismiss public policy and administrative programs as unimportant. He says simply that they are not enough "to bring order and direction to the transitional societies . . . ." He draws a contrast between communism, "still on the rise in Asia" because "it has focused its energies on political relationships and the possibilities of introducing Western principles into the political sphere," and the non-Communist effort to modernize Asia, the latter concentrating "on administrative and bureaucratic measures," with a result that the West, "as in the past under colonialism, . . . is now seen in Asia largely in the role of the administrator rather than in that of the politician." Mr. Pye concludes:

> . . . the politician in Asia, as elsewhere, is generally held to be shrewder, more subtle and flexible, less rational, less respectable and, above all, more understanding of the complexities of human motivation and behavior than the administrator. Much of the success of the Communists in Asia in filling the role of politician has been due to lack of competition, for competent non-Communists have largely ignored this role in favor of that of the administrator, or the soldier, or the leader who stands above politics.

Mr. Pye adequately describes what happens when we overconcentrate on stability and on administrative and military avenues thereto. This, I think, is a large weakness of our attempts at alliances among the politically underdeveloped states. We seem to think the whole thing can be done through fire power and an increment of productive efficiency, whereas the states concerned need above all to progress as political societies; they need to fulfill their nominal status as states.

9

THE UNITED STATES
AND THE COLONIAL DEBATE

Robert C. Good

THE APPARENT inconsistencies of America's policy on the "colonial question" are notorious. To our allies in Europe and our friends in Afro-Asia, we appear to be, alternately and sometimes simultaneously, as London's *Daily Telegraph* once wryly observed, "a pillar of society and a patron of revolution." Time and again we have been accused of a monumental talent for alienating today those whom we made friends with yesterday, while laying plans to befriend them again the day after tomorrow. Note, for example, the following:

On October 31, 1956, with Britain and France about to bomb Ismailia and Port Said, President Eisenhower told the American people: "We believe [the actions of the British and French] to have been taken in error . . . ." Three days later, Vice President Nixon observed that "for the first time in history we have shown independence of Anglo-French policies toward Asia and Africa which seemed to us to reflect the colonial tradition." And in Washington, a highly placed official commented that our break with Britain and France represented America's "second 1776, the emancipation from British and French colonialism in the Middle East."

The Arab countries, together with the entire anticolonial bloc of Afro-Asia, rejoiced at America's emancipation. Understandably,

224

Britain and France took a different view. The British press spoke of a Britain "united in anti-Americanism." One hundred and twenty Conservative members of Parliament subscribed to a motion deploring the policies of the United States. The French press spoke with bitter sarcasm of the new "Moscow-Cairo-Washington axis."

But less than four months later, everything seemed to reverse itself. The occasion for the reversal was the annual United Nations debate on Algeria. Eighteen Afro-Asian states had introduced a resolution that recognized "the right of the people of Algeria to self-determination." The anticolonial bloc, which a few weeks before had rejoiced at America's liberation from Anglo-French colonialism, spoke with passion about French colonialism in Algeria. Everyone wondered where the recently "emancipated" American government would stand. But when Ambassador Henry Cabot Lodge, Jr. spoke, it looked as if he were slipping on the shackles that would bind us once more to the "colonialism" of Britain and France. He said the United States was opposed to the eighteen-power resolution demanding self-determination for Algeria, and indeed to any proposal that would "constitute intervention in matters essentially within the domestic jurisdiction of France."

In France and Britain, there was rejoicing. The prodigal son had returned. The French paper *Le Monde,* often suspicious of American policy, declared that the United States had "expressed itself with perfect clarity and with loyalty toward its French ally, for which public opinion will be grateful." Understandably, the Arab-Asian countries took a different view.

The dilemma that has produced this apparent policy-schizophrenia has been acute. As we shall see, however, our policy on the colonial question has been much more consistent than one would suspect judging by the many contradictions into which it has led. We shall return shortly to the colonialism dilemma and the several patterns of our response to it. First, a word about those pleasant years when there was no dilemma.

I.   The Assault on Colonialism and the Retreat

Historically, the ideology of the United States has been intensely anticolonialist, McKinley, Beveridge, and T. Roosevelt to the contrary notwithstanding. Our first great state paper was a vigorously anticolonial document: "When in the course of human events it becomes necessary for one people to dissolve the political bonds which have connected them with another . . . ."—here were invoked the right of dissent, of self-determination, of revolution.

We were anticolonial by principle, but also by interest. American security forbade the extension of European colonialism in the Western Hemisphere and American trade sought to open doors closed by preferential trading relations imposed by the European colonial system. So we endorsed the right of men to political freedom. Yet, beyond the Western Hemisphere, we did not have the power at first, nor the inclination later on, to do much more than talk about our convictions. As Henry Clay once explained, "far better is it for ourselves . . . and the cause of liberty, that, adhering to our pacific system and avoiding the distant wars of Europe, we should keep our lamp burning brightly on this Western Shore, as a light to all nations, than to hazard its utter extinction amid the ruins of fallen . . . republics in Europe."[1]

During World War II, official American anticolonialism seemed to grow more vigorous in proportion as the opportunities for terminating colonial control multiplied. The Japanese had swept Southeast Asia clear of Western colonial administration. Once the Japanese in turn had been swept out, the United States was prepared to grant independence to the Philippines. Why shouldn't the European colonial powers follow suit? After all, explained Roosevelt to Queen Wilhelmina of the Netherlands, "it was American arms that would be liberating those colonies from the Japanese."[2]

Roosevelt was a vigorous anticolonialist. "There has never been, there isn't now, and there never will be," he declared to the White House Correspondents Association in 1941, "any race of people on earth fit to serve as masters over their fellow men . . . . We believe that any nationality, no matter how small, has the in-

---

[1] Interestingly enough, Dulles has kept alive important elements of this theme in his liberation policy. As an essential part of his "dynamic peace" ("Dynamic Peace," *Department of State Bulletin,* May 6, 1957, p. 718), Dulles sees us providing "an example which demonstrates the blessings of liberty," and so creating "a climate in which despotism would shrink."

[2] Elliott Roosevelt, *As He Saw It* (New York, 1946), p. 223.

herent right to its own nationhood."[3] Roosevelt seemed quite prepared to dismantle substantial parts of the French empire. He
pointed out to Morocco's Sultan that "outside interests" (the
French) should not be allowed "to drain off the country's resources."[4] He assured Ibn Saud he would use every means short
of outright force to see that the French honored their pledge to
grant independence to Syria and Lebanon.[5] His repeated prescription for French Indochina was international trusteeship. Indeed,
for a time, the State Department with Roosevelt's blessing seriously
considered advocating a vast "new deal" for colonial peoples everywhere, a trusteeship system to include all colonial territories.

It was, however, the British who bore the main force of F.D.R.'s
assault on colonialism. The Atlantic Charter spoke of "the rights
of all peoples to choose the form of government under which they
will live." "Great Britain signed the Atlantic Charter. I hope they
realize the United States government means to make them live up
to it," Roosevelt once said.[6] At Argentia and Washington, at Casa-
blanca and Quebec, at Malta and Yalta, Roosevelt pressed his
attack on "the archaic, medieval Empire ideas" of the British.
"Mr. President," the British Prime Minister finally exploded, "I
believe you are trying to do away with the British empire."[7]

Yet, F.D.R., for all his determination, was obliged to retreat
from his vigorous anticolonial stand. Two considerations caused
the retreat. First, the Joint Chiefs of Staff were unalterably opposed
to any trusteeship system that would weaken our control of the
strategic islands of the Pacific, held as mandates by the Japanese
and now being conquered at such tremendous sacrifice by American forces.[8] Second, the alliance would stand only so much strain.
Cordell Hull's lament was notable because it forewarned so clearly
one of the limits which, in the years to come, would be imposed on

---

[3] F. R. Dulles and G. E. Riginger, "Anti-Colonial Policies of F.D.R.,"
Political Science Quarterly, 70 (March 1955), 1-18.

[4] Elliott Roosevelt, *op. cit.,* p. 110.

[5] *Ibid.,* p. 245.

[6] *Ibid.,* p. 122.

[7] Chester Wilmot, *The Struggle for Europe* (New York, 1952), p. 635.

[8] Henry L. Stimson and McGeorge Bundy, *On Active Service—In Peace
and War* (New York, 1947), pp. 599 ff.

America's policy on colonial questions: ". . . we could not press [our European allies] too far with regard to the South Pacific in view of the fact that we were seeking the closest possible co-operation with them in Europe. We could not alienate them in the Orient and expect to work with them in Europe."[9] Returning home from Yalta, F.D.R. chatted with newsmen about the possibility of an international trusteeship for Indochina. But, mused the President, ". . . it would only make the British mad. Better to keep quiet just now."[10]

The colonialism dilemma was already discernible. In the years when we wielded little power in world affairs, we were pleased to call ourselves anticolonial—and to announce these sentiments loudly to the world. We could deplore with impunity. We had great convictions, but little responsibility. But now we were obliged to leave "these Western shores," to join our heretofore latent power with that of our allies, and to effect that accommodation of principles and interests necessary to the maintenance of the Grand Alliance. On the colonial question, there began to emerge a conflict between old convictions and new responsibilities. And so began our retreat.

When the representatives of the United Nations gathered at San Francisco to write the Charter of the new world organization, the United States did not line up with the anticolonial nations against the colonial bloc but, as Ralph Bunche later reported, assumed the role of mediator, "attempting . . . to bring together the divergent points of view of the interested nations."[11] Though we fulfilled our pledge to grant independence to the Philippines, we also adopted a "hands off" policy with respect to the claims of Indochinese nationalists against the French. While applauding British efforts to bring independence to South Asia, we were at the same time the very soul of circumspection (until December 1948) in the conflict between the nationalists and the Dutch in the East Indies. Indeed, in the light of F.D.R.'s assault on the colonial question during the war, our behavior in the immediate postwar years looked more like a

---

[9] Cordell Hull, *The Memoirs of Cordell Hull* (New York, 1948), Vol. 2, p. 1599.

[10] Allan B. Cole (ed.), *Conflict in Indo-China and International Repercussions* (Ithaca, N. Y., 1956), p. 48.

[11] *Department of State Bulletin*, December 30, 1945, p. 1040.

rout than a retreat. In this connection, the cases of Indochina and the Dutch East Indies bear closer analysis.

Roosevelt had made no secret of his distaste for French policies in Indochina. "France has milked it for one hundred years," he once wrote to Hull. "The people of Indochina are entitled to something better than that."[12] During the closing months of the war, the nationalist Viet Minh made friendly contacts with Americans in Kunming, China. Though we never officially endorsed their claim for eventual independence, American OSS agents by the end of the war had established such cordial relations with Viet Minh nationalists as to evoke from French Commissioner Jean Sainteny the complaint that Americans opposed the French "in the name of an infantile anticolonialism which blinded them to almost everything."[13]

But by the end of 1945, it had become quite clear that the declamations of Roosevelt and the friendly gestures of the American OSS toward the nationalists in Indochina were not to be translated into official policy. The French returned to Indochina; they fought the Indochinese in Cochin China; they signed an agreement with the Viet Minh's new Republic of Viet Nam; they broke the agreement, and by the end of 1946 the war had begun in earnest. All the while, the United States kept its distance and in February 1947 Secretary of State George Marshall went no further than to express his hope that "a pacific basis of adjustment of the difficulties would be found."[14]

Unlike Indochina, the nationalist revolt in the Dutch East Indies was the subject of frequent debates in the Security Council of the United Nations, where a posture of indifference was unthinkable. The problem was first discussed in February 1946 at the request of the Ukrainian S.S.R., which condemned the military operations of British occupation troops, assisted by certain Japanese detachments, against the guerrilla forces of the newly proclaimed Republic of Indonesia. The Council chose to take no action, and Mr. Stettinius spoke the mind of the majority when he noted that the British presence in the Dutch East Indies to disarm the Japanese and to restore

---

[12] Ellen Hammer, *The Struggle for Indochina* (Stanford, Calif., 1954), p. 43.

[13] *Ibid.*, p. 43.

[14] *Ibid.*, p. 202.

order was entirely justifiable; that the difficulties confronting the British were indeed regrettable but after all "the war has left us with many tangled situations"; that the Dutch significantly had accepted nationalism as a healthy development and were even now attempting to arrive at an agreement with the nationalists on a very liberal basis.[15]

The "very liberal" agreement between the nationalists and the Dutch to which Mr. Stettinius had referred was finally initialed in November 1946 at a small hill station in Java named Linggadjati. It stated the principles according to which independence for the Indies would be achieved. But so widely divergent were the interpretations of its provisions by either side that Linggadjati proved to be more a truce than a basis for permanent settlement. Friction increased, and in July 1947, the Dutch resorted to military measures—a "police action" designed to "restore order." Again the Security Council was seized of the issue.

The opposing sides were ably and eloquently represented. The extremely articulate Mr. Van Kleffens argued for the Netherlands that this was not war, but an action made necessary by the "evasive, unconstructive, and unco-operative" Republic of Indonesia, "divided within itself," and "not obeyed by those under its *de facto* authority." With order restored, said Mr. Van Kleffens, negotiations leading to the implementation of the right of self-determination could be resumed. Most important, he asserted, it must be understood that under the Linggadjati Agreement full sovereignty continued to reside with the Netherlands until such time as the federal government of the United States of Indonesia was brought into being, of which the Republic was to be but one constituent part. This being the case, the present dispute was a matter of domestic jurisdiction and the Charter did not apply.[16] Relations with their own colonies foremost in mind, Britain, France, and Belgium contributed elaborate variations on this theme.

The anticolonial position was impassioned. "What then are you upholding?" responded China's Ambassador Tsiang to the colonial

---

[15] *Security Council Official Records,* First Year, 16th meeting, February 11, 1946, pp. 235-36.

[16] *Ibid.,* Second Year, 171st meeting, July 31, 1947, pp. 1644-45; and *The New York Times,* August 13, 1947.

powers, who had argued that the United Nations had no jurisdiction. "You are upholding the freedom to wage colonial war as you please."[17] Mr. Pillai of India recalled the West's great democratic slogans, which had provided justification for the recent war and which, he said, Asians had taken at face value. "There is no more basis for the ownership of colonies," he continued. Indeed, "the fact that foreign armies are functioning on Asian soil is itself an outrage against Asian sentiment."[18] Far from being fully sovereign in the Indies, argued the Philippines' General Romulo, the Netherlands itself under Linggadjati had granted *de facto* recognition to the Republic including the islands of Java, Madura, and Sumatra.[19] In these debates, Australia and Syria, together with the Communist countries, strongly supported the nationalists. And what of the United States?

If we tipped the scales in favor of one side or the other in the debates subsequent to the first "police action" of the Dutch, we did so only slightly. For the most part, we occupied a position squarely in the center of the balance. At one extreme, Australia demanded a strong Security Council resolution calling for settlement by arbitration. At the other extreme, the colonial powers insisted that the United Nations was not competent to act at all. But the United States occupied a middle position, successfully urging a moderate resolution calling upon the parties to cease firing and to settle their disputes by peaceful means.[20] While we voted for an "anticolonial" measure to invite a representative of the Republic of Indonesia to participate in the Council debate (which was approved), we also voted for a "procolonial" resolution to hear representatives of the Dutch-sponsored East Indonesian and Borneo governments (which was not approved).[21] It is true that we voted for an Indonesian proposal (presented to the Council in a Russian resolution) providing for a United Nations Commission to supervise the imple-

---

[17] *Security Council Official Records,* Second Year, 172nd meeting, August 1, 1947, p. 1685.

[18] *Ibid.,* 192nd meeting, August 22, 1947, p. 2156.

[19] *Ibid.,* 185th meeting, August 15, 1947, p. 2023.

[20] *Ibid.,* 172nd meeting, August 1, 1947, p. 1658.

[21] *Ibid.,* 181st and 184th meetings, August 12 and 14, 1947, pp. 1940 and 1992.

mentation of the cease-fire, a resolution strongly opposed by the colonial powers and actually vetoed by France.[22] But we then supported a plan, originating in part with the Netherlands and concurred in by France, which requested "the Governments members of the Council which have career consular representatives in Batavia to instruct them to prepare jointly . . . reports on the situation in the Republic of Indonesia . . . ."[23] This resolution was adopted, as was a resolution incorporating an American idea to make available to the disputants a Good Offices Committee "consisting of three members of the Council, each party selecting one, and the third to be designated by the two so selected."[24] Both anticolonial and colonial representatives voted in favor.

When the debate turned to the repeated violations of the original cease-fire resolution, the United States noted a strong presumption on the part of many representatives to find the Dutch guilty. "I do not think," said Mr. Austin, ". . . it is fair to assume that everything the Netherlands does has evil motives." Wasn't it conceivable that the Netherlands' representative had a point, "that the Indonesian Republic cannot control the area, and that bands of lawless and wicked men are preying on the populace?"[25] The United States had been named middleman on the three-man Good Offices Committee, and our public posture in the Security Council reflected exactly this intermediary role. When, following the Renville Agreements (January 1948), new frictions produced the threat of renewed violence, and when anticolonial and colonial claims and accusations again fouled the air of the Security Council chamber, the United States once more took its customary stance. Said Mr. Jessup, "We are not sitting in judgment on a case in which one or the other party has brought about a failure of negotiations . . . . It would be most unfortunate if the Security Council forced the Committee of Good Offices, at various stages of a delicate negotiation, to take sides with one party or the other, to keep reporting back to

---

[22] *Ibid.,* 194th meeting, August 25, 1947, pp. 2199-2200.

[23] *Ibid.,* p. 2200.

[24] *Ibid.,* p. 2209.

[25] *Ibid.,* 195th meeting, August 26, 1947, p. 2231.

the Security Council the fact that they think this side is right in this contention and that side is right in that contention." [26]

On the colonial question, these years (1945 through 1948) were essentially years of retreat from the clarion-clear anticolonialism that once seemed about to become the policy of Roosevelt's wartime administration. It may be, as competent observers have pointed out, that our "passive attitude toward Vietnamese aspirations for independence . . . contributed to the [later] havoc . . ." [27] and that our role as impartial mediator in the early years of the Dutch-Indonesian dispute, exerting pressures on both sides presumably on an objective basis, simply made each side take offense at American meddling. [28] Be that as it may, our policies of "hands off" in the one case and "fence-straddling" in the other are best understood as initial reactions to a dilemma the shape of which gradually was beginning to emerge.

II. Colonialism and the American Dilemma

We were for national self-determination, but perhaps had underestimated both the resistance of the colonial powers to changes in the *status quo* and the determination of the colonial peoples to effect such changes immediately—and the willingness of each side to use force. We were for national self-determination, but also for the economic recovery of Western Europe. The Dutch lived by trade. One major source of trade, the German hinterland, was moribund. The remaining source was the Dutch East Indies. As an unusually frank statement by an important Netherlands Commissioner in the Indies revealed, the Dutch were fighting with the Indonesian Republic because they "were going bankrupt" without access to the rich products of the islands. [29] The French case was even more serious, for France held the key to the economic recovery of Europe. French arguments must have seemed persuasive: that the loss of Viet Nam would have serious effects throughout the empire

---

[26] *Ibid.,* Third Year, 323rd meeting, June 17, 1948, pp. 38-39.

[27] Ellen Hammer, *op. cit.,* p. 316.

[28] H. A. Steiner, "Post-War Government and Politics of the Netherlands East Indies," in T. Cole and J. H. Hallowell (eds.), *Post-War Governments of the Far East* (Gainesville, Fla., 1948), p. 630.

[29] AP dispatch, *The New York Herald Tribune,* August 4, 1947.

and ultimately disastrous effects on the French economy; that undue American pressure might topple the "Third Force" French government; and that Ho Chi Minh's regime was Communist-controlled. Since, at this time, there were no pressing security reasons to intervene decisively in Southeast Asia, and since European stability had become a major objective of American foreign policy, why not take at face value the colonial powers' repeated promises gradually to expand self-government in their colonies by the process of orderly negotiation? Under these circumstances, American nonintervention might be the most prudent course. And if we were required to intervene, it would be only to facilitate such negotiations, certainly not to attempt to alter the *status quo*.

By the end of 1948, however, events were set in motion that served both to sharpen the horns of the colonial dilemma and to force the United States toward renewed involvement in the colonial question. First, on December 19, 1948, the Dutch unabashedly violated the will of the Security Council and launched a new "police action" against the Republic of Indonesia, thus revealing more clearly than before the recalcitrance of the colonial power and the apparent justice of the nationalists' case. Second, during 1949, the Communist Chinese completed their conquest of the mainland, entirely transforming the problem of defense for all of Southeast Asia, but most immediately for Indochina. Indeed, questions of military security were gaining paramountcy everywhere, from the NATO shield in Europe established in 1949 to the defense of Korea undertaken in 1950. Third, the "emancipation debate" between colonial and anticolonial powers began to grow in intensity, both within and outside the United Nations. Apart from discussions in the Trusteeship Council, the only "colonial question" given full airing in the United Nations down to the close of 1948 was the Indonesian dispute.[30] Beginning in 1949 with the debates concerning the former Italian colonies (Britain and France hoped to remain in Libya), the United Nations became the arena for the public debate of a broadening range of colonial problems.

---

[30] Questions such as Palestine, Kashmir, and Hyderabad might more appropriately be classified as postcolonial disputes; they involved conflicts among the next of kin over the political legacy left by the recently deceased colonial power.

The principal protagonists in this debate were four in number. There were, first, the colonial powers, which were chronically short on raw materials and dollars and habitually long on arguments that only by maintaining their colonial systems in some form could they make up their economic deficiencies and provide the strategic requirements for stable, strong partners in defense of the free world. The Afro-Asian anticolonial bloc was the second protagonist. If the colonial powers believed that the maintenance of the colonial system was necessary to collective defense, the anticolonial bloc would seek the liquidation of that system regardless of collective defense. The crisis of the time in Asia, Prime Minister Nehru once declared, is not communism vs. anticommunism, but colonialism vs. anticolonialism.[31] As the strength and scope of liberated Afro-Asia has grown, so too has the vehemence of its attack on colonialism. When, in January 1949, nineteen Asian nations met at New Delhi to discuss the Indonesian dispute, Nehru opened the proceedings by declaring ". . . as long as any form of colonialism exists in Asia, and elsewhere, there will be conflict and a threat to peace . . . ."[32]

The third protagonist was the Communist bloc. When addressing Afro-Asia, the Soviets have made the anticolonial cause their own and repeatedly have linked the United States to the colonial bloc; but when addressing Europe, the Soviets have attempted to raise fears that the United States may in fact be the worst enemy of the colonial powers. "The United States," noted Russia's Mr. Arutiunian during the Indonesian debate, ". . . was playing an increasingly important part in the colonies of the European countries. It was attempting to evict those countries from their colonies and establish its own economic and political rule over them."[33]

The United States, the fourth protagonist, was caught in between

---

[31] Norman D. Palmer, "Indian Attitudes Toward Colonialism," in Robert Strausz-Hupé and Harry W. Hazard (eds.), *The Idea of Colonialism* (New York, 1958), p. 271.

[32] Richard J. Kozicki, "The United Nations and Colonialism," in Robert Strausz-Hupé and Harry W. Hazard, *op. cit.,* p. 416.

[33] *General Assembly Official Records,* 4th session, 249th meeting, November 21, 1949, p. 292.

colonial and anticolonial antagonists. Withdrawal was becoming increasingly difficult. Heated debates and frequent votes in the United Nations tended to narrow the possibilities for demonstrating strict neutrality. The demand of European allies and Afro-Asian friends to know where the United States stood could not forever be put off. And strategic necessities more and more frequently demanded actions that had strong overtones of colonial or anti-colonial bias.

Yet the dilemma was monumental. Our history linked us both to colonial Europe and to an intensely anticolonial sentiment. Our interests and responsibilities, which were universal and not parochial, required that we relate ourselves both to the West and to the Afro-Asian world. The Soviet threat compounded the dilemma. It could be argued that we should support our European allies in their colonial policies on the assumption that European strength, so necessary to the defense of the West, depended upon the economic and strategic benefits of the colonial system. Yet, in so doing, we ran the risk of alienating Afro-Asia, which then could turn only to the Soviet Union to protect its interests, thereby placing in peril the very source of Europe's strength. In the midst of the United Nations debate of 1951, Sir Mohammad Zafrulla Khan of Pakistan said:

> . . . let me state that our experience in this Organization has been that we hear a great deal about freedom, democracy and the self-determination of peoples from the group which might be called the Western States; but whenever we have had to deal concretely with the freedom, liberty, independence and self-determination of a particular people, that role is, by and large, with rare and noble exceptions, abandoned by the Western States. We have on such occasions always found the East European States in the same lobby with us. We have been forced emphatically to take note of it time after time. . . .[34]

Yet, if we supported Afro-Asian demands for early independence for the colonies, the ensuing chaos might serve Soviet interests equally well. The fears of many Europeans were summarized by André Siegfried when he accused the United States of "encouraging

---

[34] *Ibid.*, 6th session, 354th Plenary meeting, December 13, 1951, p. 265.

rebellion among the subject races and thus creating disorder from which the Soviet Union may profit . . . ."[35]

Our key officials have practiced a complex verbal alchemy trying to transmute these contradictions into rational policy. We were firm in our principled espousal of self-determination, but regularly qualified it with adjectives like "eventual," and reservations concerning "timing and procedure."[36] Who better than the United States understood when men rose up to demand independence, but the independence we were interested in must come by "orderly evolution and not . . . [by] violent revolution."[37] We appreciated everybody's position and sympathized with everyone's sentiments—those of the Afro-Asians because after all "we ourselves [were] the first colony in modern times to have won independence,"[38] and those of our European allies because we understood "the complicated problems which arise in preparing a people for stable and viable self-government in the complex world of today."[39] With one eye on Afro-Asia, we wondered at times if our position with respect to the movement for self-government had not become "unnecessarily ambiguous";[40] and with the other eye on Europe, we occasionally were moved to confess to our allies that of course we could not "blindly disregard their side of the colonial question without injury to our own security."[41]

But the alchemy did not take and the contradictions remained. "It is no secret," Assistant Secretary Henry Byroade once said, in a remarkably frank disclosure, "that these problems confront America with a dilemma." He advocated a "middle-of-the-road policy

---

[35] Sir Alan Burns, *In Defense of Colonies* (London, 1957), p. 133, footnote.

[36] See, for example, Harry S. Truman, *Memoirs* (Garden City, N. Y., 1952), Vol. I, pp. 237-38.

[37] George V. Allen, *Department of State Bulletin,* April 30, 1956, p. 718.

[38] John Foster Dulles, *Department of State Bulletin,* June 21, 1954, p. 936.

[39] Dean Acheson before the U.N. General Assembly, October 16, 1952, *Official Records,* 7th session, 380th Plenary meeting, p. 42.

[40] John Foster Dulles, *Department of State Bulletin,* June 15, 1953, p. 834.

[41] Henry A. Byroade, *Department of State Bulletin,* November 16, 1953, p. 657.

which will permit us to determine our position on practical issues on their merits as they arise."[42] As far as it goes, this is in fact a reasonably accurate description of what has taken place. Since the end of 1948, the pattern of our response to the "practical issues" represents a broad spectrum ranging from support of the anti-colonialist position (Indonesia and Suez); through an admixture of colonialism and anticolonialism (Indochina), active neutrality (Cyprus) and silent neutrality (West Irian); to support of the colonialist position (French North Africa).

The question now arises, has there been any logic at all under-lying these different responses, or has rational policy completely succumbed to the pull and tug of the conflicting claims and de-mands of Europe on the one hand and Afro-Asia on the other? The evidence seems to indicate that underlying all surface incon-sistencies, there has been a rather consistent substratum: the de-mands of defense.[43] Our policy in the emancipation debate has regularly related itself, not first and foremost to the claims of the colonial or the anticolonial bloc, but to the immediate requirements of defense both in the locality of the colony itself and in the metro-pole. Sometimes, this relationship between colonial and defense policy has been only a negative one in the sense that our position in the emancipation debate could be determined by other criteria (national self-determination, for example) so long as these did not contravene defense necessities. But much more frequently, the rela-tionship has been a positive one in that our posture on the colonial

---

[42] *Ibid.*, p. 659.

[43] The term "defense" is used in this discussion to describe policies rang-ing from simple calculations of armed strength to broader military con-siderations such as alliance systems and bases. It moves even beyond pure military factors, for the term encompasses policies designed to defend against subversion and against the dangers that attend heightened Commu-nist prestige or influence in an area. The term may even include policies aimed at increasing a country's political stability on the assumption that the will to resist an external threat dissipates when internal unrest rises. Though thus broadly defined, the term "defense" is still meaningful. It serves to in-dicate that policy is oriented toward a response to Communist expansionism, rather than toward some alternate claim or consideration. And it presumes that the most immediate danger is Communist expansion resulting from the military weakness of the non-Communist world.

question has been shaped largely by defense requirements that at times have demanded support of the colonial position, at other times an alignment with the anticolonial bloc, and at still other times a policy somewhere in between the two extremes. Other motivations have been present in varying degrees at various times. This one requirement, however, defense—whether related negatively or positively to the given colonial issue—is relatively constant throughout.

III. The Emancipation Debate and the Requirements of Defense[44]

The hypothesis just stated suggests a high correlation between defense policy and colonial policy. The following cases, illustrating the many positions we have taken in the emancipation debate, tend to substantiate this thesis and to demonstrate that our apparently contradictory stands may all be understood as responses to the requirements of defense in a broad variety of situations.

INDONESIA

On December 19, 1948, the members of the United Nations Committee of Good Offices in Indonesia, obviously alarmed, sent a wire to the Security Council in New York calling upon the Council "to consider, on the basis of the utmost urgency, the outbreak of hostilities in Indonesia in violation of the Renville Truce Agreement . . . ." Though the Dutch did not know it at the time, their second "police action" against the Republic proved to be their own undoing. A radical change now occurred in the Security Council and more than anything else, it reflected a radical change in the American position.

"This is not a situation in which there can be any uncertainty . . . ," said America's Dr. Philip Jessup. ". . . my Government fails to find

---

[44] The colonial questions examined in this section are not all-inclusive but do represent a comprehensive variety of patterns. Limitations of space have precluded a full reconstruction of events in each case examined. The development of these cases in terms of dates and events is pursued only when such development aids in understanding the American position. It should be noted that this study does not include a review of the American contribution to the trusteeship debates in the United Nations.

any justification for renewal of military operations . . . ."[45] Two resolutions were quickly passed, each supported by the American delegation. The first called for a cease-fire forthwith and the immediate release of Republican political prisoners. The second, passed four days later, called upon the Dutch to release their political prisoners forthwith and to report to the Security Council within twenty-four hours. When by January 11 the political prisoners still had not been released, Mr. Jessup condemned this "most striking . . . disregard of the orders of the Security Council" indicating at the same time that he was sure the Council had no intention of approving Dutch military victories "gained as a result of open defiance of an order of the Security Council."[46]

The new look in the American position was warmly greeted by anticolonial representatives at the Council table. ". . . a most impressive, firm and realistic speech," said the Burmese delegate.[47] "Those of us who had observed the somewhat uncertain attitude of the United States delegation," said the Philippines' Romulo, "were pleasantly surprised by the new United States policy."[48]

Several delegates, however, wondered about the implications of Dutch colonial policy for the new North Atlantic alliance, then in process of formation and of which the Netherlands would be a member. Sir Benegal Rama Rau of India said: "We are naturally inclined to wonder whether under cover of the security afforded by the Pact one of the parties to it is to be allowed to create insecurity

---

[45] *Security Council Official Records,* 3rd Year, 388th meeting, December 22, 1948, pp. 43ff.

[46] *Ibid.,* 4th year, 398th meeting, January 11, 1949, p. 5.

[47] *Ibid.,* 400th meeting, January 14, 1949, p. 21.

[48] *Ibid.,* 397th meeting, January 7, 1949, p. 20. France and Belgium continued to protest the Council's lack of jurisdiction and abstained in the votes on the resolutions cited above, though the French representative did confess that Dutch action had been "brutal and shocking." The United Kingdom noted that while the question of competence never had been clarified, the Council had felt compelled to make recommendations with which the Netherlands had not complied, "a very serious challenge to the authority of the United Nations." The United Kingdom voted in favor of the first resolution, but abstained when the Council asked the Netherlands to report within twenty-four hours concerning the release of political prisoners.

elsewhere and to become a menace to world peace."[49] The use of Marshall Plan funds was even more pointedly raised by Sir Benegal.

> Indonesia and the other countries seriously affected by this development are surely justified in requesting the United States of America to consider whether it should continue to provide resources for a country which is utilizing these resources for reviving imperialism in East Asia. The magnanimous gesture implied in the Marshall Plan on the part of the United States was designed as a contribution to world peace, and one of the recipient countries is defeating the objects of the European Recovery Programme by creating conditions in another part of the world that would have serious international repercussions.[50]

The United States needed no prodding. The Economic Cooperation Administration already had suspended further allocations of the grant made to the Netherlands for the reconstruction of war damage in Indonesia, and in Congress a measure introduced by Senator Vandenberg was adopted requiring the United States to end assistance to any state against which the United Nations was taking preventive or enforcement action. Pressures were also brought to bear at the diplomatic level by H. Merle Cochran, the American member of the newly constituted United Nations Commission on Indonesia. And in April of 1949, on the occasion of the ceremonies in Washington that inaugurated the Atlantic Pact, Secretary of State Acheson impressed upon Netherlands Premier Stikker the seriousness with which the United States regarded the Indonesian situation.

The American response to the Indonesian question following December 19, 1948, was clearly anticolonial; in fact, it was American policy, as much as any other single factor, that obliged the Dutch to quit the islands. What lay behind our new, vigorous stand? There was a large measure of moral indignation, fortified by an aroused American public and rapidly rising sentiment in the newly independent states of Asia. The will of the Security Council and of its instrument, the Committee on Good Offices (on which Americans had served with distinction), had been flouted by the Netherlands. The Dutch action had touched one of our most sensitive nerves, our dislike of force; in this case force was to be doubly

---

[49] *Ibid.*, p. 30.
[50] *Ibid.*

condemned because we were sure that the possibility of a negotiated settlement had not been exhausted. Moreover, had the United States not responded with determination, it would have seriously weakened its role as leader of the Free World, leaving the Soviet Union the only great power champion of anticolonialism.[51]

These compelling reasons fortunately concurred with the requirements of defense. There was a positive relationship between an anticolonial policy and defense requirements in that the Indonesian war had now quite clearly become a hemorrhage, which it seemed could not be stanched; the Netherlands was slowly being drained, and the Dutch contribution to Europe's economic recovery and rearmament was being weakened. There was also a negative relationship in that our anticolonial posture did not violate the requirements of defense. A strong American anticolonial position obviously was unfavorable to the Dutch and would result in a net loss of Western military strength in Asia; but Dutch favor did not weigh heavily in determining Europe's future and the Indonesian archipelago was not held to be vital to the defense of Southeast Asia. In nearby French Indochina, these considerations did not obtain, and the pattern of our response to the colonial question proved to be strikingly different.

INDOCHINA

In Indochina, France seemed quite incapable of mounting political maneuvers radical enough or military campaigns powerful enough to rescue a steadily deteriorating situation. Since December 1946, French soldiers had been fighting an inconclusive, expensive war with Ho Chi Minh's Republic of Viet Nam. Since December

---

[51] Actually the U.S.S.R. remained incredulous that the capitalist United States could genuinely support the anticolonial position. It attacked the Hague Agreement, in which independence for Indonesia was secured, as a device by which the United States would come into control of the erstwhile Dutch colony; it labeled the Indonesian nationalists "a group of traitors to the Indonesian people"; it vetoed a Security Council resolution congratulating both parties on the successful completion of the Hague talks—all of which brought from the Burmese representative a searing retort condemning Soviet policy as "flippant," "insulting," and "mischievous." Russia has not since repeated this tactical error.

1947, and with equally limited success, French diplomats had been struggling to bring into being a French counterpart to Ho's Republic, a state so organized as to give to Vietnamese nationalists the appearance of independence and to French conservatives the reality of continued French control. During these years, the United States had kept its distance.

But in 1949, Indochina was transformed from a battleground in a local colonial dispute to a theater in the Cold War. It was only then that the United States became involved. Late in 1949, Red Chinese troops swept through Kwangsi and Yünnan provinces to form a common boundary with Ho's forces in northern Indochina. One month later, January 30, 1950, the Soviet Union recognized Ho's government, which, commented Secretary of State Acheson, should remove "any illusions as to the 'nationalist' nature of Ho Chi Minh's aims and reveal Ho in his true colors as the mortal enemy of native independence in Indochina . . . ."[52] The strategic implications were clear. General Jean de Lattre de Tassigny, anticipating President Eisenhower's famous "falling domino" thesis by several years and exaggerating no doubt for the sake of emphasis, said: "Southeast Asia, and even the whole of Asia, is at stake. . . . Once Tongking is lost, there is really no barrier before Suez . . . ."[53] Just as serious was the continuing drain on France. It seemed unlikely that as long as France was forced to spend one tenth of her national budget and to commit a substantial number of her fighting men to the Indochinese struggle, she could ever meet her commitments to the defense of Western Europe under the new North Atlantic Alliance.

The United States became involved in the French-Indochinese dispute only when strategic considerations demanded it. It is not surprising then that the pattern of our response was also dictated by the requirements of defense. Our policy was two-pronged. We would work with the colonial power to defeat the Communist-dominated rebel government, despite the fact that it had captured the imagination of most Vietnamese nationalists and the tacit sup-

---

[52] Ellen Hammer, *op. cit.*, p. 250.

[53] Speech before the National Press Club, September 20, 1951, as quoted in Richard P. Stebbins, *The United States in World Affairs, 1952* (Council on Foreign Relations, 1953), p. 194.

port of many Afro-Asian states. At the same time, we would in effect work against the colonial power, obliging it to create an alternative government sufficiently independent to offset the nationalist appeal of Ho's Viet Nam. If successful, Indochina would be saved from Communist military conquest, immunized against the nationalist appeal of the Viet Minh, and pacified under a genuine nationalist regime, allowing France to resume her military responsibilities in Europe.

In March 1949, negotiations between the French and ex-Annamese Emperor Bao Dai (selected by France to head the new Vietnamese state) were concluded at the Élysée Palace in Paris. Though these agreements provided for only the shadow of genuine independence, the United States expressed its hope that they would provide "the basis for the progressive realization of the legitimate aspirations of the Vietnamese people."[54] And while the French Assembly was still debating ratification of the Élysée agreements, Dr. Philip Jessup, representing Secretary Dean Acheson, stopped at Hanoi to express to Bao Dai the "confident best wishes" of the American government "for the future of the State of Viet Nam with which it looks forward to establishing a closer relationship."[55] Immediately upon the ratification of the Élysée Agreements by an unbelievably cautious French Parliament, the United States extended diplomatic recognition to Viet Nam, Cambodia, and Laos, using the occasion to stress "our fundamental policy of giving support to the . . . evolution of dependent peoples toward self-government and independence."[56] In May 1950, Mr. Acheson promised Foreign Minister Schuman economic and military aid stressing that the solution of the Indochinese problem called for not only the restoration of security but also "the development of genuine nationalism." American assistance, he said, "can and should contribute to these major objectives."[57] The pattern of our policy was thus firmly set by mid-1950.

American aid to the French-Indochinese military effort responded like a seismograph to the recurring crises of the next four years.

---

[54] *Department of State Bulletin,* July 18, 1949, p. 75.

[55] Ellen Hammer, *op. cit.,* p. 268.

[56] *Department of State Bulletin,* February 20, 1950, p. 291.

[57] *Ibid.,* June 12, 1950, p. 977.

Aid was "accelerated" immediately after the attack on Korea;[58] it was given "particularly high priority" following the disastrous "Affaire de Caobang" in October 1950 when seven French battalions were cut to pieces retreating from a border outpost;[59] it was "expanded" further following the emergency trip to Washington in June 1952 of French Minister for the Associated States, Jean Letourneau;[60] and in the fall of 1953, responding to the bold military initiative introduced by Henri-Eugène Navarre, the new Commander of French Union troops, the National Security Council agreed to double the current allocation for Indochinese military aid.[61] By the end of 1954, our total aid bill had climbed to well over $4 billion.

But concurrently, we were engaged in a desperate tug-of-war with the French, pulling them slowly and much against their will toward an expansion of autonomy for the states of Indochina. Though agreed in principle to the development of genuine national armies for the Associated States, France had done little about it. Constant American pressure coupled with the necessity to curb the drain on French Union forces finally produced the Navarre plan in 1953 which called for the immediate development of substantial national armies. At the same time, Paris declared that there was "every reason to complete [the] independence and sovereignty" of the Associated States and renewed negotiations in the fall of 1953 ostensibly to that end.

The pace of events suddenly quickened. The national congress that now convened in Viet Nam to nominate delegates for the new negotiations with the French unexpectedly repudiated the French Union and demanded that the national congress be transformed into a Constituent Assembly to draft a new constitution. France immediately warned that if Viet Nam were to question the very conception of the French Union, France would consider itself free to withdraw from the war against the Communists. At this point, the United States reversed its role and through Vice President

---

[58] Harry S. Truman, *op. cit.*, Vol. 2, p. 339.

[59] *Department of State Bulletin*, October 30, 1950, p. 704.

[60] *Ibid.*, June 30, 1952, p. 1010.

[61] Richard P. Stebbins, *The United States in World Affairs, 1953* (Council on Foreign Relations, 1955), p. 275.

Nixon, then visiting in Southeast Asia, urged the Vietnamese to take no precipitate action that might rupture relations with France. Reluctantly, the Vietnamese agreed. An astute French reporter observed that while "the United States continues to present itself as the defender of the independence and liberty of peoples, . . . it is clear that this preoccupation is now only secondary . . . ."[62] But actually our basic purpose had *not* changed. "Independence and liberty" were only instrumental to the defense of Indochina, which was our real objective. French military involvement was vital to the defense of Indochina. If then to keep the French militarily committed it became necessary to slow down the drive toward independence, this we would not hesitate to do.

At the turn of the year, the military situation in Indochina worsened despite striking increases in deliveries of American equipment. Viet Minh forces lunged deep into Laos in February and the melodramatic siege of Dienbienphu began in March. On March 9, 1954, the French Parliament gave its blessing to an attempt to end hostilities by negotiation, according to plans laid out at the Berlin meeting of foreign ministers in February. The United States feared the results would be calamitous if the French negotiated from military weakness, and our fears were compounded when, on March 20, 1954, French Chief of Staff Paul Ely arrived in Washington to report a military situation developing in Indochina so serious that the whole area might slide to sudden defeat. President Eisenhower envisaged all of Southeast Asia falling like a set of dominoes. Top policy-makers in Washington faced seriously the possibility of direct United States involvement, but then backed away toward what Mr. Dulles called a policy of "united action." We would intervene in strength only in an allied undertaking; and only if the French first conferred real independence on the Indochinese states so as to remove the taint of fighting to uphold colonialism.

On April 28, France agreed to "the total independence of Viet Nam and its full and complete sovereignty." But "united action" was not forthcoming; neither the British nor the French, on the eve of the Geneva negotiations, were inclined to jeopardize the talks by new military adventures.

---

[62] Ellen Hammer, *op. cit.,* pp. 318-19.

The Geneva talks finally produced a divided Viet Nam and a semineutralized Indochina. Consistent with its policy of building viable independent regimes in Indochina, the United States gave the strongest support to the new South Vietnamese government of Ngo Dinh Diem, offering aid directly to that government and, over French protests, preparing to take over the training of the Vietnamese army. Though one half of Viet Nam had been lost, free Indochina was on the eve of genuine independence. It is worth noting that the "anticolonial" dimension of our policy in Indochina never gained the support of neutralist Asia, as indeed it never gained the willing endorsement of France. On the eve of the Geneva conference, Nehru declared: ". . . the conflict in Indo-China is . . . a movement [the Viet Minh] of resistance to colonialism and the attempts to deal with such resistance by the traditional methods of suppression and divide-and-rule."[63]

The second prong of our policy, military defense of the area, resulted in a new collective defense arrangement. The "united action" that Mr. Dulles hoped to set in being prior to the Geneva talks bore fruit immediately after Geneva and represented a concerted attempt to place military sanctions behind the new *status quo* in Southeast Asia. The Manila Pact (SEATO), signed in early September 1954, contained a protocol that brought the area of free Indochina under its collective defense umbrella. Once again, Nehru announced his disfavor. Talk of "united action," he had said previously, "cast a deep shadow" on India's hope of constructing a "peace area" in Asia.[64] And in the "deplorable" Manila Pact, Nehru saw only a further strengthening of the "colonial" bloc.[65]

FRENCH NORTH AFRICA

The emancipation debate, which in Indochina had been a private two-part dialogue between France and the Indochinese and France and the United States, swelled to a crescendo in the public forum of the United Nations in the years following 1950. The subject was

---

[63] Allan B. Cole, *op. cit.,* p. 18.

[64] Richard P. Stebbins, *The United States in World Affairs, 1954* (Council on Foreign Relations, 1956), p. 227.

[65] *Ibid.,* p. 305.

French North Africa. The participants were some of the great
players of the international stage: Spaak of Belgium, Menon of
India, Zafrulla Khan of Pakistan, Robert Schuman of France; Al-
Jamali of Iraq. This debate has risen to moments of intense drama:
one thinks immediately of Spaak flying the Atlantic to appear before the General Assembly after seven years' absence and there to
plead with utter eloquence the case of France in the Algerian debate
of 1955. It has had moments of tense crisis: one remembers M.
Pleven's bitter announcement that he could not predict what the
ultimate effect might be of the Assembly's action in inscribing the
Algerian item on its agenda, and the shocked silence as he and the
entire French delegation walked out.

A fundamental point of conflict raised each time the debate was
resumed concerned the legal competence of the United Nations.
The colonial powers argued that France by international treaty had
assumed control of the foreign relations of Tunisia and Morocco.
Disputes between protector and protectorate thus had no international character; rather they were domestic affairs. To argue
otherwise, said Sir Gladwyn Jebb of the United Kingdom, would
mean that France, having the right to conduct the external affairs
of its protectorates, "would have to make representations to itself on
behalf of Morocco [or Tunisia], which, of course, is a manifest
absurdity."[66] Under the Charter, the United Nations had no right
to intervene in the domestic affairs of member states. For the
United Nations was created, not to change existing treaties, but
"to build an international society based on the rule of law."[67] It
was "not a court but a political body . . . [intended to] promote
peaceful solutions, and not to make them more difficult."[68] To
permit the United Nations to violate the inner sanctum of domestic
jurisdiction would turn the world organization into a "chaotic and
nondescript body in which no rule would ever be respected and any

---

[66] *Security Council Official Records,* 8th Year, 620th meeting, August 27,
1953, p. 5.

[67] *General Assembly Official Records,* 7th session, First Committee,
538th meeting, December 6, 1952, p. 201.

[68] *Security Council Official Records,* 7th Year, 575th meeting, April 10,
1952, p. 15.

individual country would be at the mercy of decisions taken by fortuitous majorities."[69]

The anticolonial bloc argued that sovereignty could not be extinguished by conquest nor eradicated by an imposed treaty; that, while sovereignty might "lie dormant for a time," a suppressed people became sovereign again "when their national movements . . . assert[ed] themselves." It was exactly by this means that some twenty members of the United Nations had reclaimed their nationhood and ended colonial domination.[70] Indeed, the United Nations had been "instituted as a means of facilitating the orderly evolution of dependent peoples toward independence."[71]

In this debate concerning the legal competence of the world organization, the United States had remained noncommittal. The basic test as to the correctness of United Nations intervention, said American delegates, was pragmatic: will consideration by the United Nations help to bring the parties to agreement? For the whole function of the deliberative organs in disputes such as Morocco and Tunisia was "to create an atmosphere favorable to a settlement . . . to be worked out by the parties directly concerned."[72] Time and again, the American representative concluded that such discussions would worsen, not improve, the situation. In this judgment, he consistently enjoyed the support of the colonial powers and the disapproval of the anticolonial bloc. But the question of competence was finally faced on its own merits when the Algerian dispute was introduced in 1955, and the United States lined up four square with the colonial bloc. Henry Cabot Lodge, Jr., argued that Algeria, different from Morocco and Tunisia, was under French law. Those who would put the Algerian item on the Assembly's agenda "sought Assembly sanction for a course of action intended to bring about fundamental changes in the compo-

---

[69] *General Assembly Official Records,* 10th session, 530th Plenary meeting, September 30, 1955, p. 181.

[70] *Ibid.,* p. 191.

[71] *Ibid.,* 11th session, First Committee, 831st meeting, February 4, 1957, p. 110.

[72] *Ibid.,* 7th session, First Committee, 539th meeting, December 8, 1952, p. 3.

sition of the French Republic." This was a clear violation of domestic jurisdiction.[73]

Indeed, though the United States repeatedly expressed its appreciation for the concerns of the Afro-Asian bloc and frequently urged France and her North African dependencies to "work out their destinies together" through negotiation, the American representatives at the United Nations supported France with remarkable consistency. Not untypical was Ambassador Jessup's observation during the height of the Tunisian dispute: "The United States trust[s] France and wish[es] to help, not to hinder, the achievement of the high purpose to which France had pledged itself."[74]

The United States has regularly voted against inscribing French North African items on the agenda of the Security Council, though it has not been as consistent in the General Assembly. Of thirteen key votes on substantive resolutions concerning French North Africa from 1951 through 1957, the United States has abstained but once, voted with the colonial powers ten times (in all ten cases, the anticolonial powers went the other way), and voted with the anticolonial bloc but twice. These two votes involved the support of mild Latin American resolutions on Morocco and Tunisia, which were passed only after severe Afro-Asian resolutions had been defeated. Many of the Afro-Asian powers voted for the mild resolutions only under protest, and in each case Britain and the Netherlands abstained.

Its stand favoring the French made the United States the target

---

[73] *Ibid.*, 10th session, General Committee, 103rd meeting, September 22, 1955, p. 12. Three months later, Secretary of State Dulles took the same position with reference to the presumably inviolate character of "Portuguese provinces in the Far East" (including Goa), which, like Algeria, are also considered integral parts of the homeland. Dulles' endorsement, which raised a furor in India, came within the context of discussions with the Portuguese Foreign Minister, which no doubt touched on the Azores airbases, leased by America from Portugal. Of course our position on both Algeria and Portuguese colonial questions has also been shaped by our own colonial posture. For we too have insisted that each metropolitan country must be allowed to determine the juridic status of its own overseas possessions; Hawaii, Alaska, and Puerto Rico have been cases in point.

[74] *Ibid.*, 7th session, First Committee, 539th meeting, December 8, 1952, p. 208.

of frequent Afro-Asian barbs. Pakistan warned that America, having barred the inscription of the Moroccan question on the Security Council's agenda, must bear responsibility for the consequent spilling of Moroccan and French blood.[75] The heritage of the Declaration of Independence, George Washington's warm response to the Sultan of Morocco (who had been the first to recognize the new American state), F.D.R.'s promises to a later Sultan, the tradition of Lincoln, the pledge of the Atlantic Charter—all were raised up to illuminate the unfaithfulness of the United States to its ancient libertarian principles. "This completely bewilders us," said Pakistan. "The United States today is acting in a fashion contrary to these great and noble avowals of policy . . . ."[76] Perfidious America would have to pay a price. "Help given to colonialism," said Syria, "was the most important factor in the determination of many countries of Asia and Africa to oppose certain Western policies . . . ."[77]

Why did the United States side with the colonial powers in the French North African question?[78] The answer indicates again the primacy of what were considered to be the requirements of defense in our approach to the colonial question. The factors are too well known to need more than a brief review. The United States was investing close to $500 million in a network of air bases in Morocco. It is axiomatic that a posture of defense creates enormous pressures to sustain the *status quo*. We had negotiated our leases with the French and, in terms of our military position, continued French control was desirable. Next most desirable was to effect

---

[75] *Ibid.*, 6th session, 354th Plenary meeting, December 13, 1951, p. 266.

[76] *Security Council Official Records,* 8th Year, 622nd meeting, September 1, 1953, p. 16.

[77] *General Assembly Official Records,* 11th session, First Committee, 832nd meeting, February 5, 1957, p. 114.

[78] It is entirely possible that our public support of France has been supplemented by what Mr. Lodge has frequently called "quiet diplomacy," designed in this case to press the French toward more liberal policies in North Africa. If this is true, then the pattern of our response to the North African question roughly parallels the "support-pressure" pattern in Indochina. In a speech delivered to the CIO on November 18, 1953, Mr. Dulles said that the United States was "pushing for self-government more than appears on the surface." We had "not given a blank check to any colonial power." (*Department of State Bulletin,* November 30, 1953, p. 743.) His reference may well have included French North Africa.

changes in the *status quo* through orderly negotiation and political evolution. Least desirable was the revolutionary violence that normally accompanied heated United Nations debates on such questions and that would only contribute to the creation of an extremist nationalism dangerous to the security of the American bases.

But we were equally concerned about our relations to France and, in turn, France's relation to the development of NATO. American policy could not publicly contravene French interests without running the risk of unseating the weak French "center" and bringing into power the radical alternatives of left or right. Just as delicate was the problem of gaining French support for the integration of German forces into NATO. The "forward strategy," designed to defend Europe as far to the east as possible and requiring the use of German troops, was first introduced at the NATO Council meeting of September 1950. Thereafter, for almost five years, France held up its full implementation. Significantly, these were precisely the years when the issues of Morocco and Tunisia were most critical. In summary, American policy on the French North African colonial question flowed principally from these considerations: the desire to maintain the security of our bases; the importance of maintaining a "center" government in France; and the necessity of purchasing French support for the rearmament of Germany.[79]

SUEZ

The pattern of the American response to the colonial question, which had ranged from an anticolonial position in Indonesia to a support of the colonialist power in French North Africa, returned again to an alignment with the anticolonialist bloc in the Suez dispute. On October 29, 1956, Israel invaded the Sinai peninsula. On October 30, Britain and France sent their joint ultimatum call-

---

[79] With reference to Algeria, it ought to be added that the United States has been appropriately impressed with the incredible complexity of the question itself, and with the consequent difficulty of formulating a "just solution." Certain Asian states—the Philippines, Thailand, and Japan, for example—have also indicated appreciation for these complexities.

ing upon Egypt and Israel to withdraw their forces to a distance of ten miles from the Canal, demanding the right temporarily to place Anglo-French troops at strategic points along the Canal, and warning of an intervention in force if either party failed to agree to these terms. On October 31, bombs began to fall on Egyptian military installations.

It may be argued that the debate, which now was joined in the United Nations, did not concern colonialism. Whether this was technically a colonial question or not is, however, almost beside the point; Afro-Asia, the Communist bloc, and even the United States debated the Suez issue as if it were, and once again colonial powers, though commanding this time almost no support, were ranged against the anticolonial bloc.

"The issue is much more than aggression against Egypt," said Yemen. "It is . . . a return to colonialism."[80] Egypt insisted the British and French had started a war "for an obsolete colonialism."[81] Indonesia found the situation reminiscent of "the cruelty and senselessness of colonial imposition and *diktat.*"[82] Syria condemned the Anglo-French desire "to satisfy their colonial . . . hunger with other people's land."[83] The Soviet Union fumed at "this policy of colonialist banditry."[84] And the American Vice President welcomed America's "declaration of independence" from "Anglo-French policies toward Asia and Africa which seemed to us to reflect the colonial tradition."[85]

In the Security Council, Henry Cabot Lodge, Jr., made it clear that the United States took vigorous exception to the Anglo-French ultimatum. He introduced a resolution calling for an Israeli withdrawal and a suspension of military, economic, and financial assistance to Israel pending its compliance. Britain announced it would

---

[80] *General Assembly Official Records,* First Emergency Special Session, 563rd Plenary meeting, November 3, 1956, p. 57.

[81] *Security Council Official Records,* 11th Year, 751st meeting, October 31, 1956, p. 5.

[82] *General Assembly Official Records,* First Emergency Special Session, 562nd Plenary meeting, November 1, 1956, p. 39.

[83] *Ibid.,* p. 16.

[84] *Ibid.,* First Emergency Special Session, 563rd Plenary meeting, November 3, 1956, p. 63.

[85] See above p. 224.

veto the resolution. Lodge pressed for a vote anyway, explaining that it would have "considerable moral effect . . . and that it represents something that we all should do."[86] An Anglo-French double veto blocked the Council, and the issue moved to the General Assembly.

On three successive occasions (November 2, 4, and 7), the United States either introduced or gave definite support to resolutions calling for a cessation of hostilities and immediate withdrawal of troops, aligning itself in each vote with overwhelming majorities against Britain, France, and Israel. On November 24, the United States voted again with a huge majority for a resolution calling upon the three to comply "forthwith" with previous resolutions admonishing a withdrawal of forces. At the same time, Ambassador Lodge rejected strenuous Belgian efforts to recast the "forthwith" resolution in somewhat less irritating language.

It is important to understand that the American reaction to the Suez invasion in no way contravened a pattern of behavior established several years before. The full story is not known of American efforts to mediate between the British and Egyptians concerning the evacuation of the Suez Canal base. Certainly, however, the interventions of Ambassador Jefferson Caffery and contacts between President Eisenhower and Prime Minister Churchill helped to move these long-stalled negotiations off dead center. Returning from the Big Three conference at Bermuda in December 1953, Mr. Churchill reported to the House of Commons that British action on Suez "will not be dictated either by the violence of our foreign enemies or by the pressure of some of our best friends."[87] But one may reasonably assume that it was exactly this combination of Egyptian mob violence and American pressure that finally moved the British to grant further concessions, even after announcing late in 1953 that they had reached the limits of compromise.

Even more striking was the character of the American contribution to negotiations resulting from the nationalization of the Suez Canal. Our role was not that of an unofficial third party to a bi-

---

[86] *Security Council Official Records,* 11th Year, 749th meeting, October 30, 1956, p. 31.

[87] Richard P. Stebbins, *The United States in World Affairs, 1953* (Council on Foreign Relations, 1955), p. 297.

lateral negotiation, as had been the case during the last years of the Suez base dispute; rather we were, with Britain and France, a participating member of the aggrieved bloc of states. Secretary Dulles spoke of Nasser's "grievous blow at international confidence," and the United States proceeded to freeze Egyptian assets in this country.

Yet, it soon became apparent that our position reflected somewhat greater support for Egypt than it did for the policy advocated by Britain and France. We were determined, as the British and French were not, to negotiate rather than to use force. When Colonel Nasser refused to consider an "international system" for the administration of the Canal with authority vested in an internationally responsible "Suez Canal Board," Britain and France asked the Security Council to approve a resolution endorsing internationalization and calling on Egypt to negotiate a "system of operation" based on it. Again Egypt denounced the plan, whereupon Mr. Dulles confessed that he found only one provision in the Western plan that was vital, namely "that the operation of the Canal should be insulated from the influence of the politics of any nation." Quite subsidiary to this principle were the "particular mechanisms," no one of which was "sacrosanct," for carrying it out.[88]

In effect, Mr. Dulles had abandoned the "mechanism" of international control. The famous "Six Principles" for governing the settlement of the Suez question, which were hammered out by the principals in the privacy of the Secretary General's office, hardly fulfilled Prime Minister Eden's demand that the Canal not be left "in the unfettered control of a single power."

Mr. Dulles, in a press conference held early in October 1956, suggested that our position *vis-à-vis* Britain and France in these matters was not unrelated to "the so-called problem of colonialism." "Now there the United States plays a somewhat independent role ... without identifying itself one hundred per cent either with the so-called colonial powers or with the [anticolonial] powers ...."[89] In practice, this position of "independence" was designed to move

---

[88] *Security Council Official Records,* 11th Year, 738th meeting, October 9, 1956, pp. 10-12.

[89] Richard P. Stebbins, *The United States in World Affairs, 1956* (Council on Foreign Relations, 1957), p. 270.

Britain and France toward an accommodation closer to Egypt's terms than either European power was willing voluntarily to go. And, in the end, we found ourselves aligned with the anticolonial bloc against, in Mr. Dulles' own phrase, "our oldest and most trusted and reliable allies."[90]

Our motivation was complex, and no service is done by over-simplifying it. But an important strand in that motivation was again the requirements of defense; this is the strand that we must now follow. Since 1951, when plans were first drafted for a Middle East Command, the United States together with Britain had been seeking a collective defense design appropriate to the exposed nations of that area. Upon return from his world-circling tour in the spring of 1953, Mr. Dulles noted with concern that "many of the Arab League countries are so engrossed with their quarrels with Israel or with Great Britain or France that they pay little heed to the menace of Soviet communism . . . ."[91] It seemed to be a fair presumption that if the British evacuation of the Canal base could be effected, Egypt's revolutionary government might look with more favor on a Middle East collective defense plan. Thus, we encouraged the British to make further concessions to Egypt, while, at the same time, offering Egypt in July 1953 both military and economic assistance once agreement was reached. Only two days after the Anglo-Egyptian treaty was signed in Cairo on October 19, 1954, Mr. Caffery indicated to Colonel Nasser the United States' readiness to fulfill its promise. For a variety of reasons, however, Nasser chose to refuse a commitment to the West, even declining Western arms, which had been offered under the terms of the Mutual Security Act. Our policy toward Egypt now entered a period of acute vacillation. Meanwhile, the Baghdad Pact (METO) was established in an effort to create a defense line along the Middle East's northern tier.

When, in the summer of 1956, Colonel Nasser nationalized the Canal, there was no reason to believe that any conceivable Western response could have purchased an Egyptian commitment to Western defense plans. The problem now was quite different: it was to

---

[90] *General Assembly Official Records,* First Emergency Special Session, 561st Plenary meeting, November 1, 1956, p. 10.

[91] *Department of State Bulletin,* June 15, 1953, p. 835.

avoid creating a situation in which the Soviet Union might expand further the considerable influence it had already achieved in the Middle East by deciding in 1954 to give unequivocal support to the Arabs in the Palestine dispute and by arranging in 1956 to make arms available to Egypt. As early as August 23, 1956, Khrushchev had warned that the Arabs would "not stand alone"; if war came as a result of the Canal dispute, there would be "volunteers."

How to meet this threat was now the main problem of collective defense in the Middle East. Britain and France arrived at one answer; the United States, at another. The Anglo-French alternative was to strike boldly, to remove Nasser, and so to block the main outlet of Soviet influence in the area. The American alternative was to move cautiously, to effect such compromises as would guarantee both European interests and Egyptian rights, and above all to avoid every provocation that would tend to strengthen Nasser's reliance on Moscow.

It is not the purpose of this analysis to assess the comparative wisdom of these alternatives. The purpose is simply to stress that the "anticolonial" posture now assumed by the United States was linked closely with the administration's view of the requirements of defense, specifically, preventing the further expansion of Soviet influence in the Middle East. That our policy was also linked to a number of other motives is not questioned. As in the case of Indonesia, the American reflex to the use of force, which looked suspiciously like aggression in American eyes, was automatic and swift, the more so because the administration was convinced that the possibilities of a negotiated settlement had not been exhausted and because our allies took this extreme step without consulting us. Just as significant was the motive power of President Eisenhower's devotion to collective security and Secretary Dulles' allegiance to world order. "There can be no law," said the President in his broadcast of October 31, "if we were to invoke one code of international conduct for those who oppose us and another for our friends."[92] Before the General Assembly, Mr. Dulles declared: "If we were to agree that whenever a nation feels that it has been

---

[92] *Department of State Bulletin,* November 12, 1956, p. 745.

subjected to injustice it should have the right to resort to force in an attempt to correct that injustice, then I fear that . . . the world would again be a world of anarchy."[93]

It is quite possible that the administration's view of Middle East defense was largely shaped by these value judgments. The least one can say is that for the administration there was a happy concurrence between the Eisenhower-Dulles view of collective security and world order on the one hand, and the demands of collective defense on the other. But these considerations do not affect our primary concern, which, once again, is only to establish that underlying the American "anticolonial" stand was a clear concept of the requirements of defense.

With the Anglo-French bombardment already underway, Mr. Dulles on the night of November 1-2 appeared before the General Assembly and said: ". . . I fear that if we do not act, and act promptly [to bring about a cease-fire] . . . there is a great danger that . . . what has been called a police action may develop into something which is far more grave . . . ."[94] The "grave" situation that Mr. Dulles wished to avoid was, of course, direct Soviet intervention. Just before mounting the rostrum on that critical night, Dulles had held an impromptu conference on the floor of the General Assembly with Canada's Lester Pearson, who had urged sufficient delay so as to bring some of the Assembly's pressure to bear on Egypt as well as on Britain and France. William R. Frye reports in summary Dulles' reply: "The best way to control the Assembly was to lead it, he felt. If the United States did not lead, the Soviet Union would—and the Russians would gain a political and psychological foothold in the Middle East from which they might not be dislodged for generations."[95]

The first requirement was to counter the threat of direct Soviet intervention, and the second, to meet the threat—if actual intervention did not materialize—of expanding Soviet influence and prestige throughout the Middle East. Beyond this, we no doubt

---

[93] *General Assembly Official Records,* First Emergency Special Session, 561st Plenary meeting, November 1, 1956, p. 10.

[94] *Ibid.,* p. 12.

[95] William R. Frye, *A United Nations Peace Force* (New York, 1957), p. 3.

were alarmed that any policy failing to deal vigorously with the Anglo-French invasion would exact an enormous cost in terms of unifying the entire Middle East in vindictive hatred against the West.[96] Equally appalling, it was true, were the consequences of our policy for NATO. Heretofore, American policy on colonial questions had discovered an area of concurrence between the defense requirements in the colonial area itself and the defense requirements of our European allies. In the Middle East of 1956, all possibilities of such concurrence seemed to have disappeared. That we opted for a policy favoring the requirements of Middle East defense, though such a policy was at the time disastrous to our allies, was based, one suspects, on the assumption that NATO could survive this mammoth shock while our influence in the Middle East would be irreparably shattered by the opposite course of action.

WEST IRIAN AND CYPRUS

In this broad review of the many patterns of the American response to the colonial question, two positions must still be explored. West Irian (West New Guinea) and Cyprus have both been on the agenda of the emancipation debate in the United Nations since 1954, and, on each, the United States has declared itself neutral. In the one case, West Irian, our position has been that of silent neutrality; in the other, Cyprus, we have assumed a policy of active neutrality. In each case, our posture again has been closely linked to the problem of defense.

The debate on West Irian has turned on the now familiar posi-

---

[96] We also expected some immediate positive returns. The support of Egypt, we reasoned, might create a situation of trust in which a lasting settlement of Suez and Palestine could be effected. Already on November 3, 1956, Ambassador Lodge was seeking to capitalize on the new American prestige. He suggested to the Assembly that a new approach to these problems be developed. That our hopes were foreordained to failure became clear when the next speaker, representing Iraq, stressed that "all the elements of appeasement have been put together" in the proposals of the United States. *General Assembly Official Records,* First Emergency Special Session, 563rd Plenary meeting, November 3, 1956, pp. 48-49.

tions of the colonial and anticolonial blocs. Indonesia, firmly supported by India, Burma, and Ceylon, has argued that continued Dutch control of the western half of New Guinea represents a vestigial and intolerable remnant of European colonialism in Asia. Under the terms of the treaty by which Indonesia gained its independence in 1950, West Irian rightfully belongs to the Indonesians. The Netherlands, solidly ranked with Belgium, France, the United Kingdom, and Australia, has interpreted recent documents as well as past history quite differently, and has invoked the ritual of Article 2, paragraph 7—those words of the United Nations Charter that forbid intervention in affairs essentially within the domestic jurisdiction of states members of the United Nations.

The United States has taken no part whatever in the debate. More than this, we have consistently abstained in all votes on substantive resolutions relating to the problem. Only a random comment dropped in an occasional press conference has broken the American silent neutrality. In one such comment, Secretary Dulles declared, "The arguments pro and con are closely balanced. We do not see a clear case to be made for either side sufficient, we think, to enable us to take a positive position on one side or another."[97]

It is perhaps not so much out of concern for our relationship with the Netherlands that we have refrained from displaying even the slightest interest in the Indonesian claim to West Irian. Rather it is because our ally, Australia, insists that continued Dutch presence in West Irian is vital to Australian security. ". . . Australia has a cardinal interest in the whole area of New Guinea and its future . . . ," said Percy Spender at the United Nations. "New Guinea represents the very key to Australia's defense."[98] At the same time, no issue in Indonesian foreign relations is more emotionally laden than that of West Irian. Before Congress in May of 1951, President Soekarno spoke with passion of this "colonial cancer in the body politic of our motherland." "The return of West Irian," he continued, "is for us the remaining part of our national political aspiration. It is the final installment on the colonial

---

[97] *Department of State Bulletin,* December 9, 1957, p. 918.

[98] *General Assembly Official Records,* 11th session, 858th Plenary meeting, February 25, 1957, p. 285.

debt."[99] Under such circumstances as these, our policymakers no doubt have concluded that discreet silence is perhaps the better part of valor.

The Cyprus dispute, which at this writing seems headed at last for a solution, represents an intensification of the same kind of problem, though within a radically new framework. For Cyprus is different from all other current colonial problems since it does not present the customary dilemma of choosing between Western colonialism and Afro-Asian anticolonialism; nor between the requirements of defense and some other claim on policy. This is because the disputants (Britain, Greece, and Turkey) are all Western, at least in the sense of belonging to NATO,[100] and because the strength and fidelity of each is considered an indispensable requirement of the collective defense of the West.

This utterly new orientation has produced some interesting developments in the emancipation debate, not the least of which is the unprecedented division of the Afro-Asian bloc on a colonial question. In this respect, it is fascinating to watch how, as passion declines, objectivity may rise to take its place. Their ties—both religious and military—with Turkey have prompted Iraq, Iran, and Pakistan to assess the Cyprus question with unaccustomed respect for the true complexities of the issue. Pakistan has spoken not only of the relevance of Turkey's "interest in the future political status of Cyprus," but also of Britain's "legitimate strategic interest . . . in the future of the island."[101] Iraq has been forced to concede that, though it is "one of the most important aims of the Charter, . . . self-determination is not by itself a solution to a complex and difficult problem."[102]

For many Afro-Asian states, a colonial problem that is non-Afro-Asian and that involves only Caucasian disputants seems hardly "colonial" at all. Ceylon once suggested, for example, that

---

[99] *Department of State Bulletin,* June 4, 1956, p. 930.
[100] Greece frequently has voted the anticolonial ticket in the U.N., and Turkey has just as frequently supported the colonial position—reflecting, of course, the alignment of each on the Cyprus question.
[101] *General Assembly Official Records,* 12th session, First Committee, 931st meeting, December 11, 1957, p. 379.
[102] *Ibid.,* 12th session, 731st Plenary meeting, December 14, 1957, p. 619.

"the matter was essentially one between the United Kingdom and the Cypriotes."[103] India, though without compromising its conviction that Cyprus should be free, has argued the inadvisability of publicly debating an issue so complex and volatile.[104] And Thailand once went so far as to declare that the Cyprus issue "did not really constitute an international dispute" and that the United Nations ought not to intervene "in the domestic affairs of a sovereign state."[105] In December 1957, Greece succeeded in bringing before the United Nations General Assembly a resolution requesting for the Cypriotes "the right of self-determination." It succeeded in gaining 31 favorable votes, but 23 voted against it, including both Pakistan and Iran, while 24 abstained. Among those voting in favor were only 12 Afro-Asian nations; 14 Afro-Asian states abstained.

This, then, was not a situation that called for a choice between colonial and anticolonial blocs, nor one that could be resolved simply by opting for that position that clearly favored the defense interests of the non-Communist world. It was a dispute within the Western camp and one that carried grave implications for defense no matter which side one favored. The only conceivable role for the United States seemed to be that of neutrality. We have persistently argued against any public debate that would "increase tensions and embitter national feelings at a time when the larger interests of all concerned were best served by strengthening existing solidarity among freedom-loving nations."[106] When votes have been taken on substantive resolutions in the United Nations, we have generally abstained. But this was an active neutrality. "Let me

---

[103] *Ibid.*, 11th session, 854th Plenary meeting, February 21, 1957, p. 269.

[104] *Ibid.*, 10th session, 521st Plenary meeting, September 23, 1955, p. 62.

[105] *Ibid.*, 11th session, 854th Plenary meeting, February 21, 1957, p. 259. This ironically made Thailand "more Catholic than the Pope," for Britain, partly to remove the stigma of colonialism from its position, took the view a few months later that "the Cyprus problem was an international one. The Greek and Turkish governments held widely differing views on the question, and the United Kingdom was endeavoring to find a solution acceptable to all concerned." *Ibid.*, 12th session, First Committee, 927th meeting, December 9, 1957, p. 345.

[106] *Ibid.*, 9th session, First Committee, 749th meeting, December 14, 1954, p. 545.

say," declared Mr. Lodge, ". . . that the United States pledges itself to continue an active interest in the Cyprus question."[107] Presumably, our active neutrality has been designed to place the United States in the role of unofficial mediator, for "there are occasions," continued Mr. Lodge, "when quiet diplomacy is far more effective than public debate, and this seems to be one of those occasions."[108]

SUMMARY

In the years of the great emancipation debate, we have not faced the major colonial conflicts on their own merits. That is, we have not asked, are we for colonialism in this particular case, or against it? Rather, as each controversial colonial issue arose, we have asked ourselves, what must be done to sustain the collective defense of the non-Communist world? We have then proceeded to let our stand in the emancipation debate be determined by our answer.

We have been pro-Europe, but not consistently so, which led Christian Pineau, in a 1956 speech before the Anglo-American Press Association in Paris, to complain that France's allies had not given full support to the French position in North Africa, that it would have been better "if the United States had pursued a policy of collaboration with the French in Viet Nam," and that taking everything into account there was "really no common French-British-American policy in the world." We have also been pro-Afro-Asia, but again so spasmodically that from Tunisia to Indonesia we have been condemned as "the accomplice of France" and accused of doing "not enough in liberating Afro-Asian countries." But the objective of our policy has not been to persuade each side that their cause was our own. Our purpose was to perform the task of constructing a defense line against Communist expansion. Take the Indochinese case: the "colonial" dimension of our strategy was not intended to convince France that we endorsed every article of French imperial policy, but rather to make French military resistance in Southeast Asia more effective. The "anticolonial" dimension of our Indochinese policy was certainly not designed to curry

---

[107] *Ibid.*, 10th session, 521st Plenary meeting, September 23, 1955, p. 61.
[108] *Ibid.*

favor with Mr. Nehru but to create a viable, non-Communist nationalism for Viet Nam. It is not surprising that we have appeared to be both "the pillar of society and the patron of revolution." But the fact is that we have aimed to be neither. Our colonial policy is not best explained as the unfortunate and schizophrenic attempt to meet the conflicting demands of both colonial and anticolonial friends. It is best explained as an adjunct to a policy designed to meet the necessities of defense in a broad range of situations that required both a variety of responses and the frequent violation of the demands of Afro-Asia or Europe.[109]

Could it have been otherwise? Probably not, given the inevitable pressure on these colonial questions of our defense responsibilities throughout the entire non-Communist world. This is not to say that we have always arrived at exactly the proper balance between defense requirements and other claims on policy such as the welfare of a colonial population or our obligations to our European allies; it is not even to suggest that our definition of the requirements of defense has always been above question. It is to insist, however, that no policy that took seriously the problem of Communist expansion could have dissolved the hard necessity of giving priority to a defense strategy, though the implementation of that strategy brought us, from time to time, into conflict with Afro-Asia or Western Europe.

Our principal weakness was perhaps not what we did, but how we talked about it. Often, we lacked the forthrightness to state clearly the problem of conflicting claims and loyalties and to define sharply our responsibilities, as we saw them, which prompted one course of action rather than another. Too frequently (the North African debates, for example), we sought to convince Afro-Asia that we were really anticolonialists when, in fact, our performance

---

[109] This conclusion perhaps ought not to be extrapolated very far beyond the major colonial controversies discussed in these pages. It surely does not apply to American policies on many of the questions debated in the Trusteeship Council, the Fourth (Trusteeship) Committee of the General Assembly, or the Committee on Information from Non-Self-Governing Territories. The present study of course is limited to American policy *vis-à-vis* the critical colonial questions discussed as political issues in the Security Council and in the First (Political) Committee of the General Assembly.

was quite otherwise. And when, in the Suez dispute, we discovered that we could in fact support the requirements of defense and be anticolonialist at one and the same time, we celebrated our emancipation from colonialism in a way that caused profound misgivings in Western Europe.

We have seemed overly anxious to prove that we were acting in behalf of some universal legal and moral order. But our policy was not really designed to the specifications of universal order—which is a good thing because to gain universal consensus such an order would have to be so vague and distant as to have no relationship to immediate problems. Consider, for example, the conflicting conceptions of order that emerge in the emancipation debate. The only order most of the anticolonial world wants, as an Indonesian delegate to the United Nations once said, is one that would do away forever with "the old-fashioned argument that considerations of military strategy outweighed the principle of self-determination." Meanwhile, the order Western Europe seeks is one that, as Mr. Eden said, does not place Europe's economic life line "in the unfettered control of a single power." The one conception of order implies total national independence; the other demands such modifications of independence as seem necessary to guarantee vital European interests in a highly interdependent world.

Our policy has expressed, not a universal legal and moral order, but the more modest, though no less noble, attempt to keep the present order from coming apart at the seams. We are trying to maintain a minimal level of security along a world-encircling border and, to do this, we find it regrettably, sometimes tragically, necessary to contradict the somewhat more parochial interests of our friends in Afro-Asia and occasionally in Europe. If we defend such policies as expressions of a universal order with the requirements of which one or the other side cannot possibly agree, we add unnecessary insult to necessary injury.

IV. The Postcolonial Era

The emancipation debate will continue. Twenty-nine Afro-Asian powers at Bandung vowed that "colonialism in all its manifestations is an evil which should speedily be brought to an end." An Indonesian leader, at the outset of his country's independence, pledged to the United Nations that Indonesian sovereignty would not be an end in itself, but an instrument "to work for the independence of all peoples who are still struggling to free themselves from colonial domination." As the bloc of newly independent states grows, so too grows the strength of its demand to end colonialism. Through the forum of the United Nations and through direct encouragement to nationalist leaders, Afro-Asia will surely keep the emancipation debate warm. Algeria and West Irian are now on the agenda. British holdings on the Arabian peninsula will not remain exempt for long. Nor will sub-Sahara Africa. The trusteeship areas are already under debate. Those areas of East Africa where substantial European populations have deeply rooted interests will be on the agenda soon. And, ultimately, the debate will spread to include those colonies (Portuguese and Spanish) that have refused to grant even the possibility of self-government. As long as the debate persists, the United States will continue, in one form or another, to face the dilemma of opposing claims.

It would be a pity if this unhappy prospect prevented us from appreciating the all-important fact that though the emancipation debate will continue, the colonial system has already largely been dismantled, and huge areas of what remains are moving toward independence at frightening speed. On October 13, 1953, the Afro-Asian bloc introduced at the United Nations a resolution that, among other things, called for an independent Morocco in five years. This "radical" resolution was rejected. But just two years and five months later, Morocco was free. The problem of colonialism is being transmuted before our eyes into the problems of the postcolonial era, and we have hardly begun to discuss the momentous implications of this change. In this brief review we can only hint at a few of these implications.

Any analysis of the problems of postcolonialism must begin by recalling the function that the colonial system once filled. Not only did it express Europe's power over archaic societies and dormant civilizations, but the colonial system provided an answer to Europe's economic necessities and a working solution to the problem of political order. The industrialized economies of the continent moved rapidly from relative self-sufficiency to a high level of dependence upon sources of raw materials and outlets for finished goods. The colonial system solved the problems of economic dependence by assuring political control of these sources and outlets, which, in turn, made the colonial areas economically dependent on Europe.

The colonial system also represented an answer to the problem of world order. Externally (Europe *vis-à-vis* the rest of the world), order was maintained by preponderant European power administered through colonial outposts. Internally (European states *vis-à-vis* one another), a tenuous order was maintained through the balance of power, colonial possessions representing important weights in the balance, and the distribution of new colonial areas constituting a means of redressing the balance without major wars among the several colonial powers (for example, the partition of Africa during the nineteenth century). In an important sense, the situation now confronting us is that of solving the problems of economic interdependence and political order in an era in which the colonial solution is manifestly no longer available, and under conditions made hazardous by the fact that Communist power stands ready to capitalize on the distress of Europe and the turmoil of Afro-Asia resulting from the breakup of that system.

Even the clear definition of the problems of the postcolonial era is difficult because we all suffer from a "colonial hangover," as Henry Byroade once put it. There is for example a strong tendency in the Afro-Asian world to continue using the vocabulary of anti-colonialism to describe what are in fact postcolonial problems. Egypt is sure "imperialism is trying to use Israel to threaten us with another aggression." Unsatisfactory relations with Tunisia are thought in Cairo to be the result of the increasing subservience of Tunisia to Western imperial designs. Tunisia for its part accuses France of continuing to treat Tunisia like a colony when the French protest the delivery of American arms to Tunis. Syria is sure that one of the most significant manifestations of continuing colonialism in the Middle East is "the policy of the colonial Powers . . . to perpetuate the division of the Arab nation into a multiplicity of states, territories and spheres of influence." These examples could be multiplied endlessly for other areas. The intense anticolonial mind-set of Afro-Asia is today more bogus than legitimate because it is out of all proportion to the actual role played by Western colonialism. But even more important, this anticolonial mentality makes it diffi-

cult for Afro-Asia to acknowledge that present economic and political difficulties are not simply the result of an attempt to resuscitate
a dying colonialism.

Actually, the anticolonialism of Afro-Asia must be understood
as a response to an array of forces that often have little relation to
any objective assessment of colonialism. It is to be explained in
part as the continuation of the "habit of opposition" to colonial
rule; in part, the political usefulness of focusing internal animosities
on an external source; in part, the psychological necessity to find a
devil on which to blame the enormous problems of domestic instability and insecurity that native political leaders now are heir to in
the postcolonial era. All of this, incidentally, suggests an interesting thesis. It is often assumed that the Afro-Asian anticolonial, and
hence anti-Western, mind-set might be softened if America itself
were to adopt a strong anticolonial stance. But if Afro-Asian anticolonialism is in part a psychological projection of inward turmoil,
it might better be neutralized by Western assistance in the attempt
to solve some of the internal problems of the new nations and to
resolve some of the economic conflicts between the industrial West
and the underdeveloped East.

The colonial powers too suffer from the "colonial hangover."
Again, there is the tendency to use the vocabulary of colonialism
to describe what are in fact postcolonial problems. Two expressions
of this are particularly significant. First, the colonial powers, especially France, are tempted to accuse the United States of moving
toward a kind of neocolonialism in what are thought to be European areas of influence. For example, we have assumed many of
the economic and military responsibilities once fulfilled by the
French Empire in Viet Nam, Laos, and Cambodia. Second, there
is the distinct possibility of tension between Britain and France as
newly independent states within the sphere of each adopt policies
unfavorable to the former metropole. When Guinea and Ghana
announced their intention to confederate, there were veiled com-
ments in France about the designs of the British Commonwealth on
the former French colony. The point is that the tendency to analyze
these problems in terms of a continuation of colonialism clouds the
real issues, which are postcolonial. In the former case, the postcolonial problem is that of shoring up weak and exposed embryonic

states that are so jealous of their new independence that they tend to sever too quickly their ties to the former metropole. In the latter case, the postcolonial problem is that of dealing creatively with West African leaders who for a variety of reasons will continue to agitate for an alternative both to tribalism and to the arbitrary administrative units that their states now represent.

Nor is the United States unaffected by the "colonial hangover." With the Afro-Asians, we too tend on occasion to use the vocabulary of anticolonialism to describe postcolonial problems. This is particularly apparent in our recurrent thrusts against the colonialism of Britain and France. Perhaps this derives from the psychological necessity to square ourselves with our anticolonial heritage and to protest our pure motives and innocent objectives in a world in which we feel compromised by the colonialism of our European allies. In any event, our happy and public disavowal of British and French "colonialism" in the fall of 1956 tended to obscure the fact that the real problem was postcolonial: namely, to develop an alternative to the now defunct colonial relationship that will give to the highly dependent economies of Europe reasonable guarantees of access to raw materials upon which their entire enterprise depends.

For the United States, the postcolonial era will provide no escape from the dilemmas that we confronted during the emancipation debate. Though changed somewhat, they will if anything be intensified, a fact which is frequently missed by both realistic and idealistic analyses. For both view the basic problem of political order in the postcolonial era as that of adding the emancipated nations to our side of the world balance, the idealists by purchasing Afro-Asian sympathy with grand schemes of economic development, the realists by adding as many of these states as possible to our elaborate network of alliances. Without questioning the utility of either economic development or alliances per se, it ought to be pointed out that the problem of political order in the postcolonial era will involve not only the maintenance of a balance with the Communist bloc, but increasingly the use of American power to redress dangerous imbalances *within* an Afro-Asia made turbulent by the emergence of countless weak and vulnerable states and quasi states.

A new and creative approach to these intricate postcolonial problems of political order and economic interdependence is not beyond the realm of the possible. But little will be done to further such an approach until Afro-Asia, Europe, and the United States have fully accepted the fact that the colonial era, as a system for organizing the political and economic life of major parts of the non-Communist world, is now all but over.

I O

SOVIET COMMITMENTS
TO COLLECTIVE ACTION

William Welch

I. Introduction

WHILE MUCH has been written, both here and in the Soviet
Union, about the Soviet network of alliances, Soviet activity in the
United Nations, and other ways in which the Soviet Union pursues
its security in concert with other nations, systematic treatments of
the subject have been conspicuous by their absence. Non-Soviet
literature typically confines itself to parts of the subject—selected
treaties, alliances, etc.—and is apt to dismiss deeper questions of
meaning by dogmatic reference to Soviet chicanery and lust for
world domination. Soviet literature, for its part, is unsatisfactory
even to the Soviets. Writing in 1956, a group of publicists headed
by a leading academician described it as so far barren of "a single
work of any importance or a symposium of essays generalizing and
offering a scientific evaluation of the activities of the U.N. and its
agencies."[1]

This paper represents an effort to lift the discussion to a more
abstract plane. It seeks first to type and describe the full range of
relevant institutional arrangements in which the Soviets participate.
It seeks second to clarify the theory through which the Soviets pub-

---

[1] E. Korovin, *et al.*, "A Letter to the Editor," *International Affairs*, 1956,
No. 12, p. 98.

licly rationalize participation in these arrangements. It seeks third to identify the ways in which the Soviets actually behave toward them. In thus centering on the forms of co-operation, it leaves out much of importance. But it hopes at least to serve as a useful introduction to more full-scale systematic treatment and to suggest the lines along which such treatment might usefully proceed.

II. Arrangements Participated In

1. TYPES

There are three ways in which one nation can enlist the co-operation of another in order to secure itself against a potential aggressor. One is to get the other to join in a common front against the aggressor: this is the method of counterpoise. The second is to get the other not to join the aggressor: this is the method of neutralization. The third is to get the other to join in a general organization for keeping the peace, which the aggressor is also free to join: this is the method of transcendence.

The Soviet Union uses all three methods.

Its use of the method of counterpoise is reflected in mutual aid arrangements contained in treaties of that name. The Soviet Union is party to nine such arrangements: eight bilateral and one multilateral. Partners in this type of co-operation are Finland, the seven Eastern European satellites, Mongolia, and Red China.

Its use of the method of neutralization is reflected in arrangements contained both in treaties of mutual aid and treaties of neutrality. Partners in this type of co-operation are all the above countries except Mongolia and, in addition, Iran and Afghanistan.

Its use of the method of transcendence is reflected in the arrangements that define the United Nations and are described in the Charter thereof. Partners in this type of co-operation are the other 81 members of that organization.

2. CONTENTS

The counterpoise and neutralization or special arrangements to which the Soviet Union is party have certain traits in common.

They are characteristically symmetrical: each partner is to do for the other(s) as he is to be done by, no more and no less.[2] They rest on an unequivocal pledge. In the fulfillment of this pledge, they allow little choice of means. Typically, they run for twenty years, and they provide that extension for additional terms shall be automatic upon failure of one party to announce withdrawal.

A. COUNTERPOISE (MUTUAL AID) ARRANGEMENTS

The bilateral mutual aid arrangements characteristically particularize the source of the threat that is to evoke co-operative action. They name as this source either Germany and other states allied with Germany directly or in any other form, or Japan and other states allied with Japan directly or in any other form. They provide for three kinds of co-operation. These are: (1) the taking and co-ordinating of all possible measures to prevent any threatened repetition of aggression by the named source; (2) the immediate rendering of all possible military and other aid in the event of military involvement with the named source upon the effort of the latter to renew her aggressive policy; and (3) consultation on all important international questions touching common interests.

---

[2] For salient characteristics, see Table on Special Arrangements, p. 274. Official sources used are as follows:

For 1926–1941:

U.S.S.R., People's Commissariat for Foreign Affairs, *Sbornik Deistvuiushchikh dogovorov, soglashenii i konventsii, zakliuchennykh s inostrannymi gosudarstvami* (Moscow, Izd. NKID, 1925 *et seq.*).

For 1941–1945 (Sept.):

U.S.S.R., Ministry of Foreign Affairs, *Vneshniaia Politika Sovetskogo Soiuza v Period Otechestvennoi Voiny* (Moscow, Gos. Izd. Polit. Lit., 1944 *et seq.*).

For 1945 (Sept.)–1950:

U.S.S.R., Ministry of Foreign Affairs, *Vneshniaia Politika Sovetskogo Soiuza* (Moscow, Gos. Izd. Polit. Lit., 1949 *et seq.*).

For 1955 (Warsaw Pact):

Pravda, May 15, 1955.

Most accessible English translations for prewar treaties are to be found in Leonard Shapiro, ed., *Soviet Treaty Series*, Vol. I (1917-1928) and Vol. II (1929-1939), published in Washington, D. C., by the Georgetown University Press in 1950 and 1955 respectively. For Warsaw Pact, see *New York Times*, May 15, 1955.

Special Arrangements in the Collaborative Pursuit of Security to Which U.S.S.R. a Party as of 1958[a]

Year set up	Partner(s)	Title of treaty[b]	Co-operation stipulated						Neutralization	
			Counterpoise (mutual aid)							
			Precipitated by aggression		Preven-tion[c]	Restora-tion[d]	Consulta-tion[e]		Neutrality[f]	Neutralism
			By:	Against:						
1927	Iran	NA & N							x[h]	x
1931	Afghanistan	NA & N							x	x
1936	Mongolia	F & MA[i]	Any country	Partners' territory		x[j]	x[k]			
1943	Czechoslovakia	F MA & PC	Germany & her allies	Partners' territory		x				x
1945	Poland	F MA & PC	"	"	x	x				x
1948	Rumania	F C & MA	"	"	x	x	x			x
1948	Hungary	F C & MA	"	"	x	x	x			x
1948	Bulgaria	F C & MA	"	"	x	x	x[m]			
1948	Finland	F A & MA	Japan & her allies	Finland only		x[l]				x[n]
1950	China	F A & MA	"	Partners' territory	x	x[o]	x			x
1955 7	European Satellites[p]	F C & MA (Warsaw Pact)	Any country	Partners' European territory		x[q]	x[r]			x[s]

[a] For sources, see footnote 2 in body of text of this chapter.

[b] Abbreviations: A—Alliance; C—Collaboration; F—Friendship; MA—Mutual Aid; N—Neutrality; NA—Non-Aggression; PC—Postwar Collaboration.

[c] Typical statement (from Rumanian Treaty): "The above Contracting Parties bind themselves to take together all measures at their disposal for the removal of any threat of the repetition of aggression on the part of Germany or any other government which might be allied with Germany directly or in any other form."

[d] Typical statement (from Rumanian Treaty): "In case one of the above Contracting Parties is drawn into military activities with a Germany which attempted to revive its aggressive policy, or with any other government which directly or in any other form is allied with Germany in a policy of aggression, then the other above Contracting Party will immediately give to the Contracting Party drawn into military activities military and other help by all means at its disposal."

e Typical statement (from Rumanian Treaty): "The above Contracting Parties will consult with one another in all important international questions touching upon the interests of both countries."

f Typical statement (from Afghan Treaty): "In the event of war or hostilities between one of the Contracting Parties and one or several third powers, the other Contracting Party undertakes to observe neutrality in regard to the former."

g Typical statement (from Afghan Treaty): ". . . Each of the Contracting Parties undertakes not to be a party, to military or political alliances or agreements with one or several powers directed against the other Contracting Party . . ."

h Applies only to the case of war in which partner is victim of aggression.

i Called a Protocol for original term of ten years, then re-enacted as Treaty.

j *Casus foederis* is simply military attack.

k Occasion for consultation limited to threat of attack.

l Applies only to the case of military aggression across the territory of Finland, in which case the commitments are as follows: (1) Finland: to fight to repel the aggressor with all means at her command, but within her borders; (2) the Soviet Union: to give necessary help, the character of which is to be determined by additional negotiation.

m Applies only to the case of threat of military attack defined in restorative article.

n In addition, the Preamble takes note of Finland's effort to stand aside from the conflicts of interest between the great powers.

o *Casus foederis* is limited in the following curious fashion: "being attacked . . . and thus being involved in a state of war."

p Albania, Bulgaria, Czechoslovakia, East Germany, Hungary, Poland, and Rumania.

q In case of armed attack in Europe on one of the parties by any state or group of states, each party, pursuant to its right of individual or collective self-defense in correspondence with Article 51 of the United Nations Charter, will render the victim immediate help, individually or by agreement with other parties, by all means, including military force, as may seem necessary to the helper.

r Applies not only to all important international questions touching common interests, but also to an occasion that, in the opinion of one of the parties, may present a threat of armed attack. Further, upon occurrence of such attack, parties are obligated to consult on means of re-establishing peace.

s The forbidden coalitions, etc., are described as those having aims that contradict the instant treaty.

The eight bilateral mutual aid arrangements currently in force do not, however, conform with equal fidelity to the pure type.[3] In three cases, variations are of minor dimensions. The Chinese arrangement contracts the main *casus foederis* from "involvement in military measures" to "attack." The Polish excludes the consultative provision. The Czech excludes both the preventive and consultative provisions.

In two cases, however, variation is of major dimensions. The Finnish arrangement is considerably more limited than the others. Not only does it exclude the preventive provision, but it confines the *casus foederis* to German aggression across Finnish borders; it restricts correspondingly the occasion for consultation; and while providing that the Finnish response to the aggression named is to be self-defense by any and all means, it envisages a more restrictive response on the part of the Soviet Union in stipulating that the latter shall render only such help as the two parties may agree to be necessary. Finally, it pays preambular tribute to the Finnish desire to remain aloof from great-power conflicts.

The arrangement with Mongolia, on the other hand, is broader. The instrument of association, which in 1936 emerged as a protocol from the chrysalis of a "dzentl'menskoye" agreement of 1934, and which in 1946 finally achieved adulthood in the form of a full-fledged treaty, generalizes the source of hostile action to be defended against rather than confining it to named opponents. Its consultative and preventive provisions may thus be activated by the threat of aggression from *any* third party, its restorative provision by actual aggression from *any* third party.

With these variations noted, it still remains generally true that the mutual aid arrangements to which the Soviet Union is party are technically speaking *narrow* in respect to the sources of hostile action to be defended against, but *broad* in respect to (a) the range of the challenges from these sources that are to provoke joint action by the parties and (b) the range of the responses thereto that the

---

[3] For very useful analyses of the treaties involved, see W. W. Kulski, "The Soviet System of Collective Security Compared with the Western System," *American Journal of International Law,* July 1950, p. 453; and P. S. Wandycz, "The Soviet System of Alliances in East Central Europe," *Journal of Central European Affairs,* July 1956, p. 177.

parties are to make. In this they disagree at almost every point
with their closest American counterparts, our bilateral arrangements with our Far Eastern associates.[4] The contrast between the
Soviet and American arrangements with their respective Chinese
allies is in this connection illuminating.[5] The Soviet arrangement
confines the source of hostile action to Japan and allies, but binds
to unlimited support in the prevention of aggression or the repulse
of an attack; the American arrangement puts no restriction on the
source, but binds only to a loose form of consultation and, in the
case of armed attack, to no more stringent action than that which
the individual party may consider necessary at the time.

The unique multilateral special arrangement to which the Soviet
Union is party is the arrangement for the defense of Eastern Europe
that was made by an association of the Soviet Union and her European satellites called the Conference of European Powers for the
Assurance of Peace and Security in Europe.[6] The Warsaw Pact,
the charter of this association, invites accession on the part of other
European countries, whatever their ideological persuasion, and it
decrees that it shall not remain in existence beyond the date of the
establishment of a General European Treaty of Collective Security.
The regional arrangement defined by the Warsaw Pact, in short,
provides for its own dissolution upon replacement by a regional
arrangement truly inclusive in character and of the transcendent
type.

The Warsaw Pact is another mutual aid pact, as indeed its label
proclaims it to be. It includes restorative and consultative provisions similar to those of the pure bilateral type. Its consultative
provision runs, for part of the course at least, in the familiar terms.
Thus, it is not far off the mark to say that the Warsaw Pact generalizes and extends to all seven European satellites the arrangements earlier and separately contracted between the Soviet Union
and five of the seven (i.e., all but Albania and East Germany).

---

[4] U.S. Department of State, *American Foreign Policy 1950-1955, Basic
Documents* (Washington, D. C., 1957), Vol. I, pp. 873-912, 945-65; here-
inafter cited as *Basic Documents*.

[5] *Ibid.*, p. 945.

[6] See Table on Special Arrangements, p. 274.

Yet the differences are worth remarking. Unlike the bilateral pacts, the Warsaw Pact has no preventive provision; its consultative provision is broader; and it provides for implementary institutions: a joint command to implement the restorative provisions and a Political Consultative Committee to implement the consultative provision and settle questions of interpretation. Finally, its restorative provision has a somewhat different configuration. This provision stipulates that, in the event of an armed attack in Europe, each signatory shall immediately, individually or collectively, give assistance to the attacked by all means that it deems necessary, military force included. In coverage, this pact is therefore broader in some respects, narrower in others, than its bilateral counterpart. It is broader in respect to source of hostile action to be defended against, extending to any source rather than merely to Germany and her allies or to Japan and hers. It is narrower in respect to type of hostile action (confined to armed attack alone) and to place of attack (confined to Europe alone); and it allows the defenders a latitude in their choice of means that is unknown in its bilateral counterparts.

The Warsaw Pact has been called a carbon copy of the North Atlantic Treaty, and its authors have been accused of plagiarism. There is something to the accusation. The Warsaw Pact is of much the same scope as the North Atlantic Treaty and binds as firmly. Its key, the restorative clause (Article 4), strides along, idea by idea, almost word by word, with the North Atlantic counterpart, Article 5. In both cases, the *casus foederis* is an armed attack; in both cases, the commitment is to render such assistance, including armed assistance, as the committed deems necessary. Yet it is only fair to point out that there are important differences of substance: the Warsaw Pact does not condition the accession of additional parties on unanimous invitation; and it lays stress on its own provisional character. Moreover, it should be reiterated that much of the substance and language also matches closely at points the substance and language of the bilateral mutual aid treaties. In short, if we are to accuse the authors of the Warsaw Pact of plagiarism, let us concede that they purloined impartially from both West and East.

B. NEUTRALIZATION ARRANGEMENTS

The neutralization arrangements to which the Soviet Union is party are of two kinds: neutrality arrangements proper, providing for abstention from helping one another's enemy in time of war; and neutralism arrangements, or arrangements providing for non-participation at all times in alliances, coalitions, etc., directed against one another's security.[7] The neutrality arrangements proper are contained in treaties of the same name. The Soviet Union is currently party to two such arrangements, with Iran and Afghanistan. The neutralism arrangements are contained both in the treaties of mutual aid (save only that with Mongolia) and the treaties of neutrality. The Soviet Union is currently party to eleven such arrangements.

Besides the arrangements noted above, the neutralization formula underlies an understanding with Austria.[8] Moreover, the Soviets would like to extend it, under multilateral sponsorship, to Germany,[9] and in this or in the familiar bilateral form to Japan.[10] Neutralization arrangements have no counterpart in the American system.

C. TRANSCENDENT ARRANGEMENTS

The single general or transcendent arrangement to which the Soviet Union currently is party, that which describes the United Nations Organization, is well enough known to require no more than the barest summary.[11] According to its Charter, the United Nations, which today is an organization near-universal in membership, has a territorial and functional authority that is also nearly

---

[7] See Table on Special Arrangements, p. 274.

[8] The U.S.S.R. agreed to sign a peace with Austria on condition Austria accept the neutrality formula, which she did in amendments to her constitution adopted October 1955. For text of understanding, see communiqué on talks with Austria, *Pravda,* April 16, 1955, p. 1.

[9] See text of 1953 Draft for German Peace Treaty, in *New Times,* 1953, No. 34 (Supplement), and of 1959 Draft, in *Pravda,* Jan. 11, 1959, p. 1.

[10] See report of interview of Molotov by Japanese newspaperman, *Pravda,* September 13, 1954, p. 1; also note of December 1, 1958 to Japan, reported in *ibid.,* December 3, 1958, p. 1.

[11] *Basic Documents,* pp. 134-61.

universal. With minor exceptions, it has jurisdiction over all matters, except those of a purely internal character, that may threaten the peace and security of the world, and here the organization itself is to be the judge. The Charter authorizes it to respond to threats by the use of the whole range of sanctions up to and including armed force. Moreover, members bind themselves to heed the recommendations of that agency (the Security Council) that is set up to carry out the functions of the organization. On the other hand, the Charter requires extraordinary majorities to set the Security Council in motion and further stipulates that the extraordinary majority include all permanent members or the great powers. Since even honest disagreements between great powers concerning the applicability of the Charter to a concrete situation may easily arise, the net effect is to balance unlimited authority with limited operability.

The Soviets would like to supplement the United Nations with regional arrangements of the same transcendent type. Since the Berlin Conference of 1954, they have been trying to get the West to join them in a collective security organization for Europe, which would supplant both the North Atlantic Treaty and the Warsaw Pact organizations.[12] They have also endorsed, albeit with less enthusiasm, a similar arrangement for Asia, which was first proposed by Chou En-lai in July 1955.[13]

3. THE PATTERN

The various co-operative arrangements in security to which the Soviet Union is party constitute a nicely balanced institutional net. At the top—its supremacy proclaimed by Article 103 of the Charter—is the transcendent arrangement defining the United Nations. Below, and acknowledging this supremacy, are the neutralization and counterpoise arrangements. At the top is the general arrangement for keeping the peace, which is aimed not only at threats to Soviet security but at any threats to anyone's security. Below are the special arrangements, directed specifically at threats to Soviet

---

[12] See note to Western powers of February 10, 1954, published in *New Times,* 1954, No. 8 (Supplement).

[13] Reported in the *New York Times,* July 31, 1955, p. 2.

security, particularly the threat of renewed pressure or renewed assault from traditional quarters. At the top is the general partnership, with virtually all the nations of the globe. Below are the special partnerships, with neighbors and, as the endpaper map shows, virtually no one but neighbors: the neutralization arrangements, extending to countries accounting for practically the entire perimeter from the Norwegian to the North Korean border; and the counterpoise arrangements, confined to countries on the relatively sensitive Western and Eastern flanks. At the top is the general arrangement, broad in jurisdiction and calling for a full-fledged response to danger but with its concrete application conditional upon great-power accord and not tightly binding. Below are the special arrangements, narrow in jurisdiction but more automatic in application and tightly binding.

This pattern contrasts markedly at several points with the American counterpart. Both the U.S.S.R. and U.S.A. belong to the United Nations. Both are centers of extensive institutional nets that include a number of counterpoise arrangements. But here the similarities end. The Soviets favor neutralization arrangements. We do not. The Soviets prefer the bilateral form of arrangement. We prefer the multilateral. While the Soviets confine their associates to countries on or close to their borders, we number among our associates countries at great distances from our shores. While the Soviets insist on tight bonds, we are content with loose ones. These differences reflect the difference between a nation that has faced clear and omnipresent danger and one that has not.

On the other hand, the resemblance of the present Soviet pattern to earlier ones is fairly close. In the thirties, when the Soviet Union first succeeded in breaking from its isolation, it was party both to the League of Nations and to an array of bilateral arrangements with neighbors or near-neighbors. Up to 1939, when it replaced the French with the German partnership, it bound France, Czechoslovakia, and Mongolia to itself through mutual aid treaties, and it bound to itself a number of other countries through neutrality and nonaggression pacts of various kinds (in Europe: Finland, the three Baltic countries, Poland, and Italy; in Asia: the three southern border countries and China). One arrangement, of course, goes back even further, for the French association of 1935-1939 not only looks forward to the alliance of 1944-1955, but also backward to the Entente of 1890. These similarities bear witness to the perdurance of common strategic interests.

III. Rationalization

The Soviets do not articulate very systematically the rationale of the co-operative security arrangements to which they are party. They leave this to the Poles.[14] In official notes and pronouncements as well as in the exegetical commentary of publicists, however, there are generalizations concerning the workings of the international order and their manipulation in the interests of peace and security. Out of these fragments of a general theory it is possible to construct a fairly coherent whole.

1. THE CHALLENGE

According to the Soviets, the bloc represents the prime threat to peace; the imperialist aggressor walks not alone, but in twos, threes, or more. Thus, blocs are also the Great Bad in the Soviet cosmology of joint defense, which, indeed, may be characterized with little exaggeration as a polemic against joint aggression.

The bloc may be identified first and foremost by its exclusiveness, which readily distinguishes it from peaceful groupings.[15] Other hallmarks are generality of target, spurious claims to fulfill a regional defense function, dominance by the leading member, and nonconformity with a system of collective security.

Blocs lead to war. In the Soviet view, blocs and war are end links in an almost unbreakable chain of causation.[16] As his first step toward conquest, the would-be aggressor induces others to join him. This new coalition then selects a particular victim who is

---

[14] For lucid statements of the Soviet case, see, e.g., Polska Akademia Nauk, *Sécurité Collective en Europe* (Warsaw, 1955; trans. of *Zagadnienia bezpieczenstwa zbiorowego na Evropie* [Warszawa, Panstwowe Wydawnictwo Naukowe, 1955]).

[15] Manfred Lachs, "Le système de sécurité collective et le problème de la sécurité et de la paix," in Polska Akademia Nauk, *op. cit.*, p. 79.

[16] For representative statement, see A. Yerusalimsky, "Military Blocs in Europe," *International Affairs*, 1955, No. 3, p. 37.

represented as a threat to the peace; the purported threat justifies the existence of the coalition. The victim now responds by forming an opposing coalition. Arms are piled up on both sides and tensions are heightened. Finally and inexorably, in the manner of a Greek tragedy, comes the dénouement—open warfare.

The Soviets adduce a wealth of historical data, primarily from the history of Europe since 1800, in support of this generalization and in "proof" of its correctness.[17] Thus they trace the Napoleonic Wars to certain (unspecified) military alliances formed by the French; World War I to the Triple Alliance of 1882; and World War II to the Anti-Comintern Pact of 1936. They lay great stress upon the inevitable character of the cycle. Once the political build-up has begun, the ultimate conflagration is practically unavoidable. It is here, in their view, that the "balance-of-power" apologists go astray. For, to the Soviets, the existence of exclusive groupings is incompatible with the maintenance of peace. The balance between opposing groups, inherently precarious, must soon be destroyed and war must be the result.

The blocs that have at one time or another allegedly threatened Soviet security make up an imposing list stretching at least as far as from Locarno to Baghdad. Indeed, it is fair to say that this list includes almost all international groupings of which the Soviet Union has not been a member. Whenever two or three have gathered together without including the Soviets, the latter have smelt a conspiracy against them.

The current threats-in-chief to the U.S.S.R., in its view, are Western European Union and NATO, and the latest period of activation of the fateful bloc-to-war cycle dates from 1947.[18] For, in that year, according to the Soviets, the West did an about-face and abandoned the wartime policy of collaboration in collective security. In that year, the United States assumed the crown of imperialist leadership once worn by Germany and Britain and started developing the policy of "positions of strength," which, for

---

[17] *Ibid., passim.*

[18] See, e.g., G. Gendel, "The Periodization of the History of Soviet Foreign Policy," *International Affairs,* 1958, No. 5, p. 71.

pardonable linguistic reasons,[19] *inter alia,* the Soviets interpret as the policy of "positions of force."

With the North Atlantic Treaty of 1949, the cycle moved into its second stage. The West asserted its purely defensive intent, grounding its proof of such intent on the alleged aggressiveness of its selected victim—this despite the fact that the West in its heart of hearts fully recognized that the "Communist menace" was a myth. The United States then accelerated the pace of its aggressive preparations. It strengthened its ascendency over its bloc partners by means of ever-increasing military and economic outlays. It raised its policy-sights, from containment to liberation. It stepped up its threats, to massive retaliation at times and places of its own choosing. It sponsored new blocs (Baghdad Pact and SEATO) and enlarged old ones (NATO, for instance, with the accession of Greece and Turkey). This assessment of American expansionism and the inexorable movement of the cycle to its climax is neatly epitomized by the Soviet interpretation of General Ridgway's trip to Turkey in 1953. Picturing the General on top of Mount Ararat (which he had in fact climbed), they represented him—in a strange amalgam of Biblical allusions—as gazing soulfully out over the Promised Land of Armenia.[20]

Finally, and most terribly, came the rearmament of West Germany and its incorporation into Western European Union and NATO. This precipitated the formation of a contra-bloc and thus the third stage of the cycle was reached. The world is witnessing the start of the final act; the parallel with the developments leading up to World War II is too deadly for anyone to miss.

2. THE RESPONSE

The challenge confronting the Soviet architects of a system of co-operative security is thus defined as a peril, which, through the operation of the familiar dialectic, has a tendency toward self-

---

[19] The single Russian word "sila" covers both our "strength," with its honorific connotation of upright firmness, and our "force," with its dishonorific connotation of suppression of a contrary will. The phrase as a whole tends in translation to acquire this second connotation.

[20] *Pravda,* September 14, 1952, p. 6.

intensification. The proper response, then, must lie along the lines of a policy that places central reliance upon measures designed to soften bloc-rivalries by seeking adjustment of differences, or which, at least, tend to weaken blocs by dislodging old recruits or discouraging new ones. Conversely, such a policy must make sparing and guarded use of direct measures of constructing contra-blocs.

Accordingly, in their theory of a proper co-operative security system the Soviets place first and major stress on the method of transcendence, or, as it is known by Soviet and non-Soviet publicists alike, the collective security method.[21] For this method, in coming to grips with the divisiveness of a bloc-ridden world, aims at the heart of the problem.

Soviet publicists define "collective security" in much the same ways as do their Western counterparts, namely, as a

> . . . principle of international law in accordance with which the disturbance of the peace from the side if only of a single state is disturbance of the common peace, and an act of aggression against one state is an act of aggression against all other states, who have the right and the obligation to come to the help of the suffering state and suppress the aggression . . . .[22]

They stress that collective security is to be distinguished by common action taken in the interests of peace by all of the states in the system rather than by certain states only.[23] They stress that the target is internal and unspecified—anyone in the group who breaks the peace. The strength of a collective security system, in their view, therefore consists of the absence of a hard and fast defense line between rival groups—there exists, rather, a shifting line between the aggressor of the moment and the rest of the countries in both groups.

However, a successful collective security system requires institutional machinery of a certain type. Specifically and most important, it requires an organization within which action is conditional upon the concurrence of the great powers. This rule, which is known to

---

[21] Manfred Lachs, *op. cit.,* p. 118.

[22] *Bol'shaia Sovetskaia Entsiklopediia,* 2d. ed., Vol. 21, p. 619.

[23] Cezar Berezowski, "Les traités d'assistance mutuelle et le système de sécurité collective," in Polska Akademia Nauk, *op. cit.,* p. 123.

the West as the veto, is known to the Soviets as the "unanimity principle"—a significant distinction of term.

The rationale for the "unanimity principle" lies in the realities of international politics. Nations are not equal in respect to the effect of their policies upon the international situation.[24] Luxembourg is not the equal of the United States, nor El Salvador of Britain. Enforcement of a decision contrary to the will of even one small power, or a few small powers, would be difficult: hence the additional requirement of extraordinary majorities. However, the decision would be foredoomed to defeat if it ran counter to the will of a great power. The unanimity principle prevents this exercise in futility. What is probably more important, it prevents the use of a collective security organization by one bloc as a weapon against another and hence the aggravation of the condition that the organization was designed to cure.

Neutralization, in the Soviet view, is the next best method of countering the divisive influences generated by blocs, but it is a lower form of the struggle for peace and the Soviets do not regard it as applicable in every case.[25] Thus they consider assumption of a neutral status quite appropriate if it means withdrawal from a bloc, but inappropriate if it means withdrawal from a collective security arrangement.[26] For example, it was quite appropriate in the late twenties and thirties for the Eastern European and Middle Eastern countries, on the one hand, and the Soviet Union, on the other, to enter into neutralist agreements.[27] For these reflected an erosion of old blocs or the frustration of new ones. But it was most inappropriate for Hungary to seek that status in 1956, for this reflected withdrawal from an incipient collective security organization.[28] Neutralism, in other words, is a sort of half-way house

---

[24] A. Sokolov, "What is Hindering International Co-operation?" *New Times*, 1946, No. 16, esp. p. 6.

[25] E. Korovin, "The Problem of Neutrality Today," *International Affairs*, 1958, No. 3, p. 36.

[26] *Ibid.*, p. 39.

[27] I. F. Ivashin, "The U.S.S.R.'s Struggle Against the Attempt to Form Anti-Soviet Blocs," *International Affairs*, 1957, No. 9, p. 27.

[28] E. A. Korovin, "Proletarian Internationalism in World Relations," *International Affairs*, 1958, No. 2, p. 28.

reserved exclusively for those traveling *toward* membership in collective security arrangements.

The Soviets regard the counterpoise method as the least satisfactory of the three because its application involves the fatal polarization process and thus defeats the true purpose of a co-operative security system. They urge that it be used only as a last resort, and then with greatest care and circumspection. Arrangements that make use of the counterpoise method must safeguard against its employment for nondefensive purposes. In the case of bilateral arrangements, the *casus foederis* must be confined to action from a single specific source. Multilateral arrangements must be truly regional in character and scope. Finally, both types of agreements must be framed in such fashion as to conform strictly to the requirements of the overarching collective security system.

The Soviets never tire of claiming that only Eastern counterpoise arrangements meet all the requirements set forth above and that they may hence lay claim to a greater degree of legitimacy than those of the West. The Soviet bilateral arrangements are trained upon specific targets; the Western arrangements are not. Moreover, the targets of the former are members of the notorious Axis and enemies of proven aggressive tendency, not partners in the common front against the Axis, as is essentially if not nominally the case with the targets of the latter.[29] Finally, only the former are in full accord with provisions of the United Nations Charter, finding express authorization in Articles 53, 106, and 107 of that document.[30] Indeed, the bilateral arrangements, as the Soviets are fond of pointing out, are part and parcel of a network, trained upon the ex-enemies, to which the West also once was a party through the Anglo-Soviet Treaty of 1942, the Franco-Soviet Treaty of 1944, and the Anglo-French Treaty of 1947—a network that is fully consonant with the Charter.

The apologia for the Warsaw Pact arrangements sounds a more defensive note, and much is made of the fact that these arrangements were forced upon socialist Europe by West German rearma-

---

[29] See, for an exemplary defense, N. Yevgenyev, "An Aggressive Treaty under the Guise of a Regional Arrangement," *New Times,* 1949, No. 16, p. 5.

[30] Cezar Berezowski, *op. cit.,* pp. 128 *seq.*

ment. Yet the Soviets find that they substantially meet the requirements too.[31] Unlike the North Atlantic Pact arrangements, with their peculiar geography that would make the Atlantic wash the shores of Greece and Turkey, the Warsaw Pact arrangements, the Soviets say, are truly regional and embrace only European states. Unlike the Atlantic Pact arrangement, they are open to all comers; and unlike the Rio and Southeast Asia arrangements, they are in full accord with Article 51 of the United Nations Charter, confining the *casus foederis* to armed attack. Finally, they are provisional arrangements, which will remain in force only until a true European collective security group is brought into existence.

All arrangements are forms, and at the best, as the Soviets fully recognize, forms exert only a modest influence on the substance of behavior. More is needed to translate policy into fact. In the case of the collaborative pursuit of security, this "more" is defined as ingredients of a truly co-operative attitude such as respect for one another's "sovereign equality," nonintervention in one another's affairs, adherence to the principle of *pacta sunt servanda,* and, in the case of the collective security organization, a spirit of reasonable compromise when attempting to settle specific disputes.[32]

The Soviets particularly stress the importance of the parties' treating one another as sovereign equals. In this connection, they never tire of quoting Lenin's dictum: "Only equals can agree; if an agreement is to be a real agreement and not just high-sounding words to cover submission, there must be effective equality of *both* parties . . . ."[33]

In the Soviet view, of course, only their special arrangements meet the requirements, Western bloc arrangements conferring equality on *one* party alone!

3. IDEOLOGICAL GLOSS

The Soviet theory of co-operative security is always, of course,

---

[31] See, e.g., M. Lachs, "The Warsaw Agreement and the Question of Collective Security in Europe," *International Affairs,* 1955, No. 10, p. 54.

[32] Manfred Lachs, "Le système . . . ," *op. cit.,* p. 65; A. Sokolov, *op. cit.,* p. 9.

[33] V. I. Lenin, *Sochineniye,* Vol. 24, p. 302.

connected up in some degree with basic ideology (though at times the cover of Marxist stereotypes is surprisingly light).

In its ideological formulation, the problem is at once more acute and more susceptible of solution. Posture in external affairs and internal social structure are closely correlated. Aggressiveness is an exclusively capitalist phenomenon. Military coalitions and "blocs" can only be capitalist in character. Socialist nations cannot, by their very nature, be other than peace-loving.[34] Hence the confrontation of the Soviet Union and surrounding blocs is a confrontation of ideological camps—one more manifestation of the Holy War.

At the same time, the peril is more restricted and easier to combat. It is more restricted because the Soviet Union has nothing to fear from the great and growing number of its socialist comrades, who by nature are impelled to exude only sweetness and light in their dealings with one another. It is easier to combat because the available resources include not only the rest of the socialist camp but also the uncommitted world, the elements of opposition in the capitalist world bred of its contradictions, and the masses everywhere. Moreover, the range of available methods is greater. Though the school solution, under the ideological formulation, still demands central reliance upon the collective security method, it permits wider use of the method of counterpoise; for, where socialist nations alone are concerned, a counteralliance has fewer objectionable features, being by nature incapable of uses that are other than defensive.

Finally, the problem is only temporary. It will be with us only for the lifetime of capitalism. It will be with us only for the duration of the period prefatory to the moment of final socialist triumph —that period to which the Soviets are pleased to give the name of coexistence.

IV. Manipulation

We now turn from what the Soviets say are the functions and workings of their co-operative security arrangements to what the

---

[34] The general point of view hardly requires documentation. See, however, Sh. Sanakoyev, "New Type of International Relations," *International Affairs*, 1955, No. 1, p. 45.

facts of their origin and use seem to say, and we find a different story. Scrutiny of these facts leads to a number of general observations.

1. IN PURSUIT OF SECURITY

In the first place, it is well to note that the Soviets do use the arrangements for purposes that have a reasonably close connection with their security. This is to say that they direct them against external forces in which they understandably see a threat to themselves. It is well to make this point at the start because there are still those who either deny the existence of Soviet fears or, while admitting their existence, deny their reasonableness.

In the case of the special arrangements, these external forces encompass all members of the groupings stigmatized as "blocs," as well as Germany and Japan. For in practice the Soviets interpret with considerable elasticity the treaty phrase bracketing with Germany or Japan "any other country directly or indirectly allied with her." They view the Chinese Treaty as applying to American "aggression" in the Far East,[35] and the Eastern European treaties to American and British "aggression" in Europe.[36] In other words, regardless of what they say about these treaties, in practice they point them against the West just as unequivocally as the West points its treaties against them.

The Free World "blocs," and the string of encircling airbases and rearmament programs through which these blocs seek to build up their strength, are objects of real and understandable apprehension to the Soviet Union. It is unreasonable to expect any other reaction on the part of a country, of whatever political coloration, that finds itself in the Soviet position and that has the Soviet experience of invasion from abroad. There is, of course, no doubt that the Soviets, through their actions, have provoked the build-up of Western defenses and thus contributed materially to their own

---

[35] See, e.g., Khrushchev's statement à propos the Quemoy crisis, reported in *Pravda,* October 6, 1958, p. 1.

[36] See, e.g., *New Times* 1948, No. 9, pp. 3-4; and, with respect to Finland, O. Kuusinen, "The Finnish Foes of Peace and Their Artifices," *New Times,* 1951, No. 25, p. 12.

encirclement. But one may grant this—as one must—and yet reject the conclusion of those who say with the late Ernest Bevin that the Soviets *know* they can trust the West and *know* that Western motives are pure. For to accept this conclusion is to expect the Soviets to display an objectivity of judgment and a generosity in accepting the self-evaluations of others which are expected of no other nation.

The Soviet use of the counterpoise arrangements to combat these threats is illustrated by its invocation of the Mongolian, Chinese, and Warsaw treaties in crises of the thirties and fifties. Under the Mongolian Protocol the Soviets moved troops into Mongolia in 1937 to defend it against the threat of Japanese incursions.[37] These troops subsequently participated in the undeclared war against Japan along the Manchurian border in 1939. Under the Chinese Treaty, the Soviets and Chinese held consultations in September 1952 with a view to intensifying preventive measures against the step-up in the Japanese threat allegedly reflected by consummation of the separate Peace Treaty of 1951.[38] As a result, Soviet troops at Port Arthur, which under the terms of the 1950 treaty had been scheduled to leave by the end of 1952, were kept at their post until 1954. Under the Warsaw Treaty (but also under other instruments), the Soviets have quartered troops in several Eastern European countries. Also under the Warsaw Pact, they have held periodic consultations in the form of meetings of the Political Consultative Committee, looking to the strengthening of Eastern European defenses. A meeting was held in Moscow in May 1958, for example, to promote and advertise solidarity.

Use of the neutralization arrangements is illustrated by Soviet resort to the Iranian Treaty to counter various and sundry Western moves connected with the creation and maintenance of the Baghdad Pact. Thus in 1955 the Soviets invoked Article 3 of this treaty (the neutralist provision) in an unsuccessful effort to forestall Iranian accession to that pact.[39] More recently, in the fall of 1958,

---

[37] *Bol'shaia Sovetskaia Entsiklopediia,* Vol. 28, p. 213.

[38] *Pravda,* September 16, 1952, p. 1.

[39] See note of November 26, 1955, in *Pravda,* November 27, 1955, p. 3. and note of February 4, 1956, in *Pravda,* February 7, 1956, p. 2.

they repeated this maneuver in an effort to head off conclusion of an ancillary American economic and military aid agreement.[40]

The counterpoise and neutralization arrangements have by virtue of their very existence, and without activation on Soviet initiative, served the Soviet interest in combating Western influences. The Chinese Treaty performed this function in spectacular fashion during the Korean conflict when it determined, or at least strongly influenced, the American decision not to bomb north of the Yalu—which action, if carried out, might have brought American military power right up to the Far Eastern borders of the Soviet homeland.[41] It is probably also correct to allege, as the Soviets do,[42] that the Finnish and Afghani treaties have contributed to keeping these countries free of close Western connections.

The Soviets, in their use of the United Nations, have also at times adhered to their interpretation (which is also that of others) of the manner in which that organization should properly function: that is, in such a fashion as to contribute directly to the security of all and indirectly to the security of each. Agreement with the majority we take to be prima-facie evidence of such usage, and the Soviet Union does on occasion agree with the majority, or at least refrains from expressing disagreement by exercise of the veto. The Soviet stand in the Suez crisis is a case in point. Moreover, resort to the veto is not to be condemned out of hand. There is little justification for the point of view of those zealous supporters of quantitative method who see in number of vetoes the perfect index of co-operativeness, and for whom, for example, the figure "86" (marking the recent Soviet veto of the Japanese proposal on the Lebanese crisis) is devastating proof of uncompromising obstructionism. The minority position may also be reasonable; this has certainly been true of the positions underlying some Soviet vetoes. In the case of the withdrawal of British and French troops from the Levant back in 1946, for instance, it was not unreasonable for the Soviets to argue that the general security interest would be poorly

---

[40] *Pravda,* November 1, 1958, p. 2.

[41] See Secretary Acheson's testimony at the MacArthur hearings of 1951, reported in the *New York Times,* June 5, 1951, p. 16.

[42] See, e.g., D. Melnikov, "Neutrality and the Current Situation," *International Affairs,* 1956, No. 2, p. 77, and *Pravda,* April 6, 1953, p. 3.

served by the flabby majority resolution—viz., a pious expression
of confidence that the parties would undertake to negotiate without
delay and the troops would be withdrawn as soon as practicable.

But the Soviets, in using for a legitimate purpose the arrangements to which they are party, do not always or even generally use
them in a legitimate or co-operative manner. Manipulation of certain special arrangements in the interests of their security—notably
those with the Eastern European satellites and Mongolia—is rarely
co-operative in any meaningful sense. Abuse of the United Nations
in pursuit of an understandable security objective is not uncommon.

Soviet theory is one thing: in practice, the relationships of the
Soviet Union with its various partners in special arrangements
commonly depart from the standard of equality. They vary from
approximate equality to approximate total Soviet control. It is
appropriate to remember, however, that control is never complete
(for absolute power is absolutely impossible); that the degree of
Soviet control over Eastern Europe has fluctuated; and that certain
of today's arrangements were also in force during periods of lesser
control. One thinks particularly of Czechoslovakia between 1943
and 1948.

In the United Nations, Soviet pursuit of legitimate security ends
through illegitimate means takes the form of a rankly discrimi-
natory attitude toward the selection of issues to be debated and
passed upon, coupled with a dictation of positions on these issues
to other Soviet bloc countries. Thus the Soviets have been quick
to seek to submit to the scrutiny of world opinion cases that are
likely to put their adversaries in a bad light—such as Suez and
Guatemala—and to promote judgment upon such cases. They have
sought to keep from scrutiny or to frustrate judgment upon cases
likely to embarrass themselves or their allies, such as Korea and
Hungary.

But although they do use the arrangements for security purposes
—by fair means or foul—the Soviets assign to them a relatively
low priority on the full list of instruments available for such purposes; and they assign to the United Nations the lowest priority of
all. In crises directly involving a vital position, at least, the special
arrangements take precedence over the United Nations, and action
outside the co-operative institutional framework takes precedence
over both.

The point is eloquently illustrated by Soviet behavior in the case of the Hungarian revolt of 1956. In this case the Soviets vociferously denied the jurisdiction of the United Nations, pleading the dispute in question was purely internal.[43] At the same time, they defended the use of their troops to quell the uprising by claiming that the troops were stationed in Hungary under Article 5 of the Warsaw Pact and that, also under the pact, the Hungarian government had a right to request their help and the Soviet government an obligation to give it.[44] This position was surprising because, on Soviet theory, regional arrangements, to keep within the terms of Article 51 of the United Nations Charter, can legally be invoked only to defend against armed attack by another state and, no more than the Charter itself, can they be used to defend against attack by nonstate forces, such as counterrevolutionary cliques.[45] In other words, in the Hungarian case the Soviets were trying to have it both ways: the action was armed attack from abroad for purposes of establishing the jurisdiction of the subordinate instrument, but internal insurrection for the purpose of denying the jurisdiction of the superior instrument. But this was not all. The dispute might fall within the scope of the Warsaw Pact, but it did not follow that Hungary was equally free to request or to refrain from requesting help under the pact. And so we find the Soviets briskly accepting the legality of Hungary's request that Soviet troops come into the fray, but temporizing in the face of the Hungarian request that they get out, and, when opposed in this and confronted with denunciation of the pact and an appeal to the United Nations, throwing legal argument to the wind and resorting to simple and unadorned *force majeure*.

---

[43] See Shepilov's speech before the General Assembly of November 19, 1956, reported in *Pravda,* November 20, 1956, pp. 3-4.

[44] It should be noted, however, that, as time went on, the Soviet Union came to tie its legal position less directly to the pact, though the pact continued to play a prominent role.

[45] E.g., G. I. Tunkin, "O Nekotorykh Voprosakh Mezhdunarodnogo Dogovora v Svyazi c Varshavskim Dogovorom," *Sovetskoe Gosudarstvo i Pravo,* 1956, No. 1, p. 100; for an attempt to escape the inconsistency noted by shifting the grounds of Soviet intervention in Hungary from the Warsaw Pact to the bilateral Soviet-Hungarian Treaty, see K. A. Baginiian, "Printsip Nevmeshatel'stva i Ustav OON," *Sovetskoe Gosudarstvo i Pravo,* 1957, No. 6, p. 69.

In a pinch, then, the United Nations yields to the more control-lable special arrangements as an instrument for protecting security, and, when the special arrangements can no longer be controlled, these in turn yield to the strong right arm of the Red Army. Col-lective action comes last, not first, and collective security last of all. The priorities of theory are turned upside down.

Yet one important caveat must be sounded in this connection. Soviet by-passing of its institutional net does not always mean abandonment of collective action. Beyond the United Nations lie the great powers in their solitary grandeur, and while, as such, they do not form a distinct and separate association, there is one dis-tinctive institution through which they do jointly operate—viz., that select committee for executing the peace established at Potsdam in 1945 and called the Council of Ministers. What is more to the point, the Soviets not infrequently turn to the great powers as though they *did* form a distinct and separate association and as though the association thus formed had the status of a court of appeal for cases which other agencies, including the United Nations, fail to settle.

The Soviets have turned to the great powers with increasing fre-quency in recent years. Always jealous of preserving the juris-diction of the Council of Ministers over the writing of the peace, the Soviets made an annual pastime of calling sessions of the Coun-cil up to 1951; in that year, the failure of a conference of deputies and the intensification of the Cold War ushered in a three-year period during which there was no contact in this forum. The death of Stalin thawed the ice somewhat—perhaps it is more correct to say that it left a treacherous layer of surface water. There then took place in rapid succession the Council meetings at Berlin in early 1954, at Vienna in May 1955, and at Geneva in the fall of 1955. In the meantime, the powers met in other capacities: in June 1953 to fashion the Korean Armistice, at the Geneva Conference of 1954 on Indochina, and at the Geneva summit conference of July 1955 on Germany. The Soviets derived no little satisfaction from the summit conference, particularly because it marked the first time since Potsdam that the leaders of the wartime coalition had gathered together.[46] They have since, as is well known, been only too eager to repeat the experiment.

---

[46] *Pravda,* August 5, 1955, p. 1.

Because the Soviets conduct their exercises in councilship and summitry with an eye cocked on propaganda potentialities, the conclusion is sometimes drawn that they have no interest in substantive achievement and in the compromise that must precede such achievement. But the results of the Korean Armistice meetings, the Geneva Conference of 1954, and the meetings on the Austrian Treaty tell another story. Although it would be a mistake to claim great importance and permanence for these results, or to interpret them as indicating a change of heart on the part of the Soviets and development of a genuine desire for lasting peace, they do at least reflect a willingness to reach temporary and local accommodations and to make tangible, if modest, concessions to this end.

2. IN PURSUIT OF OTHER ENDS

The Soviets use the arrangements for purposes reasonably closely associated with their security, but they also find other purposes for them. They use them to influence their partner's domestic or foreign policies outside the scope of the treaty proper. They use them as pawns in the great game of great-power politics. They use them for propaganda purposes, as instruments for influencing public opinion at home and abroad.

Manipulation of the Finnish Treaty illustrates the first of these ulterior uses. To quote the Yugoslav *Review of International Affairs:*

> The Soviet Government today takes advantage of this treaty as the strongest and the most efficient weapon for pressure on Finland beside the peace treaty. For instance, the disinterestedness of the Finnish Parliament for the notorious 'Law on the Protection of Peace' is a violation of friendship and co-operation; refusal of social-democratic members of the Cabinet to sign the Stockholm appeal is a violation of the treaty on friendship and co-operation! The publication of 'unfavorable truths' about the Soviet Union in Finnish papers is a violation of the treaty on friendship and co-operation! This treaty which in its texts contains the words 'co-operation' and 'friendship' has become the instrument of most ruthless interference by the Soviet Government in the internal affairs of this country.[47]

[47] Ranko Petkovic, "Finland and the U.S.S.R.," *Review of International Affairs,* Vol. 2, No. 14 (July 4, 1951), p. 15.

Typical was the charge in 1951 that the treaty had been infringed by the alleged bias of Finnish media of communications toward material putting the West in a good and the U.S.S.R. in a bad light.[48] Also in point are references to the treaty in support of the recent successful campaign to alter the composition of the conservative coalition installed after the last elections.[49]

The Warsaw Pact furnishes an instance of the second of the ulterior uses. Indeed, there are good reasons for characterizing this instrument as essentially little more than diplomatic coin counterfeited in order to buy dissolution of NATO and to merge the two European coalitions into a single collective security system. The circumstances of its origin and the logic of the Soviet position point in this direction; so does its wording; so do the apologetics that accompanied its birth and have paralleled the course of its existence.

There are countless examples of use of the arrangements for propaganda purposes and to strengthen a positive image of the U.S.S.R. in the minds both of its citizens and the world at large. The Soviets lose few opportunities to sound the tocsin on the virtues of the happy relationships supposedly reflected in their alliances. They are particularly fond of celebrating alliance birthdays. On the third anniversary of the signing of the Chinese Treaty, for instance, Mao sent a congratulatory telegram to Stalin and Stalin one to Mao, and *Pravda* reported to a breathless world that the Soviet and Chinese peoples, together with all progressive mankind, were on that day marking with a feeling of intense satisfaction this graphic demonstration of the great vitality of Leninist-Stalinist principles of foreign policy, this token of the deep and indissoluble friendship between two great peoples, this alliance whose influence on the international situation has had no equal in the history of mankind, etc.[50] But they do not by any means confine themselves to such occasions. On the occasion of Gomulka's visit to the U.S.S.R. in November 1958, for instance, the virtues of the Polish alliance came in for their share of publicity.[51]

---

[48] O. Kuusinen, *op. cit., passim.*

[49] E.g., *Izvestia,* September 19, 1958, p. 1.

[50] *Pravda,* February 14, 1953, p. 1.

[51] E.g., *Pravda,* November 1, 1958, p. 3, and Nov. 12, 1958, p. 1.

The Soviets have not slighted the United Nations in their manipulation of security arrangements for purposes only tenuously connected with security. They have consumed much of that organization's time pushing programs that, because of their singular lack of
constructiveness, must be characterized as serving propaganda purposes mainly. The self-styled "positive" proposals that they put
forward, like the disarmament proposal of 1946 and the proposal
"against the propaganda inciters of a new war" in 1949, are commonly tendentious and platitudinous, barren of precision in respect
to definition and means of execution. These they serve up year
after year and periodically gather up into one mighty program for
the preservation of peace and security, or, as the Yugoslavs have it,
one heady "resolution stew."[52]

Finally, it is to be observed that—theory to the contrary notwithstanding—the Soviets do not give favored treatment to ideological associations in constructing their network of special arrangements. In practice, they have not been indiscriminate in their
encouragement of alliances among socialist nations. For instance,
they have no bilateral mutual aid arrangement with East Germany
or Albania, and no mutual aid arrangement at all with North Korea
or North Viet Nam. Nor do they in fact reject the possibility of a
socialist "aggressor." Their alliances are not directed exclusively
against capitalist nations—for what reason can there be for reten-
tion of the Mongolian arrangement save as a possible weapon
against the Chinese Communists? They fear the construction of
anti-Soviet socialist "blocs." The activities of Tito and Dimitrov
in organizing a Balkan security system in 1947 were regarded in
precisely this light.[53]

That there is some correlation between Soviet security and Soviet
ideological associations is, of course, true. But to use the latter to
explain the former is to invert the true relationship. Soviet security
arrangements were not created to protect the socialist family; the
reverse is true, as events in Czechoslovakia in 1948 and Hungary
in 1956 testify.

---

[52] Dr. M. Skalar, "Soviet Tactics in the United Nations," *Review of
International Affairs,* Vol. 3, No. 23 (December 1, 1952), p. 9.

[53] See the denunciatory article in *Pravda* of January 28, 1948, p. 4, and
cf. P. S. Wandycz, *op. cit.,* p. 184.

V. Conclusion

Soviet participation in the collaborative pursuit of security is thus a maze of inconsistencies and contradictions. Rationalization and manipulation conform poorly. What the Soviets say they do and what they actually do have little in common. Instead of using co-operatively the institutional net, they often use it nonco-operatively. Instead of giving high priority to this net, they give it low priority, and the collective security organization the very lowest of all. Instead of confining use of the net to security purposes, they extend it to purposes at best tenuously connected with security. Instead of giving special consideration to the interests of ideological affiliates, they often treat them like ideological opponents. Behind the forms of joint action lies the reality of individual policy individually pursued. Practice stands theory on its head.

Because of these inconsistencies, there is a tendency in the West to see the essential function of Soviet participation as providing cover and concealment for a policy of unlimited expansionism. On this view, the net of Eastern European mutual aid treaties is clearly a "superstructure" or "façade," the Warsaw Pact a "simulacrum," and the United Nations a "propaganda forum." Forms are the complete antitheses of contents. Behind the forms lies an evil genie lusting for world conquest. In their shadow lurks a malevolent presence bent not on the co-operative pursuit of security but the nonco-operative pursuit of unlimited power.

Yet Soviet behavior in this field is as consonant with an essentially defensive as with an essentially aggressive motivation. On the whole, the net of alliances the Soviet Union has constructed and the specific actions it has taken under them differ little from what one would expect any nation in its position and with its experience to construct and take. So while one must discard as false much of what it has to say about the character of its activity, one must at the same time be careful not to discard offhand what it says about the objective. Though the means are not as stated, the end may be. Though Soviet behavior in the name of co-operative security is in fact not often co-operative, security may in fact be its essential goal.

INDEX

301

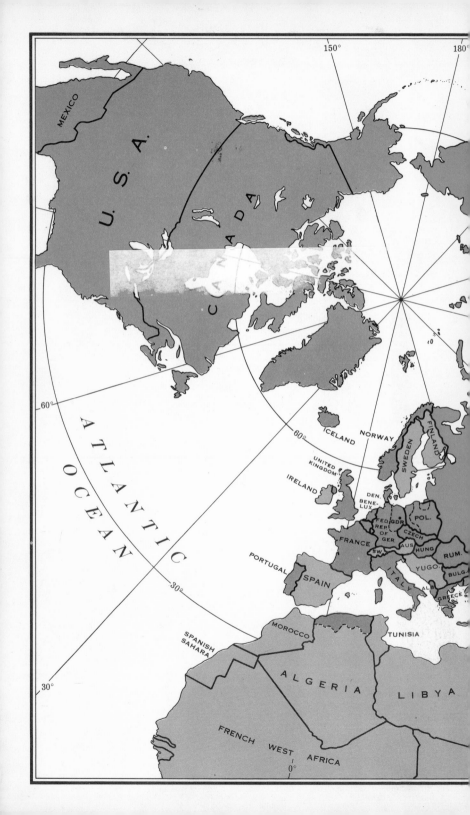